An Introduction to
AutoCAD 2000

A. Yarwood

Registered Developer

LONGMAN

Pearson Education Limited
Edinburgh Gate, Harlow
Essex CM20 2JE, England
and Associated Companies throughout the world

First published 1999

British Library Cataloguing in Publication Data
A catalogue entry for this title is available from the British Library

ISBN 0582-41913-1

Set by 24 in 10/13pt Melior
Produced by Longman Singapore Publishers (Pte) Ltd
Printed in Singapore

An Introduction to
AutoCAD 2000

Contents

List of plates

Colour plates are between pages 144 and 145.

Preface

The aim of this book is to provide a text suitable for students in Further Education or Higher Education or others such as those new to AutoCAD, wishing to learn how to use AutoCAD 2000. In line with versions of AutoCAD Release 14, AutoCAD 2000 will be published only for working in either Windows NT, Windows 95 or Windows 98 and not for other platforms. The software is now fully Windows 95, Windows 98, Windows NT and Microsoft Office compatible. Although the contents of the book will be aimed at the Windows 95 version, the book's contents will be just as suitable for those working with NT and Windows 98, despite the differences between Windows 95, Windows 98 and Windows NT – icons, some procedures etc.

The package will function in a PC preferably fitted with a Pentium 133 or faster. It will operate with a minimum of 32 Mbytes RAM, but will work better with 64 Mbytes.

Many new facilities and enhancements have been included in this latest release of AutoCAD. Among these, some details of the following will be included in this book. The size of the book is limited as to page numbers in order to keep the cost to readers down, but it is necessary to include details of some of the enhancements to emphasise the very good new technologies introduced with this release.

Improvements in speed of performance in opening and saving, zooms and pans, draw and edit operations.

Toolbars now designed as Coolbars (Microsoft Office compatibility)

Intellimouse support.

Start-up dialogue box much improved.

New Object Properties toolbar which includes a Lineweight popup list and an enhanced Layer Manager popup.

Multiple drawings on screen allowing Concurrent Command Execution – the ability to work in any one of several drawings on screen.

Multiple sessions of AutoCAD 2000 windows on screen.

Command line prompts much more specific to the required task.

The AutoCAD Design Centre introduced. This is a Windows Explorer type dialogue allowing Drop and Drag into the AutoCAD 2000 window of files, blocks, layers, linetypes, Xrefs, layers etc. from any drawing on file.

Cut/Copy/Paste from any one drawing to another while both are on screen.

Text Finder dialogue box introduced.

Enhanced Layer Properties Manager.

Enhanced Dimension Style manager which includes a Preview box showing the dimensioning style.

Enhanced Boundary Hatch dialogue box with improved Hatch Pattern palettes.

New Plot dialogue boxes, including a new Plot Progress dialogue.

Partial Open allowing details from selected layers to be brought to screen.

AutoSnap and PolarSnap enhancements.

New Dimension Style dialogue box.

Ability to amend any detail in any form of dimension through the Objects Property Manager.

Introduction of a QDIM tool, allowing quick dimensioning – creating several dimensions with a single selection of an outline.

New Property Manager which allows the editing of objects by type from screen. The updating to new properties is dynamic.

3DOrbit tool introduced.

Dynamic positioning of 3D solids on screen under digitiser movement.

Enhanced Internet features. New and improved access to and from Internet and Browsers.

Improved Object linking and embedding (OLE) features.

New Viewport dialogue boxes.

Non-rectangular viewports allowing different shapes of viewport in one AutoCAD 2000 window – e.g. square, circular, other shapes.

Enhanced DXF file save and open.

The book contains what is basically a course of work. Starting from first principles; going on to set examples and exercises in the construction of 2D drawing; proceeding on to examples and exercises in constructing 3D solid model drawings; then to examples and exercises in the rendering of 3D models. A set of four appendices, which include plotting, a glossary of tools, a glossary of computer terms, and a short list of set variables completes the contents of the book.

An 8 page insertion contains colour plates of AutoCAD screens showing 2D drawings, 3D models and renderings of 3D models. Many of the colour plates show renderings of 3D solid models which have been included as examples and exercises throughout the book.

A. Yarwood
Salisbury 1999

Acknowledgements

The author wishes to acknowledge with grateful thanks the help given to him by members of the staff at Autodesk Ltd.

Trademarks

The following are registered in the US Patent and Trademark Office by Autodesk Inc.:

Autodesk®, AutoCAD®, ACAD™, DXF™

IBM® is a registered trademark of the International Business Machines Corporation.

Windows™ is a trademark, and MS-DOS® is a registered trademark, of Microsoft Corporation.

A. Yarwood is a Registered Developer, a Master Developer and a member of the Autodesk Developer Network (ADN) with Autodesk Ltd.

Registered Developer

Chapter 1

AutoCAD 2000 for Windows 95

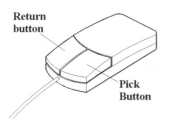

Fig. 1.1 A two-button mouse

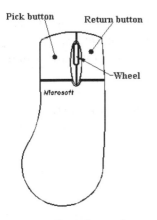

Fig. 1.2 The Microsoft Intellimouse

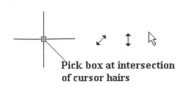

Fig. 1.3 Types of cursor

Introduction

The mouse as a digitiser

Although other types of digitiser can be used when working with AutoCAD 2000, in this book only methods of working with a two-button mouse as the digitiser are given. In general when working with a two-button mouse, the left-hand button is the **Pick** button and the right-hand button the **Return** button (Fig. 1.1).

The Microsoft Intellimouse

In particular the Microsoft Intellimouse (Fig. 1.2) can be used with AutoCAD 2000. This is a two-button mouse with a wheel between the two buttons. The wheel allows zooming, Moving the wheel forwards zooms to a larger scale. Moving the wheel backwards zooms to a smaller scale. Pressing the wheel when working in AutoCAD 2000 brings up a menu from which Object Snaps can be selected (see pages 41–3)

Terms used throughout this book

Cursor: Several types of cursor will be seen when using AutoCAD 2000. Some are shown in Fig. 1.3. Cursors can be moved under mouse control. Move the mouse and the cursor in action moves as the mouse is moved.

Left-click: Place the cursor under mouse control onto a feature and press the *pick* button of the mouse. Shown in this book in italics – *left-click*.

Right-click: Move the cursor under mouse control onto a feature and press the mouse *Return* button. Shown in this book in italics – *right-click*.

Double-click: Place the cursor under mouse control onto a feature and press the *Pick* button of the mouse twice in rapid succession. Shown in this book in italics – *double-click*.

Drag: Move the cursor under mouse control, hold down the *pick* button and move the mouse. The feature moves with the mouse movement. Shown in this book in italics – *drag*.

Drag and drop: *Drag* a feature into a new position and release the mouse button when the feature is in a required new position. Shown in this book in italics – *drag and drop*.

Docked: A feature in a position right up against the edge of the screen or against another toolbar. Shown in this book in italics – *docked*.

Select: Move the cursor onto a feature and press the *pick* button of the mouse.

Pick: The same action as select. The two terms are used throughout this book and can be regarded as having the same meaning. Shown in this book in italics – *pick*.

Pick button: The left-hand button of the mouse.

Pick box: An adjustable square associated with picking features of a construction (see Fig. 1.3).

Enter: Type the given word or letters at the keyboard. Shown in this book in italics – *enter*.

Return: Press the Return or Enter key of the keyboard (Fig. 1.4). Usually, but not always, has the same result as a *right-click* – i.e. pressing the Return button of the mouse. Shown in this book in italics – *Return*.

Esc: The **Esc** key of the keyboard. In AutoCAD 2000 pressing the **Esc** key has the effect of cancelling the current action taking place.

Tab key: The key usually on the left-hand side of the keyboard which carries two arrows.

Tool: The name given to a command in recent releases of AutoCAD.

Icons: A common graphic feature in all Windows applications – a small item of graphics representing a tool or a function of the software in use.

Tool tip: The name of the tool represented by an icon, which appears when the cursor under mouse control is placed onto a tool icon (Fig. 1.5).

Flyout: Some tool icons have a small arrow in the bottom right-hand corner of the icon. When the cursor is placed onto an icon with an arrow and the *pick* button of the mouse is held down a flyout appears (Fig. 1.6).

Default: The name given to the settings or parameters of an application as set when the software is first purchased.

Objects: Individual lines, circles etc. as drawn in AutoCAD 2000. When objects are grouped together as groups or as blocks the whole group will be treated as an object.

Entity: Has the same meaning in AutoCAD 2000 as has the word object.

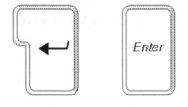

Fig. 1.4 There are usually two Enter or Return keys in computer keyboards

Fig. 1.5 A tool tip

Fig. 1.6 A flyout

Running AutoCAD 2000

When a computer running Windows 95/98 is switched on, it is usual for the Windows desktop to appear. This will often contain a number of icons (shortcut icons) representing the applications loaded on the hard disk of the computer. There are several ways in which AutoCAD 2000 can be opened from the Windows desktop window. Three methods are illustrated in Figures 1.7 and 1.8.

1. *Double-click* on the Shortcut icon representing AutoCAD 2000 (Fig. 1.7).
2. *Right-click* on the AutoCAD 2000 Shortcut icon, which brings up a menu. Then *left-click* on the name of the icon representing the AutoCAD 2000 software (Fig. 1.7).

Fig. 1.7 Two methods of opening AutoCAD 2000

3. *Left-click* on the **Start** button in the Windows 95 window. This brings up a menu, from which a second *left-click* on **Programs**, brings up a second menu. *Left-click* on **AutoCAD 2000** and from the third menu which then appears. *Left-click* again on **AutoCAD R2000** (Fig. 1.8) and the software will load.

The AutoCAD 2000 window

When the AutoCAD 2000 files have loaded, the AutoCAD 2000 window appears on the computer screen with the **Startup** dialogue

Fig. 1.8 A third method of
opening AutoCAD 2000

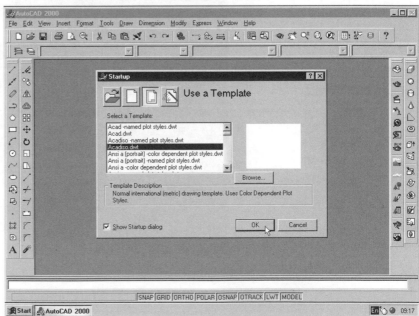

Fig. 1.9 The **Startup** dialogue
box in the AutoCAD 2000
window

box showing a list of names of AutoCAD drawing templates (file
extension ***.dwt**) – Fig. 1.9.

Left-click on the name **acadiso.dwt**, followed by another *left-
click* on the **OK** button of the dialogue box and the acadiso.dwt file
loads. The resulting computer screen is shown in Fig. 1.10.

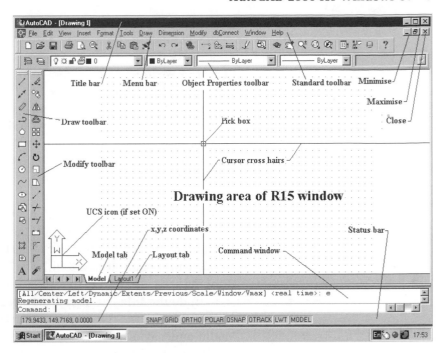

Fig. 1.10 The AutoCAD 2000 window

The parts of the AutoCAD 2000 window

Title bar: Containing the AutoCAD 2000 icon, the name **AutoCAD**, and the name of the drawing loaded into the drawing area of the AutoCAD 2000 window. Also:

> **Minimise button** – a *left-click* on the button closes the AutoCAD 2000 window, but the window is held as a button in the Windows task bar. A *left-click* on this task bar button will bring the AutoCAD 2000 window back on screen.

> **Maximise button** – *left-click* on this button and the AutoCAD 2000 window expands to fill the screen. Another *left-click* takes the AutoCAD 2000 window back to the size it was before being expanded.

> **Close button** – *left-click* on this button and the AutoCAD 2000 window disappears as it is closed.

Menu bar: *Left-click* on any of the names in this bar and the named pull-down menu appears.

Standard toolbar: Contains the icons of tools in frequent use, but not those for constructing drawings.

Object Properties toolbar: Includes panels which bring down popup lists containing details associated with layers.

Draw toolbar: Usually *docked* against the left-hand side of the AutoCAD 2000 window. Contains the icons of tools used for drawing.

Modify toolbar: usually *docked* against the **Draw** toolbar. Contains the icons of tools associated with modifying (or editing) constructions.

Cursor cross hairs: Those shown stretch across the drawing area of the AutoCAD 2000 window, but their size can be varied from the **Options** dialogue boxes. A pick box will usually be seen at the intersection of the cursor cross hairs.

Command window: A true window – can be moved or enlarged or reduced in size. The number of lines of text showing can be altered in the **Options** series of dialogue boxes, or by *dragging* the upper line of the window.

Status bar: Contains the position of the intersection of the cursor cross hairs and a number of buttons (**SNAP**, **GRID** etc.). When a tool is *picked* the Status bar changes to a **Prompt bar** with text describing the action of a selected tool.

Drawing area: the part of the AutoCAD 2000 window which does not include the title bar, menu bar, status bar, Command window or toolbars and in which all constructions are carried out.

Model and Layer tabs: The Drawing area can be altered with a *left-click* on the **Layer1** tab and revert to that shown in Fig. 1.10 with a *left-click* on the **Model** tab. This will be described later in this book.

UCS icon: if the UCS icon is set to be ON, the icon appears. If set OFF, the icon will not appear.

Windows task bar: Shows buttons describing the applications currently loaded. The Windows **Start** button is included, together with a variety of other buttons, some of which depend upon how Windows has been configured. Other items in the Task bar include the time. Place the cursor over the time figures and the date will appear in a tip box.

AutoCAD Drawing templates

In the **Startup** dialogue box, *left-click* on any of the names in the **Select a Template** list. In the Preview box to the right of the list a small illustration of the layout of each template will be seen as it is selected.

Although all the constructions described in this book can be worked in the **acadiso.dwt** template, the majority of drawings in this book have been constructed in a template which I have named **Yarwood.dwt**. When working the drawings and exercises within the pages of this book, it is probably best to construct one's own template and save it to a file name using one's own name or one's own initials.

Fig. 1.11 Selecting **Units...**
from the **Format** pull-down
menu

Creating the new drawing template

1. Setting **Limits:**
   In the Command window at the word Command:

   Command: *enter* limits *right-click*
   Reset Model space limits:
   Specify lower left corner or [ON/OFF] <0,0>: *right-click*
   Specify upper right corner or <12,9>: *enter* 420,297 *right-click*
   Command: *enter* zoom *right-click*
   Specify corner of window, enter a scale fraction (nX or nXP) or
   [All/Center/Left/Dynamic/Extents/Previous/Scale/Window/VMax/
   <real time>: *enter* a (for **All**) *right-click*
   Command:

   The drawing area is now set to the coordinate units size which is
   the same as an A3 paper size in millimetres (42 mm by 297 mm).

2. Setting **Units:**
   Left-click on the name **Format** in the menu bar (Fig. 1.11) and in the
   pull-down menu which appears, *left-click* on **Units...** . The **Drawing
   Units** dialogue box appears (Fig. 1.12). In the dialogue box, *left-
   click* on the arrow in the **Precision** panel, and again on the figure
   0 when the popup list appears. *Left-click* on the **OK** button of the
   dialogue box and note the change in the coordinate figures in the
   left-hand end of the Status bar at the bottom of the AutoCAD 2000
   window.

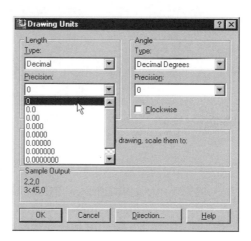

Fig. 1.12 Setting units for the
drawing template

3. Setting Grid and Snap:
   Left-click on the name **Tools** in the menu bar (Fig. 1.13) and again
   on **Drafting Settings...** in the pull-down menu which appears. The

Fig. 1.13 Selecting **Drafting Settings...** from the **Tools** pull-down menu

Drafting Settings dialogue box appears (Fig. 1.14). In the **Snap** settings area *enter* **5** in both the **X Spacing** and **Y Spacing** boxes and 10 in those of the **Grid** settings area of the dialogue box, followed by a *left-click* on the **OK** button of the dialogue box.

4. Setting screen colours:

   In the **Tools** pull-down menu (Fig. 1.13) *left-click* on **Options...** . The **Options** dialogue box appears on screen. *Left-click* on the **Display** tab in the upper part of the dialogue box and again on the **Color...** button. The **AutoCAD Color Options** dialogue box appears. In the popup list from the **Window Element** panel *left-click* on **Model tab background** and also on **Color 0** in the **Color** popup list – see Fig. 1.15. Repeat for the **Model tab pointer**, this time selecting the colour **Black** for this **Window Element**. Then *left-click* on the **Apply & Close** button of the **Color** dialogue box and again on the **OK** button of the **Options** dialogue box.

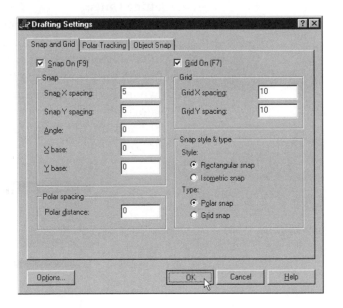

Fig. 1.14 Settings in the **Drafting Settings** dialogue box

Saving the drawing template

Left-click on **File** in the menu bar and again on **Save As...** in the pull-down menu which appears (Fig. 1.16). The **Save Drawing As** dialogue box appears. In the **File name** box *enter* a name for the template and from the **Save as Type** popup list select the ***.dwt** option, A *left-click* on the **Save** button and the drawing template has been saved to the name *entered* in the **File name** box. In this example the file has been saved to the directory **C:/AutoCAD AutoCAD 2000/ Template/Yarwood.dwt** (see Fig. 1.17).

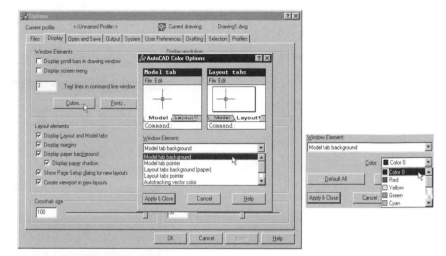

Fig. 1.15 Setting colours in the **Options** dialogue box

Dialogue boxes

As has been already shown, dialogue boxes are important in the operation of AutoCAD 2000. Several forms of dialogue box will be seen when using AutoCAD 2000. The **Select File** dialogue box, which appears on screen when **Open...** as selected from the **File** pull-down menu contains many features common to the AutoCAD 2000 dialogue boxes. Details of this box are given in Fig. 1.18.

Title bar: All AutoCAD 2000 dialogues have a title bar containing the name of the dialogue box, together with a **Close** dialogue box button (with a **X**) at the right-hand end. In many of the dialogue boxes a **Help** question mark icon is included. *Left-click* on the icon and a **?** appears with the arrow cursor. Placing this arrow and **?** over any part of the dialogue box brings up a **Help** box with text explaining the purpose of the part.

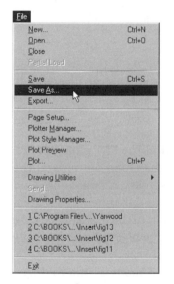

Fig. 1.16 Selecting **Save As...** from the **File** pull-down menu

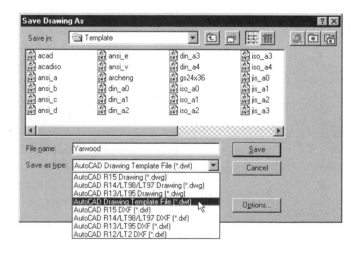

Fig. 1.17 Saving the drawing template

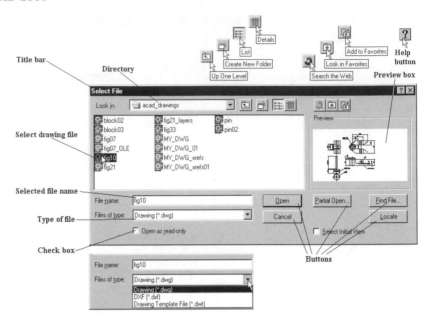

Fig. 1.18 Details of the **Select File** dialogue box

Fig. 1.19 The popup list from the **Directory** list of the **Select File** dialogue box

Directory list: *Left-click* on the arrow on the right of the panel marked **Look in:** and a popup list appears showing the names of available disks and directories. A directory name can be selected from the popup (Fig. 1.19).

Selection of a file name: When a file name is selected from the list of files, its name highlights and is repeated in the **File name:** panel. When the name appears, a *left-click* on the **Open** button and the drawing with that file name appears on screen. A *double-click* on the icon representing the file will also open the drawing to screen.

Icons: The 7 icons in the upper right-hand part of the dialogue box are displayed with their tips above the dialogue box in Fig. 1.18. Note the three Internet icons on the right.

Buttons: Buttons of this type are common to many of the dialogue boxes. Note in this example the **Partial Open...** button, new to AutoCAD 2000. A *left-click* on the **Find File** button brings up a **Browse/Search** dialogue box (Fig. 1.20).

   A *double-click* on one of the icons representing drawings in this dialogue box brings the drawing on screen.

Files of type list: A *lift-click* on the arrow to the right of the panel brings down a popup list from which the type of file required can be selected.

Preview box: A small illustration representing the drawing appears in the **Preview box** when a file name is selected from the file list. This feature will be seen in other dialogue boxes.

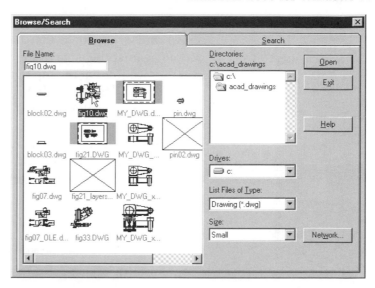

Fig. 1.20 The **Browse/Search**
dialogue box

Check box: A feature common to many dialogue boxes are small check boxes and/or check circles. When a check box is included against the name of a feature in a dialogue box, if the box contains a tick, the feature is set on. An empty check box shows the feature is set off. With check circles a dot inside the circle indicate the feature is set on. No dot and the feature is set off.

Notes

1. The **Select File** dialogue box contains many of the features common to all dialogue boxes and thus gives a reasonable representation of dialogue boxes in general.
2. In addition to dialogue boxes message boxes will sometimes be seen when operating AutoCAD 2000 – there are two types – those giving a simple message (Fig. 1.21) and those giving a warning. Before *clicking* the **OK** button of such boxes, their contents should be read and noted with care.

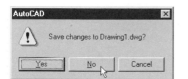

Fig. 1.21 An AutoCAD 2000
message box

Toolbars

Toolbars carry icons representing the tools used in AutoCAD 2000 for the construction, modifying, etc. of drawings created in the drawing area of the screen.

Move the cursor under mouse control over any part of a toolbar which is on screen and *right-click*. The toolbar menu appears carrying the names of all the toolbars available in AutoCAD 2000 (Fig. 1.22). *Left-click* on a toolbar name in the menu and the selected toolbar appears on screen. Those already on screen are shown with a tick on the left-hand side of a toolbar name.

Fig. 1.22 The toolbar menu

When on screen a toolbar can be *dragged* to a new position on screen and dropped in that position (Fig. 1.23). If the toolbar is *docked* against the edge of the window, the cursor must be placed over the two lines at the top of the toolbar to *drag* it away from that position. If the toolbar is being *dragged* from any other part of the screen to another, the cursor should be placed in the title bar of the toolbar.

Toolbars can be resized by moving the cursor under mouse control onto any edge, or corner of the toolbar and *dragging* the toolbar into a new shape. Figure 1.23 shows a number of examples of resizing toolbars in this way.

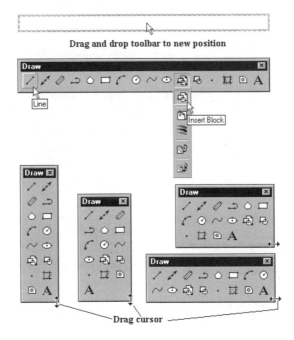

Fig. 1.23 *Dragging* a toolbar to a new position and resizing toolbars

The acad.pgp file

There are several methods by which tools can be called into action in AutoCAD 2000. One method is by *entering* an abbreviation for the tool name at the Command line. If wished, an operator can make up his/her own abbreviations or accept those held in the **acad.pgp** file found in the **Support** directory of the main directory holding all AutoCAD 2000 files. Figure 1.24 shows that part of the **acad.pgp** file which suggests how abbreviations may be *entered* into the file.

Taking the abbreviation for the **Arc** tool each abbreviation takes the form:

A,   *Arc

```
; Command alias format:
;   <Alias>,*<Full command name>

;   The following are guidelines for creating new command aliases.
;   1. An alias should reduce a command by at least two characters.
;       Commands with a control key equivalent, status bar button,
;       or function key do not require a command alias.
;       Examples: Control N, O, P, and S for New, Open, Print, Save.
;   2. Try the first character of the command, then try the first two,
;       then the first three.
;   3. Once an alias is defined, add suffixes for related aliases:
;       Examples: R for Redraw, RA for Redrawall, L for Line, LT for
;       Linetype.
;   4. Use a hyphen to differentiate between command line and dialog
;       box commands.
;       Example: B for Block, -B for -Block.
;
; Exceptions to the rules include AA for Area, T for Mtext, X for Explode.

;   -- Sample aliases for AutoCAD commands --
;   These examples include most frequently used commands.

3A,         *3DARRAY
3DO,        *3DORBIT
3F,         *3DFACE
3P,         *3DPOLY
A,          *ARC
ADC,        *ADCENTER
AA,         *AREA
AL,         *ALIGN
```

Fig. 1.24 Part of the acad.pgp
file of AutoCAD 2000

That is – the abbreviation, followed by a comma, a gap, an asterisk, followed by the full name of the tool.

If an amendment is made to the acad.pgp file, it must be saved to the **Support** directory of the directory in which the AutoCAD 2000 files are held. My acad.pgp is held in:

Progam Files/AutoCAD AutoCAD 2000/Support/acad.pgp

The acad.pgp file of AutoCAD 2000 holds abbreviations for all the tools which can be used for the construction, editing, saving, plotting etc. of drawings.

Calling tools in AutoCAD 2000

In general there are four ways in which a tool (some operators still call tools 'commands') can be called ready for the tool to be used. Figure 1.25 illustrates the four ways in which the **Line** tool from the **Draw** toolbar can be called ready to draw a line:

1. *Left-click* on **Line** in the **Draw** pull-down menu.
2. *Left-click* on the **Line** tool icon in the **Draw** toolbar.
3. *Enter* **l** (abbreviation for **Line**) at the keyboard.
4. *Enter* **line** at the keyboard.

No matter which method is used, the command is repeated in the Command window at what is known as the Command line, together with prompts, instructing the operator what his/her next operation is to be. When the tool is selected a prompt appears at the left-hand end of the Status bar informing the operator of the action of the tool.

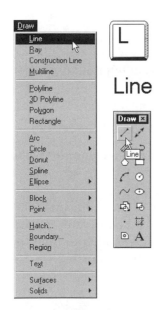

Fig. 1.25 Calling the **Line** tool

Figure 1.26 shows the Command window when the **Line** tool has been selected from either the **Draw** pull-down menu or from the **Draw** toolbar. When the tool is called by *entering* its abbreviation or its full name, the Command window shows a slightly different combination of words, but their meaning is precisely the same.

Figure 1.26 shows a line being drawn between two points on screen using AutoCAD coordinate system by which any point on screen can be defined. More about the coordinate system later (pages 16–17).

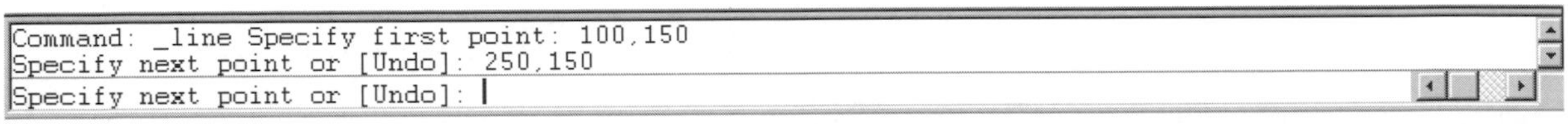

```
Command: _line Specify first point: 100,150
Specify next point or [Undo]: 250,150
Specify next point or [Undo]: |
```

Fig. 1.26 The Command window when the **Line** tool is called

The phrase **Specify first point:** which appears at the Command line is known as a **prompt**. In this book, if a description of drawing the line shown in Fig. 1.25 were to be given, it would be shown as follows:

Command: _line Specify first point: *enter* 100,150 *right-click*
Specify next point or [Undo]: *enter* 250,150 *right-click*
Specify next point or [Undo]:

Enter means type the numbers (or letters in some instances) that follow from the keyboard.

Right-click means press either the right-hand mouse button or the *Return* key of the keyboard.

Questions

1. What are the advantages of using a Microsoft Intellimouse over a standard two-button mouse?
2. What is meant in this book by the following terms:

    enter, Return, drag, left-click, right-click, double-click?

3. How are the AutoCAD 2000 files loaded into a computer when working in Windows 95/98?
4. What is an AutoCAD drawing template?
5. In the right-hand end of the Status bar of the AutoCAD 2000 window the position of the cursor is shown in coordinate numbers until a tool is selected either from the **Draw** toolbar or from the **Draw** pull-down menu. What happens in the Status bar when a tool is selected?
6. What is the purpose of the **?** button usually seen at the top right-hand corner of a dialogue box?

7. What is the difference between an AutoCAD 2000 dialogue box and an AutoCAD 2000 message box?
8. Can you name the AutoCAD 2000 file which holds the tool abbreviations?
9. Toolbars are said to be *floating* when they are not docked against either a side or the top of the AutoCAD 2000 window. How can a toolbar be *floated*?
10. In how many ways can a tool be called in AutoCAD 2000?

Chapter 2

Introduction

The AutoCAD coordinate system

Drawings can be constructed in AutoCAD in either a 2D (two-dimensional) coordinate system or in a 3D (three-dimensional) coordinate system. When working in 2D the coordinates are expressed in terms of X and Y. X units are measured horizontally and Y units vertically. Within this system, any point in the AutoCAD 2000 window can be referred to in terms of x,y. The point $x,y = 70,40$ is 70 units horizontally to the right of an origin where $x,y = 0,0$ and 40 units vertically above the origin. Figure 2.1 shows a number of 2D coordinate points in an AutoCAD 2000 window.

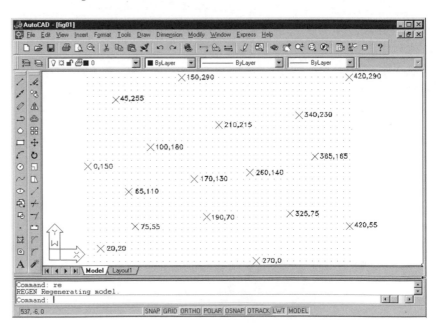

Fig. 2.1 2D Coordinate points in an AutoCAD 2000 window

Coordinates points can be measured in either positive or in negative figures. The point $x,y = 100,50$ is 100 units to the right of the origin $x,y = 0,0$ and 50 units above the 0,0. On the other hand, the point $x,y = -100,-50$ is 100 units to the left of the origin 0,0 and 50 units below the origin.

3D coordinates include a third direction measured in terms of Z. In AutoCAD 2000, positive Z is as if coming towards the operator from the AutoCAD 2000 window perpendicular to the screen. This means that negative Z is perpendicular to the screen away from the operator. 3D drawings are referred to as solid model drawings.

The coordinate reading in the prompt line of AutoCAD 2000 shows a three number coordinate e.g. $x,y,z = 70,40,0$. When taking 2D coordinates Z units are at 0, that is lying on the surface of the screen.

More about 3D coordinates in a later chapter (Chapter 15).

Methods of using tools

In Chapter 1, the four methods of calling drawing tools was given (page 13). As a revision this is repeated here:

1. *Left-click* on the name of the tool in the **Draw** pull-down menu.
2. *Left-click* on the tool icon in the **Draw** toolbar.
3. *Enter* the abbreviation for the tool at the keyboard.
4. *Enter* the full name of the tool at the keyboard.

Using the five tools – **Line**, **Polyline**, **Multiline**, **Circle** and **Arc**, examples of simple drawings involving the tools and based on the involvement of the AutoCAD coordinate system are given below.

The Line tool – a worked example (Fig. 2.3)

As shown in Fig. 2.2, the **Line** tool can be called by either a *left-click* on its name in the **Draw** pull-down menu, by a *left-click* on its tool icon in the **Draw** toolbar, by *entering* the letter **l** or *entering* the full name **line** at the Command line. When the tool is called *enter* coordinate figures at the Command line as shown:

Command: _line Specify first point: *enter* 10,280 *right-click*
Specify next point or [Undo]: *enter* 290,280 *right-click*
Specify next point or [Undo]: *enter* 290,220 *right-click*
Specify next point or [Close/Undo]: *enter* 410,220 *right-click*
Specify next point or [Close/Undo]: *enter* 410,100 *right-click*
Specify next point or [Close/Undo]: *enter* 290,100 *right-click*
Specify next point or [Close/Undo]: *enter* 290,40 *right-click*
Specify next point or [Close/Undo]: *enter* 10,40 *right-click*
Specify next point or [Close/Undo]: *enter* c (Close) *right-click*
Command:

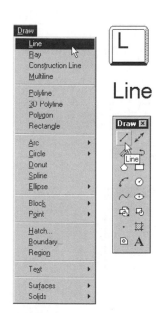

Fig. 2.2 Methods of calling the **Line** tool

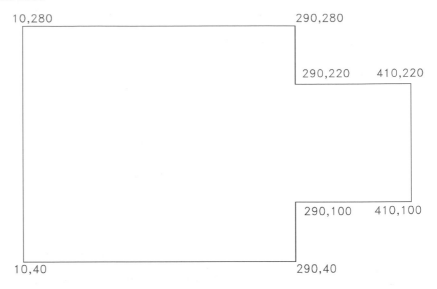

Fig. 2.3 Drawing with the **Line** tool – a worked example

The Circle tool – a worked example (Fig. 2.5)

As shown in Fig. 2.4, the **Circle** tool can be called by either a *left-click* on its name in the **Draw** pull-down menu, by a *left-click* on its tool icon in the **Draw** toolbar, by *entering* the letter **c** or *entering* the full name **circle** at the Command line. When the tool is called *enter* coordinate figures at the Command line as shown:

> **Command:_circle Specify center point for circle or [3P/2P/Ttr (tan tan radius)]:** *enter* 70,210 *right-click*
> **Specify radius of circle or [Diameter]:** *enter* 80 *right-click*

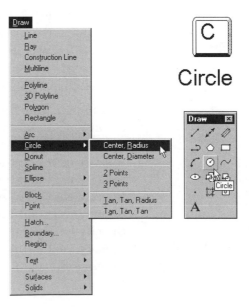

Fig. 2.4 Methods of calling the **Circle** tool

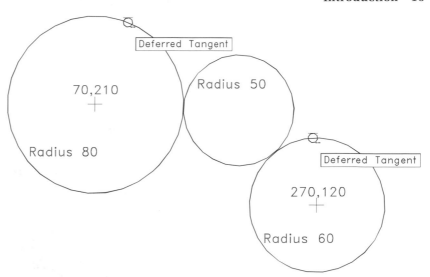

Fig. 2.5 Drawing with the **Circle** tool – a worked example

Command: *right-click*
CIRCLE Specify center point for circle or [3P/2P/Ttr (tan tan radius)]: *enter* 270,120 *right-click*
Specify radius of circle or [Diameter]: *enter* 60 *right-click*
Command: *right-click*
CIRCLE Specify center point for circle or [3P/2P/Ttr (tan tan radius)]: *enter t* (tan tan radius) *right-click*
Specify point on object for first tangent of circle: *pick* on circle
Specify point on object for second tangent of circle: *pick* the other circle
Specify the radius: *enter* 50 *right-click*
Command:

The Arc tool – worked examples (Fig. 2.7)

As shown in Fig. 2.6, the **Arc** tool can be called by either a *left-click* on its name in the **Draw** pull-down menu, by a *left-click* on its tool icon in the **Draw** toolbar, by *entering* the letter **a** or *entering* the full name **arc** at the Command line. Note the number of different methods of drawing arcs as seen when the tool is called from the **Draw** pull-down menu. When the tool is called *enter* coordinate figures at the Command line as shown:

Command:_arc Specify start point of arc or [CEnter]: *enter* 60,210 *right-click*
Specify second point of arc or [CEnter/ENd]: *enter* 140,270 *right-click*
Specify end point of arc: *enter* 240,230 *right-click*
Command: *right-click*

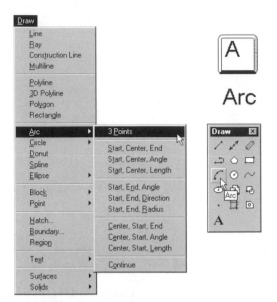

Fig. 2.6 Methods of calling the
Arc tool

ARC Specify start point of arc or [CEnter]: *enter* ce *right-click*
Specify center point of arc: *enter* 0,110 *right-click*
Specify start point of arc: *enter* 50,50 *right-click*
Specify end point of arc or [Angle/chordLength]: *enter* 20,185
   right-click
Command: *right-click*
ARC Specify start point of arc or [CEnter]: *enter* 150,70 *right-click*
Specify second point of arc or [CEnter/ENd]: *enter* en *right-click*
Specify start point of arc: *enter* 250,150 *right-click*
Specify center point of arc or [Angle/Direction/Radius]: *enter* r
   right-click

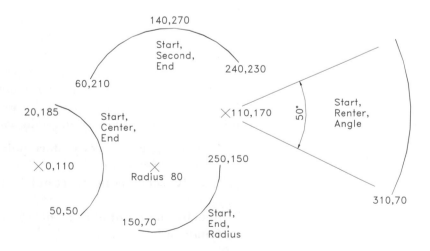

Fig. 2.7 Drawing with the **Arc**
tool – worked examples

Specify radius of arc: *enter* 80 *right-click*
Command: *right-click*
ARC Specify start point of arc or [CEnter]: *enter* 310,70 *right-click*
Specify second point of arc or [CEnter/ENd]: *enter* ce *right-click*
Specify center point of arc: *enter* 110,170 *right-click*
Specify end point of arc or [Angle/chordLength]: *enter* a *right-click*
Specify included angle: *enter* 50 *right-click*
Command:

The Polyline tool a worked example (Fig. 2.9)

As shown in Fig. 2.8, the **Polyline** (**Pline**) tool can be called by either a *left-click* on its name in the **Draw** pull-down menu, by a *left-click* on its tool icon in the **Draw** toolbar, by *entering* the letters **pl** or *entering* **pline** at the Command line. When the tool is called *enter* coordinate figures at the Command line as shown:

Command:_pline Specify start point: *enter* 40,220 *right-click*
Current line width is 0
Specify next point or [Arc/Close/Halfwidth/Length/Undo/Width]: *enter* w *right-click*
Specify starting width <0>: *enter* 1 *right-click*
Specify ending width <1>: *right-click*
Specify next point or [Arc/Close/Halfwidth/Length/Undo/Width]: *enter* 290,220 *right-click*

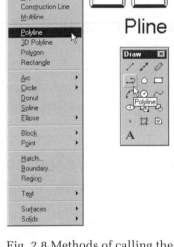

Fig. 2.8 Methods of calling the **Polyline** tool

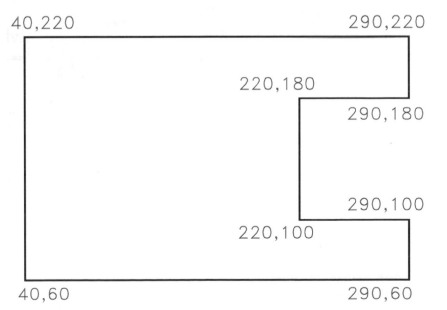

Fig. 2.9 Drawing with the **Polyline** tool – a worked example

Specify next point or [Arc/Close/Halfwidth/Length/Undo/Width]:
enter 290,180 *right-click*

Specify next point or [Arc/Close/Halfwidth/Length/Undo/Width]:
enter 220,180 *right-click*

Specify next point or [Arc/Close/Halfwidth/Length/Undo/Width]:
enter 220,100 *right-click*

Specify next point or [Arc/Close/Halfwidth/Length/Undo/Width]:
enter 290,100 *right-click*

Specify next point or [Arc/Close/Halfwidth/Length/Undo/Width]:
enter 290,60 *right-click*

Specify next point or [Arc/Close/Halfwidth/Length/Undo/Width]:
enter 40,60 *right-click*

Specify next point or [Arc/Close/Halfwidth/Length/Undo/Width]:
enter c *right-click*

Command:

The Multiline tool – worked examples (Fig. 2.11)

As shown in Fig. 2.10, the **Multiline** tool can be called by either a *left-click* on its name in the **Draw** pull-down menu, by a *left-click* on its tool icon in the **Draw** toolbar, by *entering* the letters **ml** or *entering* **mline** at the Command line. When the tool is called *enter* coordinate figures at the Command line as shown:

Command:_mline
Current setting: Justification = Top, Scale = 1.00, Style = STANDARD

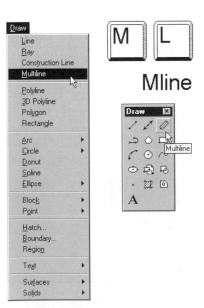

Fig. 2.10 Methods of calling the **Multiline** tool

Specify start point or [Justification/Scale/STyle]: *enter* s *right-click*

Enter mline scale <1.00>: *enter* 15 *right-click*

Specify start point or [Justification/Scale/STyle]: *enter* 0,270 *right-click*

Specify next point: *enter* 190,270 *right-click*

Specify next point or [Undo]: *enter* 190,160 *right-click*

Specify next point or [Close/Undo]: *enter* 0,160 *right-click*

Specify next point or [Close/Undo]: *enter* c *right-click*

Command:

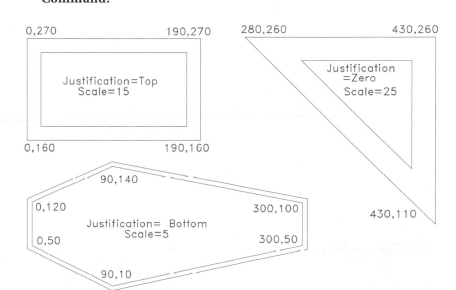

Fig. 2.11 Drawing with the **Multiline** tool – worked examples

Notes

1. To initiate the prompts such as **[Close/Undo]**, all that is necessary is to *enter* the capital letter(s) of the prompt.
2. When using the **Ttr** prompt of the **Circle** series of Command line responses, the AutoSnap and Osnap symbols and tip will be seen as shown in Fig. 2.5.
3. When using **Multiline**, if the **Justification** prompt is called, the multiline is drawn from point to point either from the **Top** of the mline, from the centre (**Zero** setting) or the **Bottom** of the mline.

Context sensitive Help

When working with any of the tools in AutoCAD 2000, pressing the **F1** key of the keyboard brings a window on screen describing how to use the tool. An example is given in Fig. 2.12, in which, while

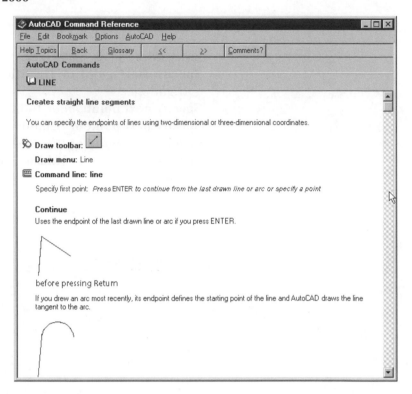

Fig. 2.12 The **Line** help
window called by pressing **F1**
while working with the **Line**
tool

Fig. 2.13 Calling for **Help** for
other topics

working with the **Line** tool, the key **F1** was pressed and the **Line** help
window appeared.

Help for other topics when using AutoCAD 2000 can be called by
selecting **AutoCAD Help Topics** from the **Help** pull-down menu
(Fig. 2.13). In particular note that **Help** from the Internet can be
called by selection from the **Autodesk on the Web** sub-menu (Fig.
2.14). To use the Web Help items, the computer must be equipped
with a modem together with a connection service system loaded into
the computer. More about the Web and Internet in Appendix A.

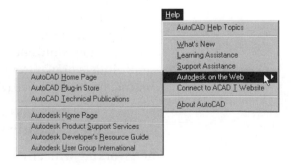

Fig. 2.14 The **Autodesk on the
Web** sub-menu from **Help**

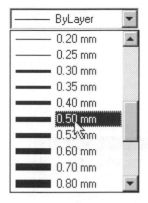

Fig. 2.15 The **Lineweight** popup list

Lineweights

Left-click on the arrow on the right of the **ByLayer** panel and a lineweight popup list appears (Fig. 2.15). *Left-click* on one of the lineweight icons (0.50 mm has been *picked* in Fig. 2.15). Then construct some outlines with the aid of the tools, **Line**, **Circle** and **Arc** with varying lineweights as shown in Fig. 2.16.

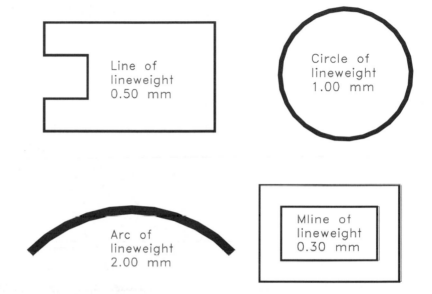

Fig. 2.16 Objects of different lineweights

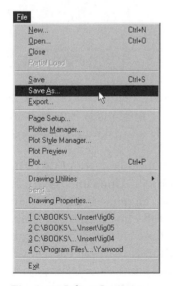

Fig. 2.17 Select **Save As...** from the **File** pull-down menu

Saving drawings to file

A few worked examples have been given in earlier pages of this chapter. Some exercises involving the drawing tools so far mentioned are included at the end of this chapter. The reader is advised to work through the worked examples and to attempt the exercises. If this advice is followed it is suggested that each drawing as it is constructed is saved to disk. As other operators may be using the computer on which the examples and exercises are worked, it is best to save the files to a floppy disk, which will probably be held in drive **a:**. Each drawing could be saved to directories such as **Chap02**, with drawing file names such as **example01.dwg**. The full file name of such a file would then be **a:\Chap02\example01.dwg**.

When AutoCAD 2000 drawings are saved to disk the extension **.dwg** will automatically be applied to the file name. However, as can be seen in Fig. 2.18, drawings can be saved in other formats if desired – in **.dwg** formats of earlier releases of AutoCAD LT and of AutoCAD, as well as in **.dxf** format in LT and AutoCAD releases. More about ***.dxf** files later (pages 190–91).

To save a drawing to a new file name, *left-click* on **Save As...** in the **File** pull-down menu (Fig. 2.17). The **Save Drawing As** dialogue box appears (Fig. 2.18). Select the disk drive and directory from the popup menu in the **Save in:** panel, *enter* the required file name in the **File name:** panel. Select the required file format (usually AutoCAD 2000) and *left-click* on the **Save** button.

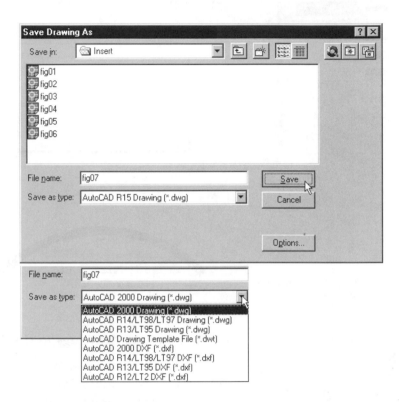

Fig. 2.18 Saving a file to the filename **Fig07.dwg** in the **Save Drawing As** dialogue box

Notes

1. The **Save** option (from the **File** pull-down menu) can be used if wished, but only if a drawing has been previously saved to a required file name. The **Save** option saves a file without bringing up a dialogue box.

2. **Call the** Options dialogue box to screen (**Options...** from **File** pull-down) and in the dialogue box, *left-click* on the **Open and Save** tab. In the **File Safety Precautions** area of the dialogue, it will be seen that an **Automatic save** can be set with a *left-click* in the check box against **Automatic save** (Fig. 2.19). The time between savings can also be set by *entering* a number for minutes between each save. Take care if using **Automatic save** because unless a drawing has already been saved to a desired file name, the naming of the drawing file may be incorrect.

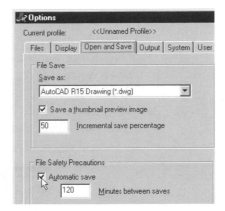

Fig. 2.19 The **Automatic save** feature of the **Options** settings

Fig. 2.20 The **Open** tool icon from the **Standard** toolbar

Opening files

Files previously saved to disk can be opened by Calling **Open...** from the **File** pull-down menu or with a *left-click* on the **Open** tool icon in the **Standard** toolbar *docked* against the menu bar of the AutoCAD 2000 window (Fig. 2.20). The **Select File** dialogue box opens (Fig. 2.21). To open a file:

1. Select the directory from the **Look in:** panel.
2. Select a file from the list of files which appears in the main area of the dialogue box.
3. The file name is repeated in the **File name:** panel.
4. A small copy of the drawing appears in the Preview panel of the dialogue box.
5. If the preview drawing appears OK, *left-click* on the **Open** button and the drawing appears in the drawing area of AutoCAD 2000.

Fig. 2.21 The **Select File** dialogue box

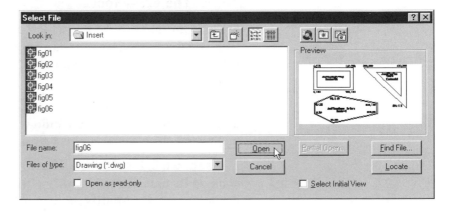

Note

When starting up AutoCAD 2000, the **Startup** dialogue box appears. One of the tool icons at the top of the dialogue box is an **Open a Drawing** tool (Fig. 2.22). A *left-click* on the tool icon brings up the **Select File** dialogue box. The icons also appear in the **Create a New Drawing** dialogue box, called to screen with a *left-click* on **New...** (**File** pull-down menu).

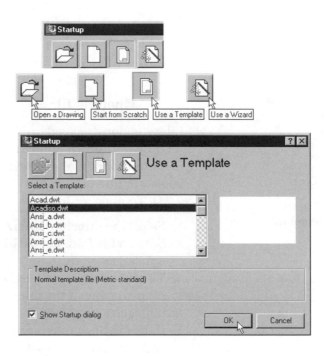

Fig. 2.22 The tool icons at the top of the **Setup** dialogue box

The Erase tool

Erase is an important tool, which most operators find themselves using on frequent occasions as errors are made while constructing a drawing. There are three main methods by which erasing can be carried out:

1. Erasing single objects.
2. Erasing objects within a window.
3. Erasing objects crossed by a crossing window.

As shown in Fig. 2.23, the **Erase** tool can be called by either a *left-click* on its name in the **Modify** pull-down menu, by a *left-click* on its tool icon in the **Modify** toolbar, by *entering* the letter **e** or *entering* the full name **erase** at the Command line. By far the easiest and quickest method of calling the tool is to *enter* **e** at the Command line.

Fig. 2.23 Methods of calling the **Erase** tool

Erasing a single object

Drawing **1** of Fig. 2.24 is an outline drawn with the **Line** tool with two circles inside the outline drawn with the **Circle** tool. To erase a single object:

Command: *enter* e *right-click*
ERASE Select objects: *pick* the object to be erased **1 found**
Select objects: *right-click*
Command:

The result is shown in Drawing **2** of Fig. 2.24.

Erasing objects within a window

Drawing **3** of Fig. 2.24 shows a window surrounding the two circles of the drawing. Erasing the objects within the window is shown in Drawing **4**.

Command: *enter* e *right-click*
ERASE Select objects: *enter* w *right-click*
Specify first corner: *pick*
Specify opposite corner: *pick* **2 found**
Select objects: *right-click*
Command:

And the two circles within the window are erased.

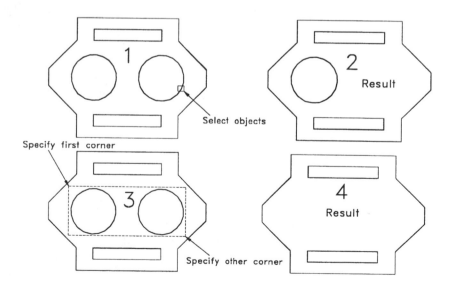

Fig. 2.24 Using the **Erase** tool

Erasing objects within a crossing window

If, instead of *entering* w (for window), **c** (for crossing) is *entered* and the corners of a crossing window then *picked*, all objects **crossed** by the lines of the crossing window are erased. Note the difference between a window and a crossing window. If a window is used it is all objects completely within the window which are erased. If a crossing window is used, it is all objects crossed by the lines of the window.

Another way of using a crossing window when erasing is to *pick* a corner to the bottom right of the objects to be erased, followed by *picking* the opposite corner to the top left of the objects.

Regen tool

Calling **Regen** regenerates the whole of a drawing, removing unwanted material such as blips or unwanted pixels. The tool will also sharpen up objects such as arcs and circles in zoomed parts of drawings. The easiest method of using the tool is to *enter* **re** at the Command line (Fig. 2.25).

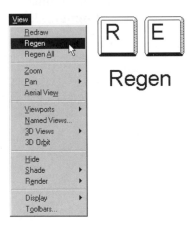

Fig. 2.25 Calling the **Regen** tool

The Esc key of the keyboard

When operating within AutoCAD 2000, pressing the **Esc** key (top left-hand corner of keyboard) – Fig. 2.26, cancels the operation currently in action. Thus if an error is made in selecting a tool, pressing **Esc** cancels the error and brings the Command line back to **Command:**. When the **Esc** key is pressed the Command line shows:

Command: *Cancel*

Fig. 2.26 The **Esc** key

Questions

1. How would you define the point $x,y = 120,90$ with respect to the origin point $x,y = 0,0$?
2. In the Status bar coordinates show up as 3 dimensional – an example would be 20,50,0. What is the meaning of the third figure **0**?
3. How would you define the point $x,y = 90, -50$?
4. What is a **Deferred Tangent** as shown in Fig. 2.5 on page 19?
5. What is set by the **Scale** prompt of the **Multiline tool**?
6. How many forms of **Justification** can be set when using the **Multiline** tool?
7. When using any tool in AutoCAD 2000, what happens if the **F1** key is pressed?
8. Why is it not advisable to use the **Save** tool before saving with the aid of the **Save As** tool?
9. How is the **Automatic Save** feature set?
10. Why is it necessary to take care when setting the **Automatic Save** feature?

Exercises

When constructing drawings in answer to the following exercises, commence by loading the template file (*.dwt file) which you saved after making settings as shown in Chapter 1. If you have not saved your own template file, load the **acadiso.dwt** template file before answering each exercise.

1. Left-hand drawing of Fig. 2.27. With the aid of the **Line** and **Circle** tools, construct the given drawing from the instructions given with the drawing.

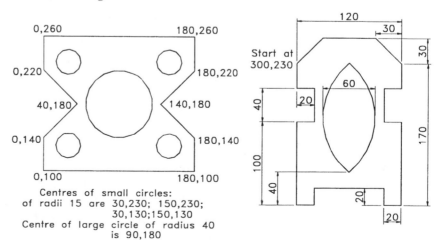

Fig. 2.27 Exercises 1 and 2

Centres of small circles:
of radii 15 are 30,230; 150,230; 30,130;150,130
Centre of large circle of radius 40 is 90,180

2. Right-hand drawing of Fig. 2.27. Construct the given drawing working to details given with the drawing. Use the tools **Line** and **Arc**.

3. With the aid of the tools **Line** and **Circle**, construct the outlines given in Fig. 2.28. You must calculate the coordinate figures for each point on the outlines with the aid of simple arithmetic.

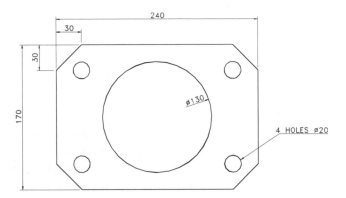

Fig. 2.28 Exercise 3

4. Left-hand drawing of Fig. 2.29. Call **Polyline** and set the **Width** to 2. Then complete the construction of the given outline.

5. The right-hand drawing of Fig. 2.29 shows three circles, the smallest tangential to the other two. The centres of the two larger circles are 115 units apart. Construct the three circles with **Lineweight** set to 1.00 mm.

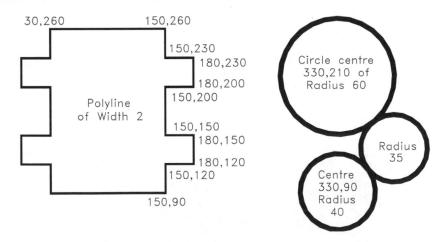

Fig. 2.29 Exercises 4 and 5

6. The top left-hand drawing of Fig. 2.30 shows two lines, each 120 units long and at right angles to each other with a circle of radius 50 units tangential to the two lines. Construct the drawing.

7. The top right-hand drawing of Fig. 2.30 shows two arcs with a 55 unit circle tangential to the arcs. Construct the drawing.

8. The lower drawing of Fig. 2.30 shows a line with an arc, touching at each end of the line. Tangential internally to the two objects are two circles each of radius 25 units. Construct the drawing.

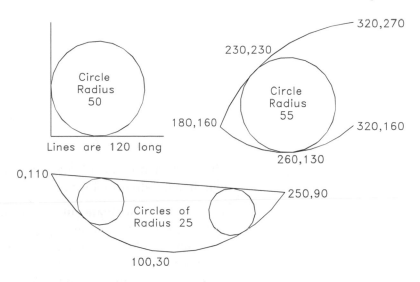

Fig. 2.30 Exercises 6, 7 and 8

9. Figure 2.31. Construct the four Multilines to the details given with each drawing.

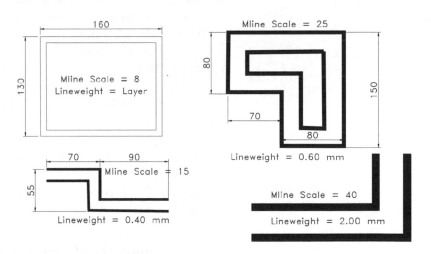

Fig. 2.31 Exercise 9

Chapter 3

Accurate construction of drawings

Introduction

There are a number of methods of operating AutoCAD 2000 by which accurate drawings can be constructed. These involve:

1. **Absolute coordinate entry:** The *entering* at the Command line, of the coordinate positions of points of each object as it is drawn. Examples of absolute coordinate entry have already been given in Chapter 1.
2. **Relative coordinate entry:** The *entering* at the Command line, of the coordinate points of the relative position of the next point to the last point of an object as it is added to a drawing.
3. **Tracking:** *Entering* the coordinate position of an end point, followed by *dragging* the rubber band associated with tools such as **Line** and **Pline** in the direction in which the object is to be drawn, then *entering* the length of the object.
4. **Snap:** *Picking* snap positions to ensure accurate x,y points on an object.
5. **Object Snaps:** Making use of object snaps by which the exact position along an object already on screen can be determined.
6. **AutoSnap:** Used in conjunction with object snaps to position objects accurately as to their position relative to previously drawn objects.
7. **Polar tracking:** To obtain accurate angular positions and lengths of objects.

Absolute coordinate entry (Fig. 3.1)

The x,y coordinates of each point on an object are *entered* at the Command line in response to the prompts appearing when a tool is called. For example; both x,y coordinates of the ends of lines, the x,y coordinates of centres of circles, x,y coordinate points on an arc.

Several examples are given in Fig. 3.1. See also the worked examples in Chapter 1.

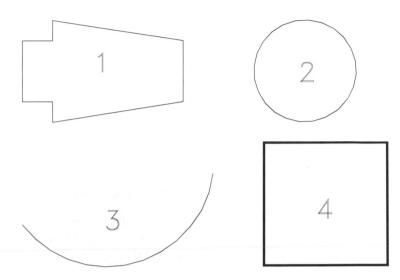

Fig. 3.1 Examples of drawing using **absolute coordinate entry**

Drawing 1

Command:_line Specify first point: *enter* 0,250 *right-click*
Specify next point or [Undo]: *enter* 30,250 *right-click*
Specify next point or [Undo]: *enter* 30,270 *right-click*
Specify next point or [Close/Undo]: *enter* 160,250 *right-click*
Specify next point or [Close/Undo]: *enter* 160,190 *right-click*
Specify next point or [Close/Undo]: *enter* 30,190 *right-click*
Specify next point or [Close/Undo]: *enter* 0,190 *right-click*
Specify next point or [Close/Undo]: *enter* c *right-click*
Command:

Drawing 2

**Command:_circle Specify center point for circle or [3P/2P/TTr
    (tan tan radius):** *enter* 280,220
Specify radius of circle or [Diameter]: *enter* 50 *right-click*
Command:

Drawing 3

Command:_arc Specify start point of arc or [CEnter]: *enter* 0,70
    right-click
Specify second point of arc or [CEnter/ENd]: *enter* 100,30 *right-click*
Specify end point of arc: *enter* 190,120 *right-click*
Command:

Drawing 4

Command:_pline Specify start point: *enter* 240,150 *right-click*
Specify next point or [Arc/Close/Halfwidth/Length/Undo/Width]:
    enter 360,150 *right-click*
Specify next point or [Arc/Close/Halfwidth/Length/Undo/Width]:
    enter 360,30 *right-click*
Specify next point or [Arc/Close/Halfwidth/Length/Undo/Width]:
    enter 240,30 *right-click*
Specify next point or [Arc/Close/Halfwidth/Length/Undo/Width]:
    enter c *right-click*
Command:

Relative coordinate entry

When constructing an outline the *x,y* coordinates of a start point are *entered* at the Command line and further points on the outline are constructed by *entering* the relative distance in terms of *x* and *y* to the start of each object as it is added to the outline. Relative coordinate entry always starts with @. Examples are given in Fig. 3.2.

Drawing 1

Command:_line Specify first point: *enter* 0,240 *right-click*
Specify next point or [Undo]: *enter* @30,30 *right-click*
Specify next point or [Undo]: *enter* @60,0 *right-click*
Specify next point or [Close/Undo]: *enter* @30,–30 *right-click*
Specify next point or [Close/Undo]: *enter* @0,–100 *right-click*
Specify next point or [Close/Undo]: *enter* @–40,0 *right-click*
Specify next point or [Close/Undo]: *enter* @–10,–30 *right-click*
Specify next point or [Close/Undo]: *enter* @–20,0 *right-click*
Specify next point or [Close/Undo]: *enter* @–10,30 *right-click*
Specify next point or [Close/Undo]: *enter* @–40,0 *right-click*
Specify next point or [Close/Undo]: *enter* c *right-click*
Command:

Drawing 2

Command:_pline Specify start point: *enter* 170,270 *right-click*
Specify next point or [Arc/Close/Halfwidth/Length/Undo/Width]:
    enter w *right-click*
Specify starting width <0>: *enter* 2 *right-click*
Specify ending width <2>: *right-click*
Specify next point or [Arc/Close/Halfwidth/Length/Undo/Width]:
    enter @180,0 *right-click*
Specify next point or [Arc/Close/Halfwidth/Length/Undo/Width]:
    enter @0,–160 *right-click*

Specify next point or [Arc/Close/Halfwidth/Length/Undo/Width]: *enter* @–40,0 *right-click*
Specify next point or [Arc/Close/Halfwidth/Length/Undo/Width]: *enter* @0,–30 *right-click*
Specify next point or [Arc/Close/Halfwidth/Length/Undo/Width]: *enter* @–100,0 *right-click*
Specify next point or [Arc/Close/Halfwidth/Length/Undo/Width]: *enter* @0,30 *right-click*
Specify next point or [Arc/Close/Halfwidth/Length/Undo/Width]: *enter* @–40,0 *right-click*
Specify next point or [Arc/Close/Halfwidth/Length/Undo/Width]: *enter* c *right-click*
Command:

Drawing 3:

Command:_line Specify first point: *enter* 0,180 *right-click*
Specify next point or [Undo]: *enter* @40<45 *right-click*
Specify next point or [Undo]: *enter* @180<350 *right-click*
Specify next point or [Close/Undo]: *enter* @0,-30 *right-click*
Specify next point or [Close/Undo]: *enter* @180<190 *right-click*
Specify next point or [Close/Undo]: *enter* @40<135 *right-click*
Specify next point or [Close/Undo]: *enter* c *right-click*
Command:

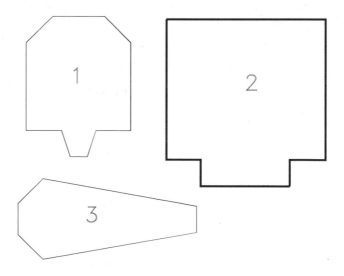

Fig. 3.2 Examples of drawing using **relative coordinate entry**

Notes

1. It is important to understand that, whether working in absolute or relative coordinate units methods of construction:

positive X units are horizontally to the right
negative X are horizontally to the left
positive Y units are vertically upwards
negative Y units are vertically downwards.

2. When constructing from point to point with the aid of the relative coordinate units method, coordinate figures must be preceded by @.
3. When using the relative coordinate units method of construction, angle figures must be preceded by <. The default direction in which angles in degrees are measured in AutoCAD 2000 is counter-clockwise (anticlockwise) as shown in Fig. 3.3.

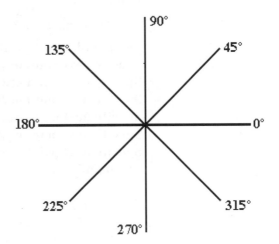

Fig. 3.3 Counter-clockwise (the default) measurement of angles

Tracking

When working with tools such as **Line** and **Polyline** as each **Specify next point** is seen at the Command line, a rubber-banded line positioned at the last point can be *dragged* in the drawing area of the AutoCAD 2000 window. If a figure is *entered* at the Command line, followed by a *right-click* as the rubber-band line is *dragged* in any direction, the line becomes fixed at the length of the number *entered*. Figure 4.4 shows examples of simple constructions created using the tracking method.

Drawing 1

Left-click on the **ORTHO** button in the Status bar to set **Ortho** on. Or press the key **F8** which will also set **Ortho** on or off. When **Ortho** is set on, the rubber band of **Line** or **Pline** is restrained to move either horizontally or vertically.

Command:_line Specify first point: *enter* 0,260 *right-click*
Specify next point or [Undo]: *drag* the rubber band to the right and *enter* 180 *right-click*
Specify next point or [Undo]: *drag* the rubber band vertically down and *enter* 100 *right-click*
Specify next point or [Close/Undo]: *drag* the rubber band to the left and *enter* 60 *right-click*
Specify next point or [Close/Undo]: *drag* the rubber band upwards and *enter* 30 *right-click*
Specify next point or [Close/Undo]: *drag* the rubber band to the left and *enter* 60 *right-click*
Specify next point or [Close/Undo]: *drag* the rubber band down and *enter* 30 *right-click*
Specify next point or [Close/Undo]: *drag* the rubber band to the left and *enter* 60 *right-click*
Specify next point or [Close/Undo]: *drag* the rubber band to the right and *enter* c *right-click*
Command:

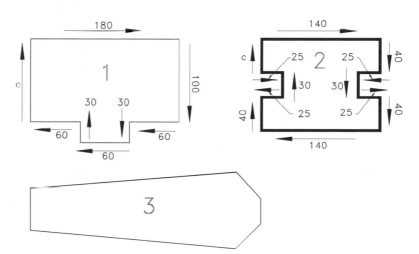

Fig. 3.4 Examples of drawing using **tracking**

Drawing 2

Using the same method and with the aid of the **Polyline** tool set to **Width** of **2**. Construct the outline **Drawing 2**.

Drawing 3

This example uses a combination of the relative coordinate units methods and tracking. With **Ortho** set on:

Command:_line Specify first point: *enter* 0,80 *right-click*
Specify next point or [Undo]: *drag* down and *enter* 50 *right-click*
Specify next point or [Undo]: *enter* @250<355

Specify next point or [Close/Undo]: *drag* upwards and *enter* 30 *right-click*
Specify next point or [Close/Undo]: *enter* c *right-click*
Command:

With Snap set

Fig. 3.5 Calling **Settings...** from the *right-click* menu of **OSNAP**

Right-click on any one of the buttons along the Status bar. The right-click menu shown in Fig. 3.5 appears. *Left-click* on **Settings...** in the menu. The **Drafting Settings** dialogue box appears on screen. *Left-click* on the **Snap and Grid** tab of the dialogue box. Make settings as shown in Fig. 3.6. Note in particular the check circle against **Grid Snap** is set on (dot in the circle). Note **Snap** is set to 5 (X) and 5 (Y).

Fig. 3.6 The **Grid and Snap** settings from the **Drafting Settings** dialogue box

When **Snap** is set in this manner, when the cursor is moved under mouse control, the cursor snaps from each 5 units position to the next – either horizontally or vertically. With **Snap** set to 5, the cursor will not move smoothly across the screen, but jumps across each 5 unit area.

With **Snap** set in this way, coordinate points can be *picked* on the screen and providing the coordinate numbers at the left-hand end of the Status bar are followed, accurate drawings can be constructed providing all measurements are based in multiples of 5 units. Or, a start point for an outline can be *picked* from a snap point and the remainder of the outline constructed using one of the methods outlined above.

Snap can be toggled on/off either with *left-clicks* on the **SNAP** button in the Status bar or by pressing the **F9** key of the keyboard.

Grid

Figure 1.10 (page 5) shows the AutoCAD 2000 window with a pattern of grid points showing at 10 units intervals both horizontally and vertically. Grid can be set on either by pressing the key **F7**, which toggles **Grid** on/off, or by a *left-click* on the **GRID** button in the Status bar, which also toggles **Grid** on/off.

In this book most drawings are based on an AutoCAD 2000 window set to **Limits** 0,0 and 420,297. Setting **Grid** smaller than 10 in this window will cause the drawing area to be too cluttered with grid points. **Grid** can be set as seen from the **Drafting Settings** dialogue box (Fig. 3.6).

Fig. 3.7 The buttons in the Status bar

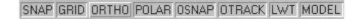

Object Snaps (Osnaps) and AutoSnap

To make full use of the **Object Snaps** feature, the **OSNAP** button in the Status bar should be set on with a *left-click* which 'pushes' the button in. In Fig. 3.7 the **OSNAP** button is set on.

Fig. 3.8 Calling **Options** from the right-click menu in the Command window

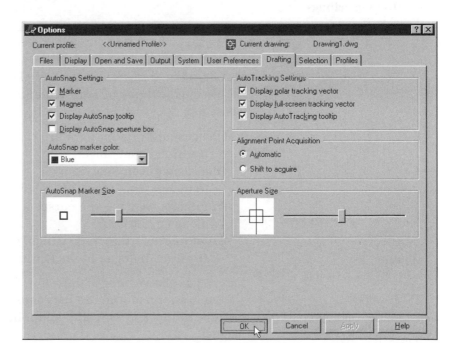

Fig. 3.9 **AutoSnap** settings in the **Options** dialogue box

Right-click with the cursor positioned in the Command window. A right-click menu appears (Fig. 3.8). In the menu *left-click* on **Options...**. The **Options** dialogue box appears. In the dialogue box *left-click* on the **Drafting** tab and in the **Drafting** dialogue which then appears, make settings as shown in Fig. 3.9. These settings ensure that the **AutoSnap** feature is fully on.

Now call the **Drafting Settings** dialogue box back on screen. *Left-click* on the **Object Snaps** tab, followed by setting all the **Object Snap Modes** on as indicated in Fig. 3.10 (ticks in their check boxes).

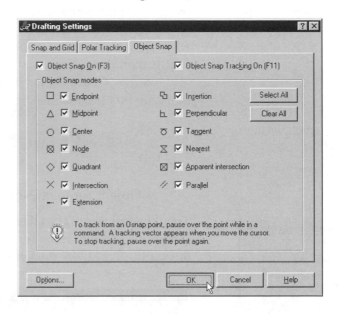

Fig. 3.10 Setting **Object Snaps** in the **Drafting Settings** dialogue box

When **OSNAP** is set on – either with a *left-click* on the **OSNAP** button in the Status bar or pressing key **F3**, full use can be made of the various features of both **AutoSnap** and **Object Snap** systems. These are:

> **Object snap/AutoSnap** tooltip showing the name of the selected position on an object.
>
> **Object snap/AutoSnap** marker – an icon which varies according to the position along the selected object.
>
> **AutoSnap** magnet – the cursor locks onto the position selected along an object.
>
> **AutoSnap** aperture box which can be varied in size in the **Drafting** dialogue of the **Options** dialogue box.

Figure 3.11 shows three of these four features. The Magnet cannot be shown in an illustration. In the example given in Fig. 3.11 the snap features are locked onto the endpoint of a line by the AutoSnap magnet.

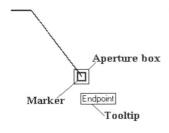

Fig. 3.11 The features of **Object snap/AutoSnap**

An example of using Object snaps/AutoSnaps

Figure 3.12 shows an example of the construction of outlines involving the use of snaps. After drawing the two circles and the right-hand vertical line, other lines were added by determining the exact positions of further lines on the existing objects by having both **Object snaps** and **AutoSnap** set on as described above.

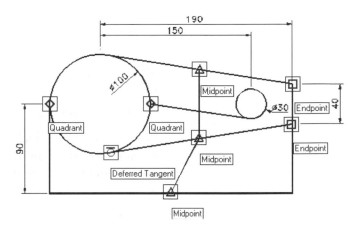

Fig. 3.12 An example of using **Object snaps/AutoSnap**

Figure 3.13 is another example which includes the **Center** tooltip of the **Osnaps/AutoSnap** which is not included in Fig. 3.12.

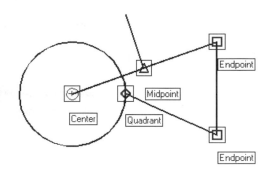

Fig. 3.13 Another example of the use of **Osnaps/AutoSnaps**

Notes

1. If the **AutoSnap** features are turned off in the **Drafting** dialogue of the **Options** dialogue box, only the **Osnap** marker and tooltip will be displayed at the selected point along an object providing **OSNAP** is set on (button in Status bar).
2. When an Osnap marker and tooltip are displayed at a selected point, pressing the **Tab** key of the keyboard repeatedly will cycle the marker icons and tooltips on that object – for example – pressing **Tab** when selecting an endpoint of a line the Osnap markers will cycle through midpoint, the other endpoint, nearest

etc. Pressing **Tab** when selecting a quadrant on a circle, will cycle through center, nearest, each quadrant in turn.

3. If desired, abbreviations for the snap points, along an object can be used. Among those most commonly in use:

> **end** – endpoint
> **mid** – midpoint
> **cen** – center
> **qua** – quadrant
> **int** – intersection
> **tan** – tangent
> **nea** – nearest
> **per** – perpendicular

An example would be:

> **Command:_line Select first point:** *enter* end *right-click*
> **of** *pick* the end of an object on screen
> **Specify next point or [Undo]:** *enter* mid *right-click*
> **of** *pick* near the middle of another object on screen

And so on from object to object using abbreviations for the osnap points.

Polar Tracking

Call the **Drafting Settings** dialogue box to screen, *left-click* on the **Polar Tracking** tab and make settings for **Polar Tracking** as shown in Fig. 3.14.

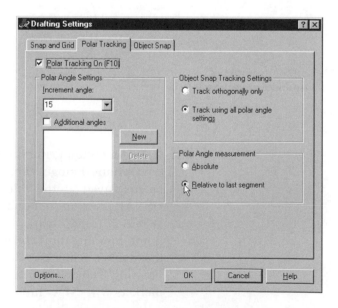

Fig. 3.14 **Polar Tracking** settings in the **Drafting Settings** dialogue box

Polar Tracking can be toggled on/of either with *left-clicks* on the **POLAR** button in the Status bar or by pressing the key **F10** of the keyboard. When set on, in addition to the **AutoSnap** features appearing during the addition of objects to a drawing, the **Polar Tracking** tooltip appears. This occurs when the rubber band attached to the last selected point is *dragged* at angles as set in the **Polar Tracking** section of **Drafting Settings**. Figure 3.15 gives examples of a variety of **Polar Tracking** tooltips at a variety of angles. Note the distance from the last selected point is given in addition within the tooltip. This distance varies as the object is *dragged* to a new position.

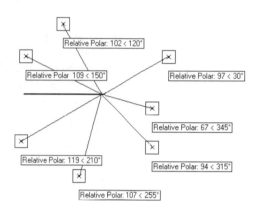

Fig. 3.15 **Polar Tracking –** tooltips

Notes

1. Any or all of the features described in this chapter can be used in conjunction with one another when a drawing is being constructed on screen.
2. When using **Polar Tracking**, if a figure for the length of a line or pline is *entered* at the keyboard, followed by a *right-click* the line will appear on screen at the angle shown in the tooltip and the *entered* length long.
3. When using the **AutoSnap** features, it is possible to *enter* figures for a distance and angle as the cursor is moved under mouse control. Figure 3.16 shows the tooltip from an **Endpoint**. If new figures for length and angle are *entered* when such a tooltip is showing, the line assumes its *entered* length and angle. For example, if instead of the **71 < 45** showing in Fig. 3.26 being accepted, new figures such as **100 < 40** are *entered,* the line will automatically appear on screen at the new line and angle length. But remember the *entered* angle will be relative to the line from which the length and angle are being *entered*.
4. **Polar Tracking** can be set to other angles if required.

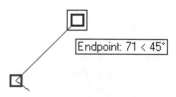

Fig. 3.16 An example of length and angle included in an **Endpoint** tooltip

5. When working with **Osnaps**, **AutoSnap** and **Polar tracking**, the setting of the **Snap** interval may be largely ignored. The three tools take precedence over **Snap**

An example of Polar Tracking (Fig. 3.17)

With **POLAR** set on, and using the tooltip to inform of the direction of the line, start at 80,110:

Command:_line Select first point: *enter* 80,110 *right-click*
Select next point or [Undo]: *drag* the cursor vertically upwards and *enter* 80 *right-click*
Select next point or [Undo]: *drag* the cursor until the tooltip shows an angle of 315 and *enter* 40 *right-click*
Select next point or [Undo]: *drag* the cursor until the tooltip shows an angle of 300 and *enter* 100 *right-click*
Select next point or [Undo]: *drag* the cursor until the tooltip shows an angle of 30 and *enter* 100 *right-click*
Select next point or [Undo]: *drag* the cursor until the tooltip shows an angle of 315 and *enter* 40 *right-click*

And continue in this manner, using the angle shown in the Polar tool tip, but *entering* the length of each line as the work proceeds. Remember the angle is relative to the last line. Some of the tooltips are shown in Fig. 3.17.

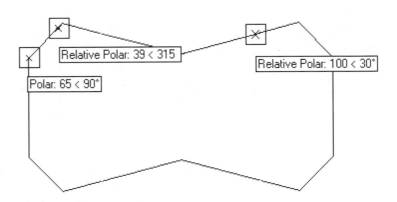

Fig. 3.17 An example of using **Polar Tracking**

Questions

1. What is the difference between drawing an outline using the **absolute coordinate entry** method and using the **Relative coordinate entry** method?

2. When should an **X** coordinate figure be negative, when *entering* x,y coordinates?

3. When should a **Y** coordinate figure be negative, when *entering x,y* coordinates?
4. In which direction are angles measured by default in AutoCAD 2000? Call the **Drafting Units** dialogue box to screen. Can you see how to change the direction of measuring angles in the dialogue box?
5. How is **Snap** set?
6. Can you name the four parts of **AutoSnap** when all features are in action?
7. In the Status bar there is a button named **OTRACK**. Have you tried setting it on? What is its action?
8. What do you believe is the quickest way to call the **Options** dialogue box to screen?
9. What is a right-click menu?
10. What are the abbreviations for the osnaps: Endpoint; Midpoint; Tangent; Nearest; Perpendicular?

Exercises

When constructing the answers to these exercises start by loading your template. If you haven't created your own template file, use the **acadiso.dwt** template.

Make use of what you consider to be the most appropriate method of accurate construction method when producing the drawings in answer to the exercises.

1. Construct the outline given in Fig. 3.18

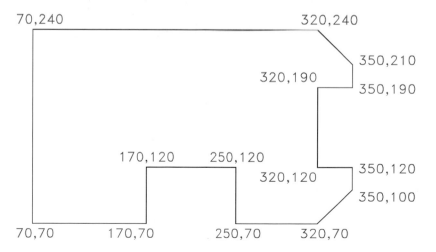

Fig. 3.18 Exercise 1

2. Construct the outline given in Fig. 3.29

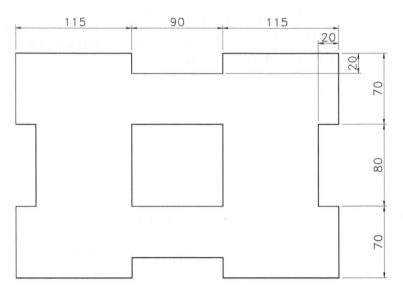

Fig. 3.19 Exercise 2

3. With the aid of the **Line** (or **Polyline**), **Circle** and **Arc** tools construct the drawing given in Fig. 3.20.

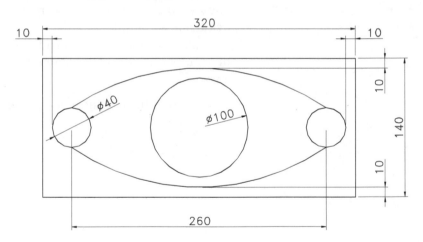

Fig. 3.20 Exercise 3

4. Construct the drawing given in Fig. 3.21.

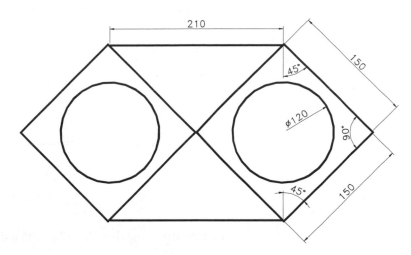

Fig. 3.21 Exercise 4

5. Construct the arrow outline given in Fig. 3.22.

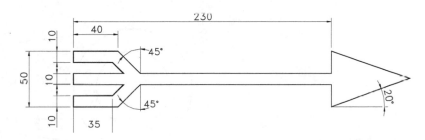

Fig. 3.22 Exercise 5

6. Construct the drawing Fig. 3.23 with the aid of the tools **Line** (or **Polyline**), **Circle** and **Arc**.

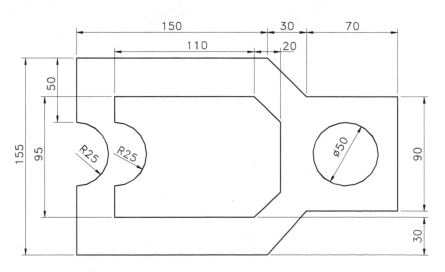

Fig. 3.23 Exercise 6

7. With the aid of **Line** (or **Polyline**), **Circle** and **Arc**, construct the drawing given in Fig. 3.24.

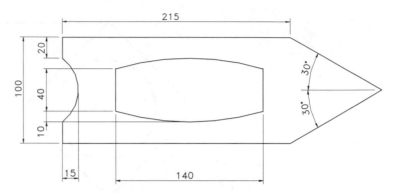

Fig. 3.24 Exercise 7

8. Construct the drawing Fig. 3.25 using the **Circle** and **Polyline** tools.

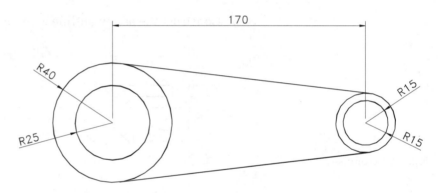

Fig. 3.25 Exercise 8

Chapter 4

2D drawing tools

The Draw tools

The **Draw** tools can be selected either from the **Draw** toolbar, where they are held in the form of tool icons, or from the **Draw** pull-down menu which is brought on screen with a *left-click* on **Draw** in the menu bar. The **Draw** toolbar is usually *docked* against the left-hand side of the AutoCAD 2000 window, unless an operator has changed the default AutoCAD 2000 window layout.

Figure 4.1 shows the tool icons in the **Draw** toolbar, including those from the **Insert Block** flyout, together with the name of the tools in the **Draw** pull-down menu.

Throughout this book, when the use of any tool is being described, an illustration showing the four methods of calling the tool will be included – from a toolbar, from a pull-down menu, by *entering* the tool name or its abbreviation at the Command line.

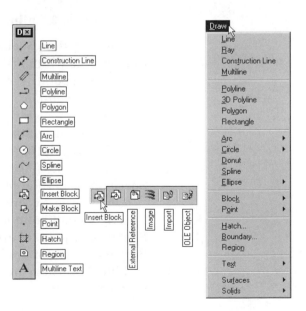

Fig. 4.1 The tools from the **Draw** toolbar and from the **Draw** pull-down menu

Not all of the **Draw** tools will be described in this chapter. The **Line**, **Polyline**, **Arc** and **Circle** tools have been briefly described in earlier chapters. More details about using the **Polyline** are given below. The tools **Construction Line**, **Hatch**, **Multiline Text**, **Insert Block** (and the tools on its flyout), **Make Block** and **Region** are best described in later chapters.

The Polyline tool

To call the **Polyline** tool, either *left-click* on its name in the **Draw** pull-down menu, or *left-click* on its tool icon in the **Draw** toolbar, or *enter* **pl** or **pline** at the Command line (Fig. 4.2)

Example 1 – pline arc (Figure 4.3, drawing 1)

Command:_pline Specify first point: *pick* 0,210
Current line width is 0
Specify next point or [Arc/Close/Halfwidth/Length/Undo/Width]: *enter* a *right-click*
Specify end point of arc or [Angle/CEnter/CLose/Direction/Halfwidth/ Line/Radius/Second pt/Undo/Width]: *enter* s *right-click*
Specify second point on arc: *pick* 80,260
Specify end point of arc: *pick* 190,210
Specify end point of arc or [Angle/CEnter/CLose/Direction/Halfwidth/ Line/Radius/Second pt/Undo/Width]: *right-click*
Command:

Example 2 – pline arc (Figure 4.3, drawing 2)

Command:_pline Specify first point: *pick* 0,130
Current line width is 0
Specify next point or [Arc/Close/Halfwidth/Length/Undo/Width]: *enter* w *right-click*
Specify starting width <0>: *enter* 1 *right-click*
Specify ending width <1>: *enter* 10 *right-click*
Specify next point or [Arc/Close/Halfwidth/Length/Undo/Width]: *enter* a *right-click*
Specify end point of arc or [Angle/CEnter/CLose/Direction/Halfwidth/ Line/Radius/Second pt/Undo/Width]: *enter* s *right-click*
Specify second point on arc: *pick* 90,170
Specify end point of arc: *pick* 220,130
Specify end point of arc or [Angle/CEnter/CLose/Direction/Halfwidth/ Line/Radius/Second pt/Undo/Width]: *right-click*
Command:

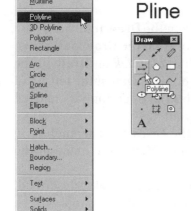

Fig. 4.2 Methods of calling the **Polyline** tool

Example 3 – pline arc (Figure 4.3, drawing 3)

Command:_pline Specify first point: *pick* 0,50
Current line width is 0
Specify next point or [Arc/Close/Halfwidth/Length/Undo/Width]: *enter* w *right-click*
Specify starting width <0>: *right-click*
Specify ending width <0>: *enter* 20 *right-click*
Specify next point or [Arc/Close/Halfwidth/Length/Undo/Width]: *enter* a *right-click*
Specify end point of arc or [Angle/CEnter/CLose/Direction/Halfwidth/Line/Radius/Second pt/Undo/Width]: *enter* s *right-click*
Specify second point on arc: *pick* 110,100
Specify end point of arc: *pick* 215,50
Specify end point of arc or [Angle/CEnter/CLose/Direction/Halfwidth/Line/Radius/Second pt/Undo/Width]: *enter* l *right-click*
Specify next point or [Arc/Close/Halfwidth/Length/Undo/Width]: *pick* 340,50
Specify next point or [Arc/Close/Halfwidth/Length/Undo/Width]: *right-click*
Command:

Example 4 – pline arc (Figure 4.3, drawing 4)

Command:_pline Specify first point: *pick* 345,260
Current line width is 0
Specify next point or [Arc/Close/Halfwidth/Length/Undo/Width]: *enter* w *right-click*
Specify starting width <0>: *right-click*
Specify ending width <0>: *enter* 25 *right-click*

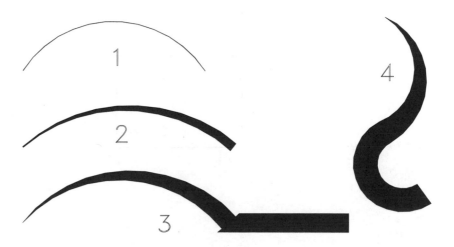

Fig. 4.3 Examples of polyline arcs

Specify next point or [Arc/Close/Halfwidth/Length/Undo/Width]:
   enter a *right-click*
Specify end point of arc or [Angle/CEnter/CLose/Direction/Halfwidth/
   Line/Radius/Second pt/Undo/Width]: *enter* s *right-click*
Specify second point on arc: *pick* 380,200
Specify end point of arc: *pick* 345,140
Specify end point of arc or [Angle/CEnter/CLose/Direction/Halfwidth/
   Line/Radius/Second pt/Undo/Width]: *pick* 385,75
Specify next point or [Arc/Close/Halfwidth/Length/Undo/Width]:
   right-click
Command:

Notes (Fig. 4.4)

1. If a mistake is made while constructing a pline, the **Undo** prompt
   undoes the error.
2. If the **Close** response of polyline is used a polyline which is
   partially open is closed (Drawings **1** and **2**).
3. To draw a circle using **Polyline** use the **Arc** prompt to construct a
   semicircle and the **Close** prompt to complete the circle (Drawing **3**).
4. The plines in Fig. 4.3 on page 53 are filled with whatever colour is
   current when the pline is drawn. If the set variable **FILL** is set off,
   only the outlines of plines will be seen on screen. To turn **FILL** off:

Command: *enter* fill *right-click*
Enter mode [ON/OFF] <ON>: *enter* off *right-click*
Command:

And then when plines are drawn they appear as in the examples
Fig. 4.5.

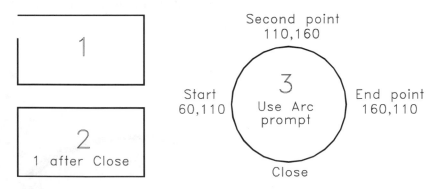

Fig. 4.4 Notes on **Polyline**

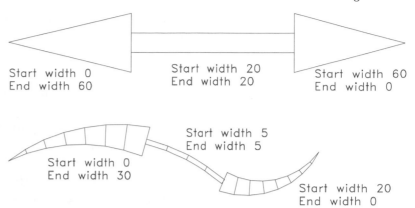

Fig. 4.5 Examples of plines
with **FILL** set off

The Polygon tool

To call the **Polygon** tool, either *left-click* on its name in the **Draw**
pull-down menu, or *left-click* on its tool icon in the **Draw** toolbar, or
enter **pol** or **polygon** at the Command line (Fig. 4.6).

Examples – polygon (Fig. 4.7)

Figure 4.7 shows a number of polygons created with the tool. The
radius of each of the polygons shown in that illustration is 60.

Command:_polygon Enter number of sides <4>: *enter* 5 *right-
click*
Specify center of polygon or [Edge]: *pick* 60,230
**Enter an option [Inscribed in circle/Circumscribed about circle]
<I>:** *right-click*

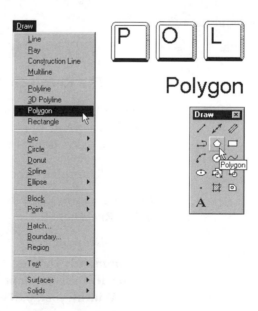

Fig. 4.6 Methods of calling the
Polygon tool

Specify radius of circle: *enter* 60 *right-click*
Command:

Notes

1. If the response to the prompt **Specify center of polygon or [Edge]:** is e (Edge), the next response will be **Specify first point of edge:** followed by **Specify second point of edge:**. When both ends of the edge have been *picked* or *entered* as coordinates, the polygon appears.
2. As can be seen in Fig. 4.7, if the **Inscribed in circle** option is chosen, the angles of the polygon touch the circle. If the **Circumscribed about circle** option is chosen the edges of the polygon touch the circle.

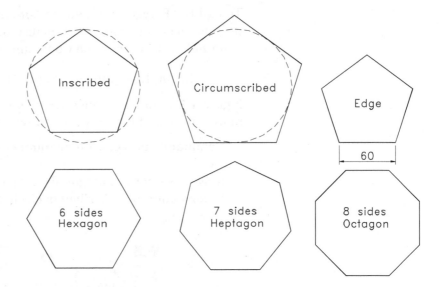

Fig. 4.7 Examples of the use of the **Polygon** tool

The Rectangle tool

To call the **Rectangle** tool, either *left-click* on its name in the **Draw** pull-down menu, or *left-click* on its tool icon in the **Draw** toolbar, or *enter* **rec** or **rectang** at the Command line (Fig. 4.8).

Examples – rectangle (Fig. 4.9)

Figure 4.9 shows four examples of outlines constructed with the aid of the **Rectangle** tool.

Drawing 1

Command:_rectang
Specify first corner point or [Chamfer/Elevation/Fillet/Thickness/ Width]: *pick* 0,270

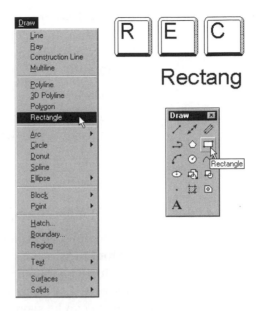

Fig. 4.8 Methods of calling the **Rectangle** tool

Specify other corner point: *pick* 160,260
Command:

Drawing 2

Command:_rectang
**Specify first corner point or [Chamfer/Elevation/Fillet/Thickness/
Width]:** *enter c right-click*
Specify first chamfer distance for rectangles <0>: *enter* 15 *right-click*
Specify second chamfer distance for rectangles <0>: *right-click*

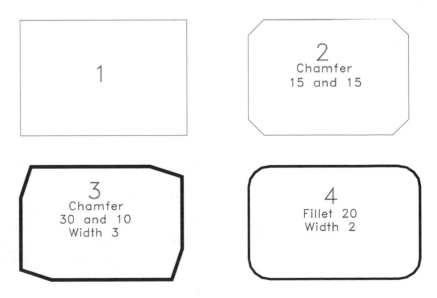

Fig. 4.9 Examples of the use of the **Rectangle** tool

Specify first corner point or [Chamfer/Elevation/Fillet/Thickness/Width]: *pick* 220,270
Specify other corner point: *pick* 370,160
Command:

Drawing 3

Set chamfer distances to 30 and 10, then *enter* **3** for the **Width**, followed by *picking* two points for the corners of the rectangle.

Drawing 4

Set **Fillet radius** to 20 and **Width** to **2**.

Another example – rectangles (Fig. 4.10)

If the two prompts of the **Rectangle** Command line sequence **Elevation** and **Thickness** are used, the resulting rectangles are 3D (three-dimensional) model drawings. If the resulting drawings are placed in one of the 3D Isometric viewing points, the 3D aspect of the rectangles can be seen. See Fig. 4.10. An Isometric view can be set with a *left-click* on **View** in the menu bar, followed by another on **3D Views** in the resulting pull-down menu.

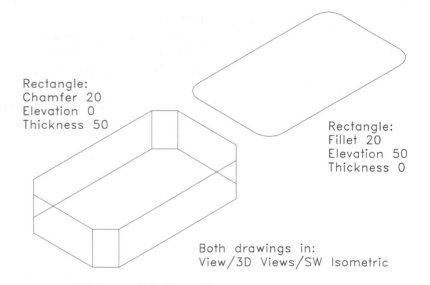

Rectangle:
Chamfer 20
Elevation 0
Thickness 50

Rectangle:
Fillet 20
Elevation 50
Thickness 0

Both drawings in:
View/3D Views/SW Isometric

Fig. 4.10 Isometric views of rectangles constructed using **Elevation** and **Thickness** prompts

The Spline tool

To call the **Spline** tool, either *left-click* on its name in the **Draw** pull-down menu, or *left-click* on its tool icon in the **Draw** toolbar, or *enter* **spl** or **spline** at the Command line (Fig. 4.11).

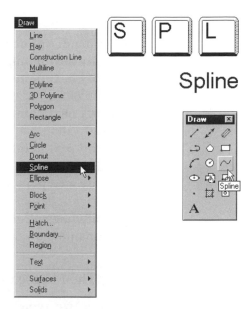

Fig. 4.11 Methods of calling the **Spline** tool

Examples – spline (Fig. 4.12)

Drawing 1

Command:_spline Specify first point or [Object]: *pick* 0,200
Specify next point: *pick* 90,270
Specify next point or [Close/Fit tolerance]<start tangent>: *pick* 170,200
Specify next point or [Close/Fit tolerance]<start tangent>: *pick* 260,270
Specify next point or [Close/Fit tolerance]<start tangent>: *pick* 350,200
Specify next point or [Close/Fit tolerance]<start tangent>: *right click*
Specify start tangent: *right-click*
Specify end tangent: *right-click*
Command:

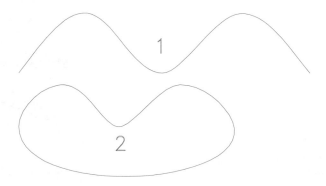

Fig. 4.12 Examples of the use of the **Spline** tool

Drawing 2:

Command:_spline Specify first point or [Object]: *pick* 0,80
Specify next point: *pick* 60,130
Specify next point or [Close/Fit tolerance]<start tangent>: *pick* 120,80
Specify next point or [Close/Fit tolerance]<start tangent>: *pick* 190,130
Specify next point or [Close/Fit tolerance]<start tangent>: *pick* 260,80
Specify next point or [Close/Fit tolerance]<start tangent>: *enter* c *right-click*
Specify tangent: *pick* 0,20
Command:

The Ellipse tool

There are two types of ellipse possible in AutoCAD 2000 – the default type – a true ellipse and an ellipse which is a polyline. An advantage of using the second type of ellipse is that it can be acted upon by the tool **Polyline Edit** (**Pedit**), which, if required, can edit the width of the elliptical line (see page 208). Which ellipse is used depends upon the setting of the set variable **PELLIPSE**:

Command: *enter* pellipse *right-click*
Enter new value for PELLIPSE <0>: *enter* 1 *right-click*
Command:

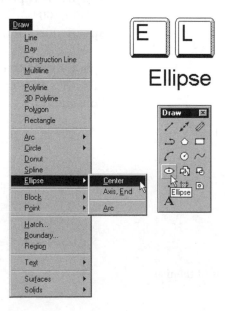

Fig. 4.13 Methods of calling
the **Ellipse** tool

When set to 0 true ellipses will be drawn.

To call the **Ellipse** tool either *left-click* on its name in the **Draw** pull-down menu, *let-click* on its icon in the **Draw** toolbar, or *enter* **el** or **ellipse** at the Command line (Fig. 4.13).

Examples – ellipse (Fig. 4.14)

Drawing 1

Command:_ellipse
Specify axis endpoint of elliptical arc or [Center]: *pick* 20,230
Specify other endpoint of axis: *pick* 190,220
Specify distance to other axis or [Rotation]: *enter* 40 *right-click*
Command:

Drawing 2

Command:_ellipse
Specify axis endpoint of elliptical arc or [Center]: *enter* c *right-click*
Specify center of ellipse: *pick* 320,220
Specify endpoint of axis: *pick* 220,220
Specify distance to other axis or [Rotation]: *pick* 320,250
Command:

Drawing 3

Command:_ellipse
Specify axis endpoint of elliptical arc or [Center]: *pick* 20,100
Specify other endpoint of axis: *pick* 190,220
Specify distance to other axis or [Rotation]: *enter* r *right-click*
Specify rotation around major axis: *enter* 45 *right-click*
Command:

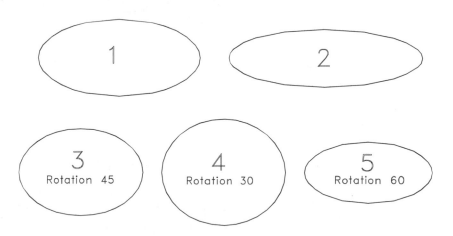

Fig. 4.14 Examples of the use of the **Ellipse** tool

Drawing 4

As **Drawing 3** but with **Rotation** *entered* as 30.

Drawing 5

As **Drawing 3** but with **Rotation** *entered* as 60.

Notes

1. The longest axis of an ellipse is its **major axis**. The smaller axis is its **minor axis**. See Fig. 4.15.
2. Ellipses can be regarded as circles which are viewed so as to see the full circle and then rotated on one of the diameters (major axis) so that, from the same viewing point the diameter at right angles to that of rotation (minor axis) becomes apparently shorter. In AutoCAD 2000 the angle through which the circle is rotated is the figure *entered* in response to the **Rotation** prompt.
3. Figure 4.15 shows these details – **Drawing 1** the two axes; **Drawings 2** and **3** the points in response to the **Ellipse** prompts; **Drawing 4** angles of rotation.

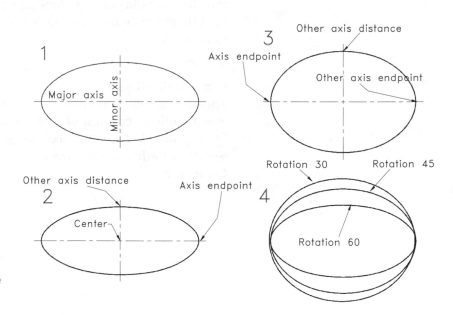

Fig. 4.15 Parts of an ellipse and the meaning of the **Ellipse** prompts

The Point tool

Before calling the tool choose a point style from the **Point Style** dialogue box (Fig. 4.16), which is called to screen by selecting **Point Style...** from the **Format** pull-down menu (Fig, 4.17). Most of the point styles are shown in Fig. 4.19.

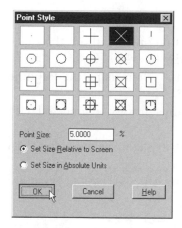

Fig. 4.16 The **Point Style** dialogue box

To call the **Point** tool, either *left-click* on its name in the **Draw** pull-down menu, or *left-click* on its tool icon in the **Draw** toolbar, or *enter* **po** or **point** at the Command line (Fig. 4.18).

After selecting the required point style, remembering to set the point size in the **Point Size:** box of the dialogue box, call the tool and the Command line will show:

Command:_point
Current point modes: PDMODE=2 PDSIZE=-10
Specify a point: *pick* or *enter* a coordinate
Command:

Notes

1. **PDMODE** is the number given to the position of the point style in the **Point Style** dialogue box, or a combination of the positions of 2 point styles. Thus **PDMODE=0** is a dot – the first of the point styles.

2. **PDSIZE** is the size *entered* in the dialogue box against **Point Size:**. A negative figure denotes a size in relative to the screen. A positive figure denotes a size in units.

Fig. 4.17 Calling **Point Style...** from the **Format** pull-down menu

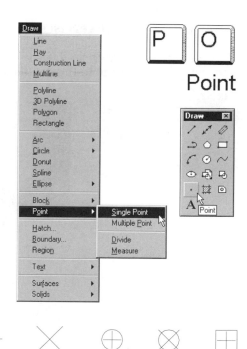

Fig. 4.18 Methods of calling the **Point** tool

Fig. 4.19 Point styles selected from the **Point Style** dialogue box

Questions

1. How can polylines be drawn in outline only, without the space between the outlines being coloured?
2. Have you tried the **Halfwidth** prompt when using the **Polyline** tool? If you have, what is the result?
3. Have you tried responding to the various prompts connected with drawing polyline arcs?
4. How many sides has a pentagon? A hexagon? A heptagon? An octagon?
5. Two types of ellipse can be drawn in AutoCAD 2000. What are they?
6. How can the types of ellipse be set?
7. What is the effect of using the **Rotation** prompt of the **Ellipse** Command line sequence?
8. What does **PDMODE=4** mean when using the **Point** tool?
9. What does **PDMODE=5** mean when using the **Point** tool?
10. What are the tool abbreviations for the following tools:

    Polyline; **Polygon**; **Rectangle**; **Spline**; **Ellipse**; **Point**?

Exercises

1. Figure 4.20 is a pline made up from two segments. Construct the pline to the details given with the drawing.

Pline:
Start width 25
End width 25
Start 170,290
End 170,218

Pline:
Start width 25
End width 0
Arc:
Start 150,230
Second 240,165
End110,125

Fig. 4.20 Exercise 1

2. Construct the two plines given in Fig. 4.21 to the details given with the drawing.

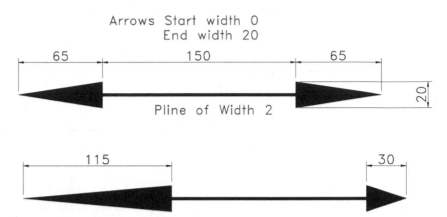

Fig. 4.21 Exercise 2

3. Figure 4.22 is a drawing of a metal plate. Construct the drawing using only the **Polyline** tool with **Width** set to **0.7**.

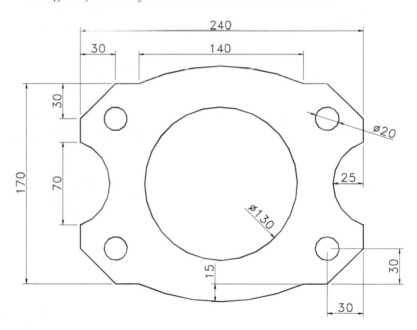

Fig. 4.22 Exercise 3

4. Figure 4.23 shows 6 hexagons surrounding a central hexagon. Construct the drawing with the aid of the **Polygon** tool.

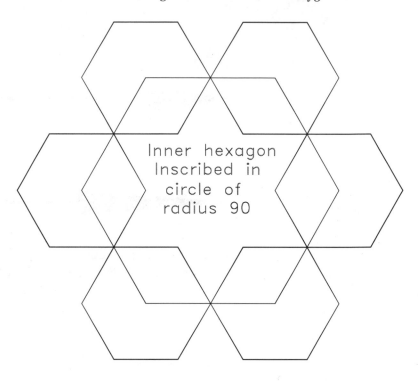

Inner hexagon
Inscribed in
circle of
radius 90

Fig. 4.23 Exercise 4

5. Figure 4.24 shows 4 ellipses all of the same major and minor axes lengths. Construct the given drawing to the sizes given with the drawing.

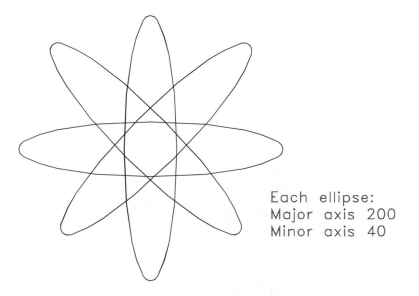

Each ellipse:
Major axis 200
Minor axis 40

Fig. 4.24 Exercise 5

6.   Figure 4.25 is a drawing of a plate with 4 circular holes and an elliptical hole cut through its surface. Make an accurate drawing of the plate to the sizes given with the drawing.

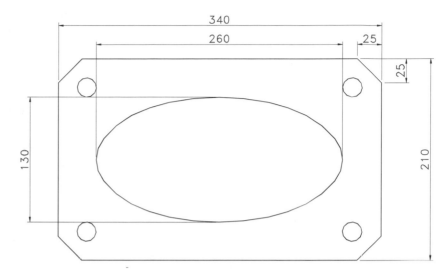

Fig. 4.25 Exercise 6

7.   Construct the drawing Fig. 4.26 to the sizes given with the drawing and using only the **Polyline** tool with **Width** set at **1**.

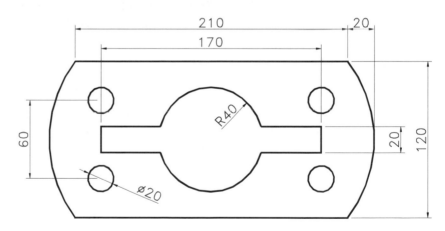

Fig. 4.26 Exercise 7

8.   The drawing Fig. 4.27 was constructed using the tools **Polygon**, **Ellipse**, **Circle** and **Rectangle** (Fillet 30). Making full use of osnap, make an accurate copy of the drawing.

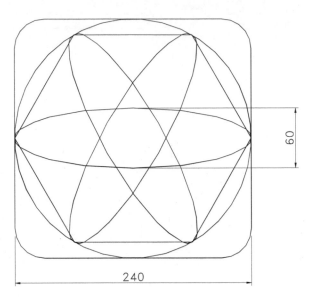

Fig. 4.27 Exercise 8

9.   Figure 4.28. The drawing has been constructed using **Polygon**, **Circle** and **Point**. Construct the given drawing to the sizes shown, selecting the point style from the **Point Style** dialogue box.

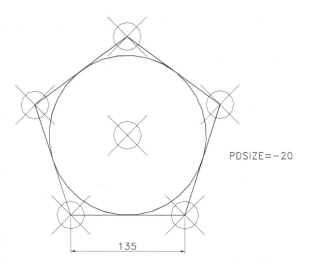

Fig. 4.28 Exercise 9

10. A revision exercise involving **Circle**, **Line** and the **osnap** tangent. Construct the drawing Fig. 4.29 to the sizes given with the drawing.

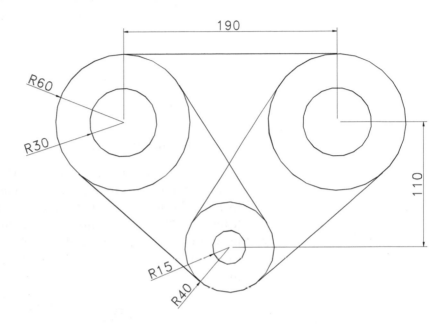

Fig. 4.29 Exercise 10

Chapter 5

The Modify tools

Introduction

The tools from the **Modify** toolbar are for the modification or editing of objects or groups of objects on screen. Figure 5.1 shows the tools in both the toolbar and the pull-down menu. Later in this book (Chapter 17) it will be shown that some of the **Modify** tools can be used for the modification of 3D solid drawing models, but for the time being, we are only concerned with their value in editing 2D drawings.

Fig. 5.1 The **Modify** toolbar and **Modify** pull-down menu

When AutoCAD 2000 is started, the **Modify** toolbar is usually *docked* against the **Draw** toolbar on the left-hand edge of the AutoCAD 2000 window. However, if an operator previously using the computer has changed its position, it may be found elsewhere or have to be called from the **Toolbar** *right-click* menu.

Note

The **Erase** tool was described in Chapter 2, so will not be included here. The **Modify** tool **Explode** is best left until later Chapters.

The Copy Object tool

For copying an object or objects in groups from one place on screen to another.

To call **Copy Object** either *left-click* on its tool icon in the **Modify** toolbar or on the name **Copy** in the **Modify** pull-down menu, or *enter* **cp** or **copy** at the Command line (Fig. 5.2)

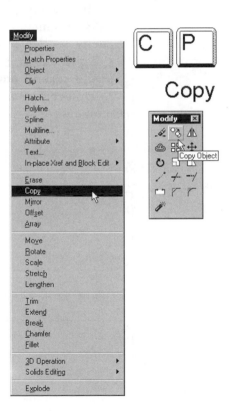

Fig. 5.2 Methods of calling **Copy Object**

Examples – copy (Fig. 5.3)

Drawing 1 and 2

Command:_copy Select objects: *pick* **1 found**
Select objects: *right-click*
Specify base point or displacement, or [Multiple]: *pick*
**Specify second point of displacement or <use first point as
    displacement>:** *pick*
Command:

Drawings 3 and 4

Command:_copy Select objects: *pick* **1 found**
Select objects: *right-click*
Specify base point or displacement, or [Multiple]: *enter* m *right-
    click*
Specify base point: *pick*
**Specify second point of displacement or <use first point as
    displacement>:** *pick*
**Specify second point of displacement or <use first point as
    displacement>:** *pick*
**Specify second point of displacement or <use first point as
    displacement>:** *pick*
**Specify second point of displacement or <use first point as
    displacement>:** *right-click*
Command:

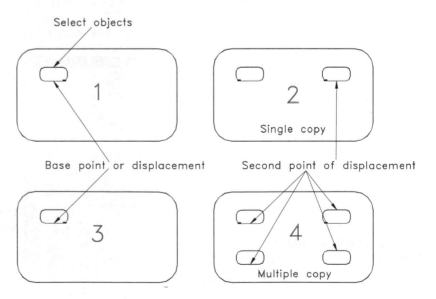

Fig. 5.3 Examples of the use of
Copy

The Mirror tool

To call **Mirror** either *left-click* on its tool icon in the **Modify** toolbar or on the name **Mirror** in the **Modify** pull-down menu, or *enter* **mi** or **mirror** at the Command line (Fig. 5.4)

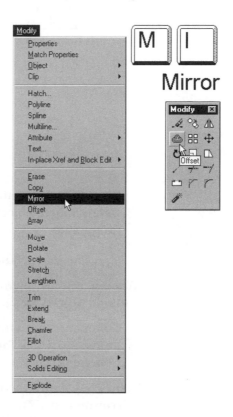

Fig.5.4 Methods of calling **Mirror**

Examples – mirror (Fig. 5.5)

Drawings 1 and 2

Command:_mirror Select objects *pick* **1 found**
Select objects: *right-click*
Specify first point on mirror line: *pick*
Specify second point on mirror line: *pick*
Delete source objects [Yes/No]: <N>: *right-click*
Command:

Drawings 3 and 4

Command:_mirror Select objects *enter* w (Window) *right-click*
Specify first corner: *pick* **Specify opposite corner:** *pick* **4 found**
Select objects: *right-click*
Specify first point on mirror line: *pick*

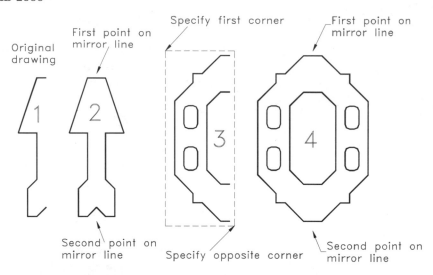

Fig. 5.5 Examples of using
Mirror

Specify second point on mirror line: *pick*
Delete source objects [Yes/No]: <N>: *right-click*
Command:

The set variable MIRRTEXT

When using the **Mirror** tool on text, care must be taken to set the variable **MIRRTEXT to** 0 or **1**. To set the variable:

Command: *enter* mirrtext *right-click*
Enter new value for MIRRTEXT <0>: *enter* 1 *right-click*
Command:

Figure 5.6 shows the results of each of these settings when using **Mirror** on text.

MIRRTEXT=1   I=TXƎTЯЯIM
MIᴚᴚ⊥EX⊥=I

Fig. 5.6 Examples of setting
the variable **MIRRTEXT**

MIRRTEXT=0   MIRRTEXT=0
MIRRTEXT=0

The Offset tool

To call **Offset** either *left-click* on its tool icon in the **Modify** toolbar or on the name **Offset** in the **Modify** pull-down menu, or *enter* **o** or **offset** at the Command line (Fig. 5.7).

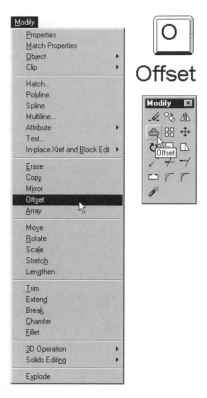

Fig.5.7 Methods of calling
Offset

Examples – offset (Fig. 5.8)

Each of the examples given in Fig. 5.8 have used the same procedure as follows:

Command:_offset
Specify offset distance or [Through] <0>: *enter* number *right-click*

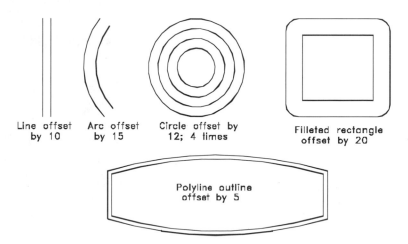

Fig. 5.8 Examples of using
Offset

Select object to offset or <exit>: *pick*
Specify point on side to offset: *pick*
Select object to offset or <exit>: *right-click*
Command:

Note

The **Through** response can be answered by *picking* 2 points on screen the distance apart by which the offset is to take place.

The Array tool

To call **Offset** either *left-click* on its tool icon in the **Modify** toolbar or on the name **Array** in the **Modify** pull-down menu, or *enter* **ar** or **array** at the Command line (Fig. 5.9).

Two types of array are possible:

Rectangular Array: In which objects or groups of objects are arrayed in parallel rows and columns.

Polar Arrays: In which objects or groups of objects are placed in a circular or part circular array around a central point.

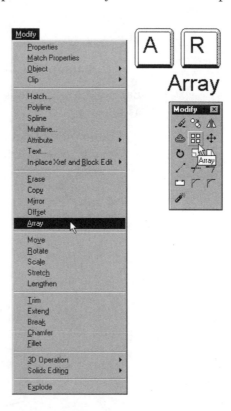

Fig. 5.9 Methods of calling
Array

Example – rectangular array (Fig. 5.10)

Construct **Drawing 1** which is a polyline, hence is a single closed object.

> **Command_array Select objects:** *pick*
> **Enter the type of array [Rectangular/Polar] <R>:** *right-click*
> **Enter the number of rows (---) <1>:** *enter* 4 *right-click*
> **Enter the number of columns (| | |) <1>:** *enter* 5 *right-click*
> **Enter the distance between rows or specify unit cell (---)** *enter* −70 *right-click*
> **Specify the distance between columns (| | |):** *enter* 80 *right-click*
> **Command:**

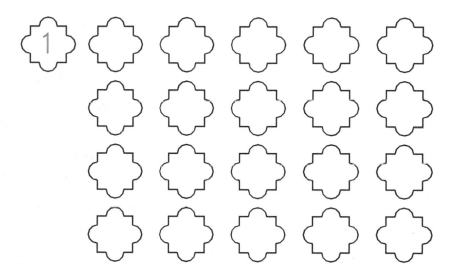

Fig. 5.10 An example of a Rectangular **Array**

Example – Polar array (Fig. 5.11)

Drawing **1** shows the objects to be arrayed.

> **Command_array Select objects:** *enter* w (window) *right-click*
> **Specify first corner:** *pick* **Specify opposite corner:** *pick* **3 found**
> **Select objects:** *right-click*
> **Enter the type of array [Rectangular/Polar] <R>:** *enter* p *right-click*
> **Specify center point of array:** *pick* or *enter* 170,160 *right-click*
> **Enter the number of items in the array:** *enter* 8 *right-click*
> **Specify the angle to fill (+=cw, −=ccw) <360>:** *right-click*
> **Rotate arrayed objects ? [Yes/No] <Y>:** *right-click*
> **Command:**

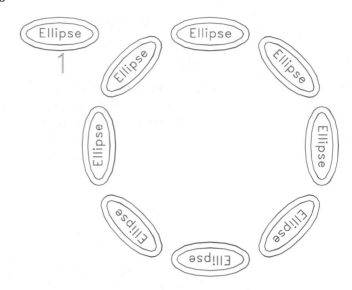

Fig. 5.11 An example of a
Polar **Array**

Second example – Polar array (Fig. 5.12)

Command_array Select objects: *enter* w (window) *right-click*
Specify first corner: *pick* **Specify opposite corner:** *pick* **3 found**
Select objects: *right-click*
Enter the type of array [Rectangular/Polar] <R>: *enter* p *right-click*
Specify center point of array: *pick* or *enter* 170,160 *right-click*
Enter the number of items in the array: *enter* 5 *right-click*
Specify the angle to fill (+=cw, –=ccw) <360>: *enter* –180 *right-click*
Rotate arrayed objects ? [Yes/No] <Y>: *enter* n *right-click*
Command:

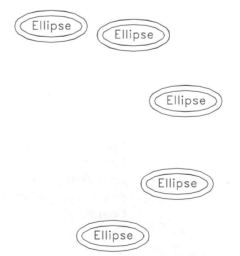

Fig. 5.12 A second example of
a Polar **Array**

Note

In this second example of a polar **Array** (Fig. 5.12), the angle to be filled with the array was given as −180. Because the default angle rotation in AutoCAD 2000 is counter clockwise, the negative figure ensures the rotation is clockwise.

The Move tool

To call **Move** either *left-click* on its tool icon in the **Modify** toolbar or on the name **Move** in the **Modify** pull-down menu, or *enter* **m** or **move** at the Command line (Fig. 5.13).

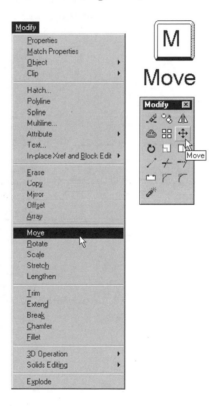

Fig. 5.13 Methods of calling **Move**

Example – move (Fig. 5.14)

In this example the main outline is a rectangle with corners filleted at 15. The object to be moved is made from four arcs in a closed polyline.

> **Command:_move Select objects:** *pick*
> **Select objects:** *pick*
> **Specify base point or displacement:** *pick* **Specify second point of displacement or <use first point as displacement>:** *pick*
> **Command:**

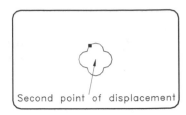

Fig. 5.14 An example of a
Move

The Rotate tool

To call **Rotate** either *left-click* on its tool icon in the **Modify** toolbar
or on the name **Rotate** in the **Modify** pull-down menu, or *enter* **ro** or
rotate at the Command line (Fig. 5.15).

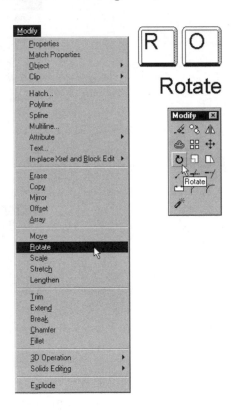

Fig. 5.15 Methods of calling
Rotate

Example – rotate (Fig. 5.16)

Drawing **1** of Fig. 5.16 is a polyline. Its arrow was drawn with start
width 25 and end width 0, followed by a circle of width 1. The
drawing is a single closed polyline.

Command_rotate
Current positive angle in UCS: ANGDIR=counterclockwise
     ANGBASE=0

Select objects: *pick* **1 found**
Select objects: *right-click*
Specify rotation angle or [Rotation]: *enter* 30 *right-click*
Command:

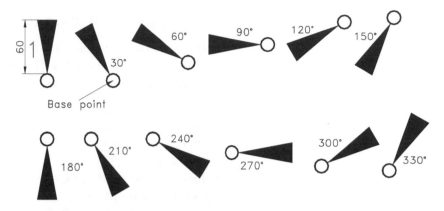

Fig. 5.16 Examples of **Rotate**

Note

Figure 5.16 shows the same object rotated through multiples of 30°
angles from 0° (or 360°) to 330°. If a negative number is given in
response to **Specify rotation angle** the rotation will be clockwise.

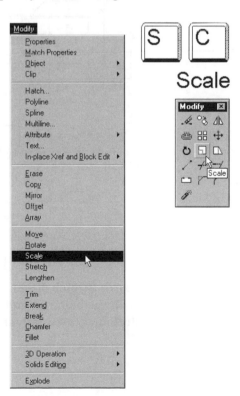

Fig. 5.17 Methods of calling
Scale

The Scale tool

To call **Scale** either *left-click* on its tool icon in the **Modify** toolbar or on the name **Scale** in the **Modify** pull-down menu, or *enter* **sc** or **scale** at the Command line (Fig. 5.17).

Example – scale (Fig. 5.18)

Drawing **1** is a drawing which is to be scaled to 0.5 size (drawing **3**); 1.25 (Drawing **4**) and **scale 1.5 (Drawing** 5). In each case the entries in response to prompts of the **Scale** Command line sequence are similar:

Command_scale
Select objects: *pick* top left of the drawing **Opposite corner:** *pick* **2 found**
Select objects: *right-click*
Specify base point: *pick*
Specify scale factor or [Reference]: *enter* 0.5 *right-click*
Command:

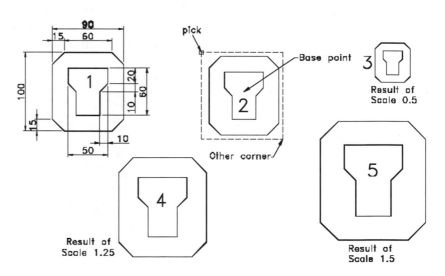

Fig. 5.18 Examples of **Scale**

The Stretch tool

To call **Stretch** either *left-click* on its tool icon in the **Modify** toolbar or on the name **Stretch** in the **Modify** pull-down menu, or *enter* **s** or **stretch** at the Command line (Fig. 5.19).

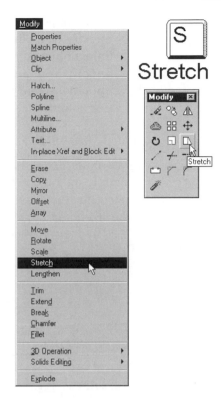

Fig. 5.19 Methods of calling **Stretch**

Examples – stretch (Fig. 5.20)

Command:_stretch
Select objects to be stretched by crossing-window or crossing-
      polygon

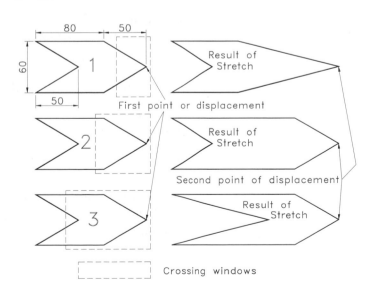

Fig. 5.20 Examples of **Stretch**

Select objects: *enter* c (crossing) *right-click*
Specify first corner: *pick* **Specify opposite corner:** *pick* **1 found**
Select objects: *right-click*
Specify base point or displacement: *pick*
Specify second point of displacement: *pick*
Command:

Examples – stretch (Fig. 5.21)

The examples in Fig. 5.21 show the difficulties when attempting to stretch an object involving arcs. Unless some care is taken in selecting the crossing window, quite severe distortions can occur in the stretched object(s).

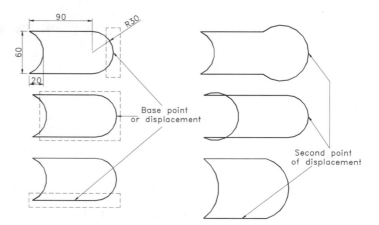

Fig. 5.21 Further examples of **Stretch**

The Lengthen tool

To call **Lengthen** either *left-click* on its tool icon in the **Modify** toolbar or on the name **Lengthen** in the **Modify** pull-down menu, or *enter* **len** or **lengthen** at the Command line (Fig. 5.22).

Examples – lengthen (Fig. 5.23)

Command:_lengthen
Select an object or [DElta/Percent/Total/DYnamic]: *pick*
Current length is 155
Select an object or [DElta/Percent/Total/DYnamic]: *enter* de *right-click*
Enter delta length or [Angle]: <0>: *enter* 50 *right-click*
Enter delta length or [Angle]: <0>: *right-click*
Command:

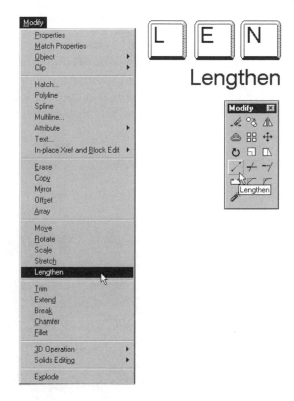

Fig. 5.22 Methods of calling
Lengthen

Note

Pick the end of the object towards which the delta lengthening is to take place.

Figure 5.22 shows the results of responding to the prompts **DElta** (Drawing **1**), **Percent** (Drawing **3**) and **Total** Drawings **2** and **4**).

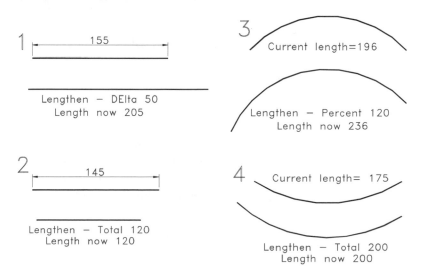

Fig. 5.23 Examples of using
Lengthen

The Trim tool

To call **Trim** either *left-click* on its tool icon in the **Modify** toolbar or on the name **Trim** in the **Modify** pull-down menu, or *enter* **tr** or **trim** at the Command line (Fig. 5.24).

Trim is a tool which will be used frequently. Because of this, several examples of its use are given below.

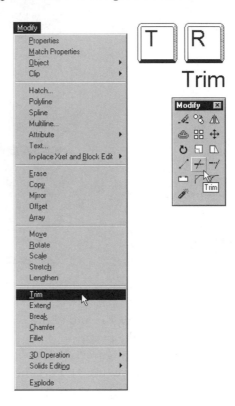

Fig. 5.24 Methods of calling **Trim**

Examples – trim (Fig. 5.25)

Drawings 1 and 2: trim – simple

Command:_trim
Select cutting edges: (Projmode = UCS, Edgemode = No extend)
    pick
Select objects: *pick* **1 found**
Select objects: *right-click*
<Select object to trim>/Project/Edge/Undo: *pick*
<Select object to trim>/Project/Edge/Undo: *right-click*
Command:

The result is given in drawing **2**.

Drawings 3 and 4: trim – using a fence

Command:_trim
Select cutting edges: (Projmode = UCS, Edgemode = No extend)
    pick
Select objects: *pick* **1 found**
<Select object to trim>/Project/Edge/Undo: *enter* f (fence) *right-*
    click
First fence point: *pick*
Undo/<Endpoint of line>: *pick*
Undo/<Endpoint of line>: *right-click*
Command:

The result is given in drawing **4**.

Drawings 5 and 6: trim – using the Edge prompt

Command:_trim
Select cutting edges: (Projmode = UCS, Edgemode = No extend)
    pick
Select objects: *pick* **1 found**
<Select object to trim>/Project/Edge/Undo: *enter* e *right-click*
Extend/No extend/<No extend>: *enter* e (Extend) *right-click*
<Select object to trim>/Project/Edge/Undo: *pick*
<Select object to trim>/Project/Edge/Undo: *right-click*
Command:

The result is given in drawing **6**.

Drawings 7 and 8: trim – using the Edge prompt

Repeat the sequence for drawings **5** and **6** but trimming both
horizontal lines to the extension of the cutting edge. The result is in
drawing **8**.

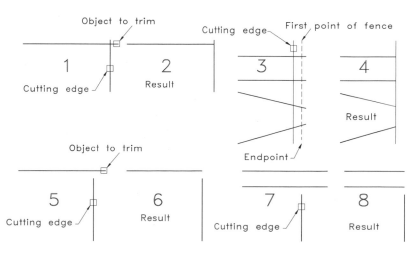

Fig. 5.25 Examples of using
Trim

Example – trim to complete an outline (Fig. 5.26)

Drawing 1: Construct drawing **1** with the aid of the **Pline** and **Circle** tools.

Drawing 2: Call **Trim**. *Pick* the pline as a cutting edge. Because the pline is a single object the circles can all be trimmed back to the pline.

Drawing 3: Select each semicircle in turn and trim the pline portions back to the semicircles.

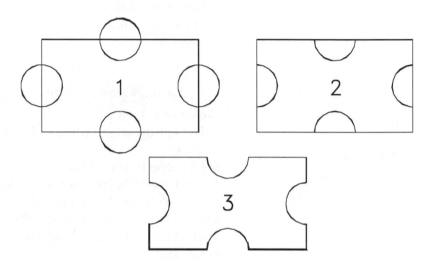

Fig. 5.26 An example of using **Trim** to construct an outline

The Extend tool

To call **Extend** either *left-click* on its tool icon in the **Modify** toolbar or on the name **Extend** in the **Modify** pull-down menu, or *enter* **ex** or **extend** at the Command line (Fig. 5.27).

Examples – extend (Fig. 5.28)

Command:_lengthen
Current settings: Projection=UCS Edge=Edge extend
Select boundary edges
Select objects: *pick* **1 found**
Select objects: *right-click*
Select objects to extend or [Project/Edge/Undo]: *pick*
Select objects to extend or [Project/Edge/Undo]: *right-click*
Command:

Drawing **1** to **8** of Fig. 5.28 show a variety of examples of using this series of prompts and responses when using **Extend**.

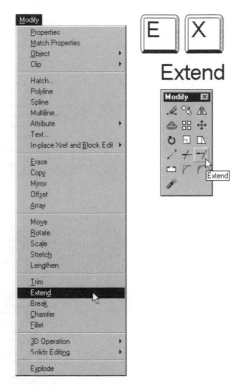

Fig. 5.27 Methods of calling **Extend**

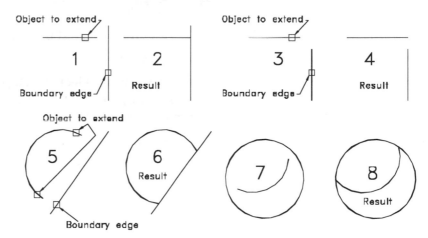

Fig. 5.28 Examples of using **Extend**

The Break tool

To call **Break** either *left-click* on its tool icon in the **Modify** toolbar or on the name **Break** in the **Modify** pull-down menu, or *enter* **br** or **break** at the Command line (Fig. 5.29).

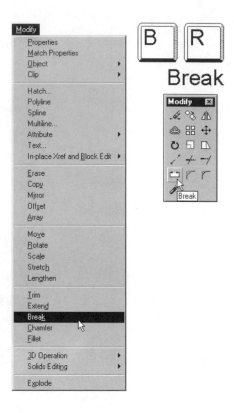

Fig. 5.29 Methods of calling **Break**

Examples – break (Fig. 5.30)

Drawing 1

Command:_break Select object: *pick* the line at **First point**
Enter second point (or F for First point): *pick* the **Second point**
Command:

And the line breaks.

Drawing 2

Command:_break Select object: *pick* the line at **First point**
Enter second point (or F for First point): *pick* the **Second point**
Command:

And the arc breaks.

Drawing 3

Command:_break Select object: *pick* the line at **First point**
Enter second point (or F for First point): *pick* the **Second point**
Command:

And the circle breaks.

Drawing 4

Command:_break Select object: *pick* the line at **First point**
Enter second point (or F for First point): *pick* the **Second point**
Command:

And the circle breaks.

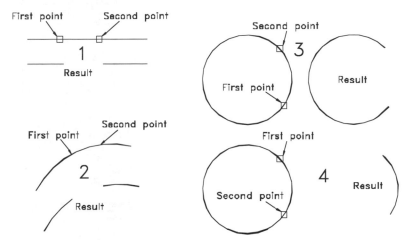

Fig. 5.30 Examples of using **Break**

Note

The default direction for the effects of **Break** in AutoCAD 2000 is counter clockwise (anticlockwise). In drawing **4** the points were picked in a clockwise direction, the circle breaks leaving the smaller arc. In drawing **3**, because the points were *picked* in a counter clockwise direction, the larger of the arcs remains after **Break** has been used.

The Chamfer tool

To call **Chamfer** either *left-click* on its tool icon in the **Modify** toolbar or on the name **Chamfer** in the **Modify** pull-down menu, or *enter* **cha** or **chamfer** at the Command line (Fig. 5.31).

Examples – chamfer (Fig. 5.32)

Drawing 1

Command:_chamfer
(TRIM mode) Current chamfer dist 1 = 10, Dist2 = 10
Polyline/Distance/Angle/Trim/Method/<Select first line>: *enter* d *right-click*
Enter first chamfer distance <10>: *enter* 20 *right-click*
Enter second chamfer distance <10>: *enter* 20 *right-click*
Command: *right-click*

Fig. 5.31 Methods of calling **Chamfer**

(TRIM mode) Current chamfer dist 1 = 10, Dist2 = 10
Select first line or [Polyline/Distance/Angle/Trim/Method]: *pick*
Select second line: *pick*
Command:

The result is given in drawing **2**.

Drawing 3

Command:_chamfer
(TRIM mode) Current chamfer dist 1 = 10, Dist2 = 10
Polyline/Distance/Angle/Trim/Method/<Select first line>: *enter*
    p *right-click*
Select 2D polyline: *pick*
4 lines were chamfered
Command:

Drawing 4

Command:_chamfer
(TRIM mode) Current chamfer dist 1 = 10, Dist2 = 10
Select first line [Polyline/Distance/Angle/Trim/Method]: *enter* t
    right-click

Enter Trim mode option [Trim/No Trim] <Trim>: *enter* n *right-click*

Select first line [Polyline/Distance/Angle/Trim/Method]: *enter* p *right-click*

Select 2D polyline: *pick*

4 lines were chamfered

Command:

Drawing 5

Command:_chamfer

(TRIM mode) Current chamfer dist 1 = 10, Dist2 = 10

Select first line [Polyline/Distance/Angle/Trim/Method] *enter* a *right-click*

Specify chamfer length on first line <10>: *enter* 20 *right-click*

Specify chamfer angle from first line <0>: *enter* 60 *right-click*

Command: *right-click*

CHAMFER (TRIM mode) Current chamfer length = 20, Angle = 60

Select first line [Polyline/Distance/Angle/Trim/Method]: *enter* p *right-click*

Select 2D polyline: *pick*

4 lines were chamfered

Command:

Drawing 6

In this example the **Polyline** prompt was not *entered* and each pair of lines selected separately.

Several examples of the uses of this tool have been given because the tool may be used frequently by many operators.

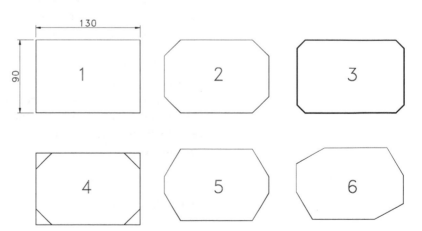

Fig. 5.32 Examples of using **Chamfer**

The Fillet tool

To call **Fillet** either *left-click* on its tool icon in the **Modify** toolbar or on the name **Fillet** in the **Modify** pull-down menu, or *enter* **f** or **fillet** at the Command line (Fig. 5.33).

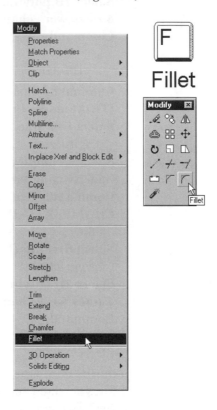

Fig. 5.33 Methods of calling **Fillet**

Examples – fillet (Fig. 5.34)

Because of similarities between using **Chamfer** and **Fillet**, only one set of Command lines prompts and responses is given below.

Drawing 1

Command:_fillet
Current settings: Mode = TRIM, Radius = 20
Select first object or [Polyline/Radius/Trim]: *pick*
Select second object: *pick*
Command:

Drawing 2

An example involving the **No Trim** option.

Drawing 3

An example involving the *picking* of a polyline.

Fig. 5.34 Examples of using
Fillet

Questions

1. When using the **Scale** tool, what is the purpose of the **Reference** prompt in the Command line sequence of the tool?
2. Can the **Stretch** tool be used to stretch a circle?
3. What is the purpose of the **Dynamic** prompt of the **Lengthen** Command line sequence?
4. When using the **Trim** tool, what is the purpose of the **Edgemode** prompt of the Command line sequence?
5. The **Trim** tool is one which you will probably use very often. What advantage is there in using a fence or crossing window to trim a series of objects projecting beyond a line?
6. There are similarities between the prompt sequences of **Chamfer** and **Fillet**. Can you describe them?
7. What is the **No Trim** mode for either **Chamfer** or **Fillet**?
8. If you try to chamfer two separate plines meeting at a corner what happens?
9. Have you tried chamfering or filleting lines which do not meet with **Chamfer** distances or **Fillet** radius set to **0**?
10. Have you tried chamfering or filleting crossing lines with **Chamfer** distance or **Fillet** radius set to **0**?

Exercises

1. Construct a 'face' somewhat like that in the left-hand drawing of Fig. 5.35 with the aid of the **Circle** and **Line** tools.

    Then with the aid of the **Extend** tool, extend objects as shown in the right-hand drawing of Fig. 5.35.

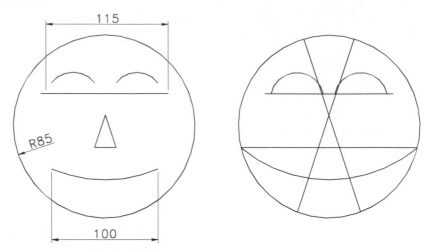

Fig. 5.35 Exercise 1

2. Construct the left-hand drawing of Fig. 5.36 with the aid of the **Circle** and **Line** tools.

Then **Trim** the lines and circles as shown in the right-hand drawing.

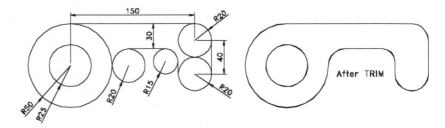

Fig. 5.36 Exercise 2

3. **Copy** your answer to exercise **2** three times and, with **Scale** alter the scales of the drawing as shown in Fig. 5.37.

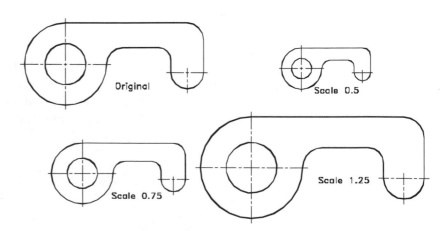

Fig. 5.37 Exercise 3

4. Construct the upper of the two drawings in Fig. 5.38 with the aid of **Circle** and **Line**.

   Then, using the **Trim** tool, trim parts of the drawing as shown in the lower drawing of Fig. 5.38.

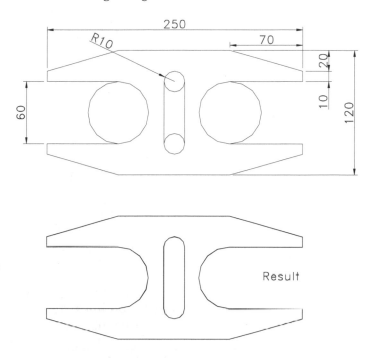

Fig. 5.38 Exercise 4

5. Construct the left-hand drawing of Fig. 5.39 to the sizes as shown using the **Polyline** tool. The upper four sided outline is separate from the circle.

   Then, with the aid of the **Array** tool, polar array the upper outline 12 times around the circle.

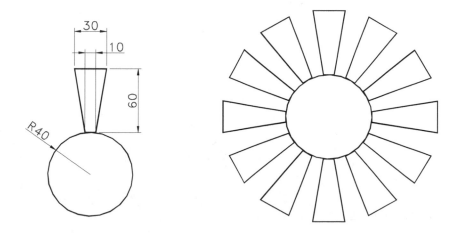

Fig. 5.39 Exercise 5

6. Construct the upper left-hand drawing of Fig. 5.40 to sizes as shown using the **Polyline** tool. Multiple **Copy** the outline 4 times.

   Then, using the **Stretch** tool, stretch the copies to the new sizes as shown in Fig. 5.40.

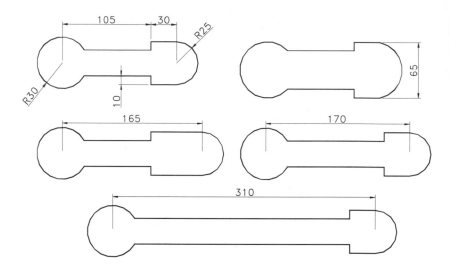

Fig. 5.40 Exercise 6

7. Construct the outline shown in Fig. 5.41 to the sizes as shown. Then **Copy** the outline twice.

   With **Chamfer** set to distances of 15 chamfer all corners of the outline (drawing **2** of Fig. 5.42).

   With **Fillet** set to radius 15, fillet all corners of the second of the copies (drawing **3** of Fig. 5.42).

   Construct drawing **4** of Fig. 5.42 to sizes as shown using **Circle** and **Arc** tools. Then with the **Trim** tool trim the outline to give drawing **5**.

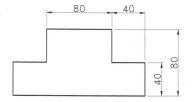

Fig. 5.41 Outline for exercise 7

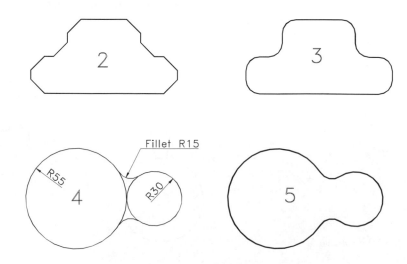

Fig. 5.42 Exercise 7

8. With **Arc** and **Line** construct drawing **1** of Fig. 5.43. **Copy** the two objects (drawing **2**). With **Fillet** (radius 20) Fillet the two objects as shown in drawing **2**.

   Construct the outline drawing **3** with **Line** and **Arc** tools. Then with **Fillet** set to radius 20, fillet its corners as shown in drawing **3A**.

   Construct the four arc outline given in drawing **4** of Fig. 5.43. **Copy** the drawing and with **Fillet** set to radius 20, fillet the four corners as shown in drawing **4A**.

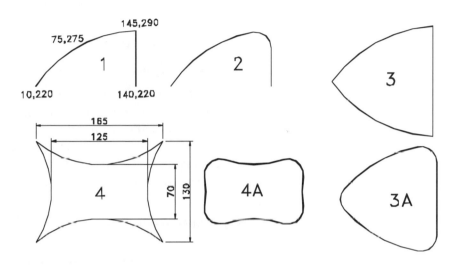

Fig. 5.43 Exercise 8

Chapter 6

Menus and text

Introduction

Two types of menus can be called into the AutoCAD 2000 window:

Pull-down menus: Which appear when one of the menu titles is selected with a *left-click* on its name in the menu bar. Pull-downs can also be called by holding down the **Alt** key of the keyboard and pressing the underlined letter in the menu name in the menu bar. Thus, pressing **Ctrl** and **O** brings the **Format** pull-down menu on screen, because the **o** in **Format** is underlined.

All the pull-down menus are shown in Fig. 6.1.

Right-click menus:
1. Which appear according to the settings of either the set variable **shortcutmenu** or the set variable **mbuttonpan** with a *right-click* when tools are in use, or when the wheel of an Intellimouse is pressed down.
2. Which appear with a *right-click* in the Command window, on one of the buttons in the Status bar, on either the **Model** or one of the **Layout** tabs, or on the arrow tabs next to the **Model** tab.
3. With a *right-click* in any toolbar on screen, which brings the toolbar menu on screen.

Set variables

Many of the functions in AutoCAD 2000 depend upon settings made in response to calling a set variable. There are a very large number of set variables associated with AutoCAD 2000. Those which might affect the use of AutoCAD 2000 for readers of this book are given in an Appendix D on page 305. When consulting this appendix it must be remembered that only a selection of all available variables are given in this appendix.

Fig. 6.1 All the pull-down
menus of AutoCAD 2000

The set variable SHORTCUTMENU

To set the variable, at the Command line:

> **Command:** *enter* shortcutmenu *right-click*
> **Enter new value for SHORTCUTMENU: <0>:**

The figure entered depends upon the following:

> Disable right-click menus: *enter* **0** – no right-click menus
> Enable default right-click menus: *enter* **1** – Fig. 6.2.
> Enable Edit mode right-click menus: *enter* **2** – Fig. 6.3.
> Enable Command mode right-click menus: *enter* **4** – Fig. 6.4.

Enable Command mode menus when options are available at the Command line: *enter* **8**

Fig. 6.2 The default right-click menu appearing when **shortcutmenu** is set at **1**

Fig. 6.3 The Edit mode right-click menu appearing when **shortcutmenu** is set at **2**

In addition adding together the figures will enable some, or all of the right-click menus. Thus *entering* **3** enables default and edit mode right-click menus. *Entering* **15** enables all the right-click menus.

Notes

Fig. 6.4 The Command mode right-click menu appearing when **shortcutmenu** is set at **4**

1. Edit mode is obtained when an object on screen is selected with a *left-click* on the object. Grips (small *pick* box squares) appear along the object (see Fig. 6.3). The object becomes editable and a *right-click* brings the Edit mode menu on screen its contents depending upon the last tool called.
2. Command mode operates during tool operations of any kind.

The set variable MBUTTONPAN

This variable can be set to **0** (on) or **1** (off). When set on (**0**), when the wheel of an Intellimouse is pressed a menu allowing selection of osnaps and point filters comes on screen (Fig. 6.5).

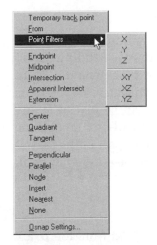

Fig. 6.5 The menu appearing with pressing the Intellimouse wheel when **mbuttonpan** is set to **0**

Fig. 6.6 The right-click menu from the Command window

Fig. 6.7 The right-click menu from any button in the Status bar

Note

It is up to the operator which right-click menus he/or she wishes to use, in fact some operators may wish not to use them at all.

The set variable AUTOSNAP

Another set variable is **autosnap** by which settings for **AutoSnap**, **PolarSnap** and **Osnaps** can be set. As was shown in pages ?? to ??, these settings can be made in dialogue boxes – **Drafting Settings** and **Options**. If setting from the Command line:

Command: *enter* autosnap *right-click*
Enter new value for AUTOSNAP <0>:
Requires an integer between 0 and 63
Enter new value for AUTOSNAP <0>:

The following values or the sums of the values can be set:

Disable all snaps: *enter* **0**
Turn on AutoSnap markers: *enter* **1**
Turn on AutoSnap tooltips: *enter* **2**
Turn on AutoSnap magnet: *enter* **4**
Turn on PolarSnap tracking: *enter* **8**
Turn on Osnap tracking: *enter* **16**
Turn on tooltips for **PolarSnap** and **Osnaps**: *enter* 32

Add all together giving **63** and all snaps are operating.

Other right-click menus

Command window: *Right-click* anywhere in the Command window and a menu appears (Fig. 6.6). It is most likely that **Options...** in this menu will be the most frequently chosen name in this menu because it is probably the easiest way to call the **Options** dialogue box in which so many settings can be made (see page 10).

Status bar buttons: *Right-click* in any of the buttons in the Status bar and the menu (Fig. 6.7) appears. A *left-click* on **Settings...** in the menu brings the **Drafting Settings** dialogue box on screen. In addition the feature represented by the button can be turned on/off, but it is probably easier to *left-click* on the button to toggle the feature on/off.

Remember also toggling from function keys – **F3** – Osnaps; **F7** – Grid; **F8** – Ortho; **F9** – Snap; **F10** – Polar; **F11** – Otrack.

Status bar tabs: *Right-click* on any tab in the Status bar – those marked with an arrow, the **Model** tab, or the **Layout** tabs and a menu (Fig. 6.8) appears. More about these tabs and the menu later in this book (Chapter 17).

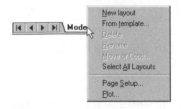

Fig. 6.8 The right-click menu
from any of the tabs in the
Status bar

Text

The addition of text to drawings is important in all technical
documents. AutoCAD 2000 includes two methods of adding text to
a drawing – **Multiline Text** and **Single Line Text** (or **Dynamic Text**).
In addition selection can be made from a large number of type fonts
which can be used when placing text. Fonts can be placed at any
height, in upright position, upside down, vertically, in an oblique
(sloping) position, upside down, justified in any part of the text. If
the Windows Truetype fonts are used, they can be *entered* in **bold**,
italic, or underlined.

Multiline Text

To call **Multiline Text**, either select **Multiline Text** from the **Draw**
toolbar or from the **Draw** pull-down menu, or *enter* **t**, **mt** or **mtext** at
the Command line (Fig. 6.9).

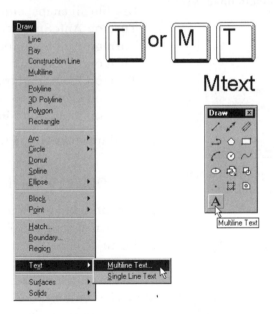

Fig. 6.9 Methods of calling
Multiple Text

When the tool is called:

1. **Command:_mtext Current text style: TIMES Text height: 20**
   Specify first corner: *pick* (or *enter* coordinates and *right-click*)
   Specify other corner or [Height/Justify/Line spacing/Rotate/Style/
   Width]: *pick* (or *enter* coordinates and *right-click*) and the box
   Fig. 6.10 appears on screen

2. When the **opposite corner** has been *picked* the **Multiline Text
   Editor** appears on screen (Fig. 6.11). In Fig. 6.11, the **Character**
   popup list is shown, from which a suitable text font can be chosen.

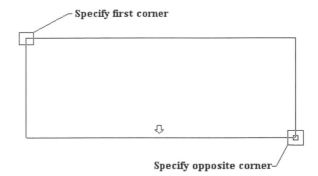

Fig. 6.10 The text box which
appears when **Mtext** is called
and the box corners specified

Fig. 6.11 The **Multiline Text
Editor** with the **Character**
popup list showing

3. Having selected a suitable font and *entered* its height in the **Font
   Height** box of the editor, text can then be *entered* in the edit area of
   the dialogue box as indicated in Fig. 6.12.

Fig. 6.12 *Entering* the desired
text in the edit area of the
Multiline Text Editor

4. When the text has been *entered left-click* on the **OK** button of the
   dialogue box and the text appears in the area outlined when corners
   of the area for text were selected.

Figure 6.13 shows all the text fonts normally available from the
popup list in the **Character** area of the dialogue box.

Fonts

In general two types of text fonts can be selected from the AutoCAD
2000 list shown in Fig. 6.13:

AutoCAD SHX fonts: Those shown in Fig. 6.13 with an icon
   representing a pair of dividers.

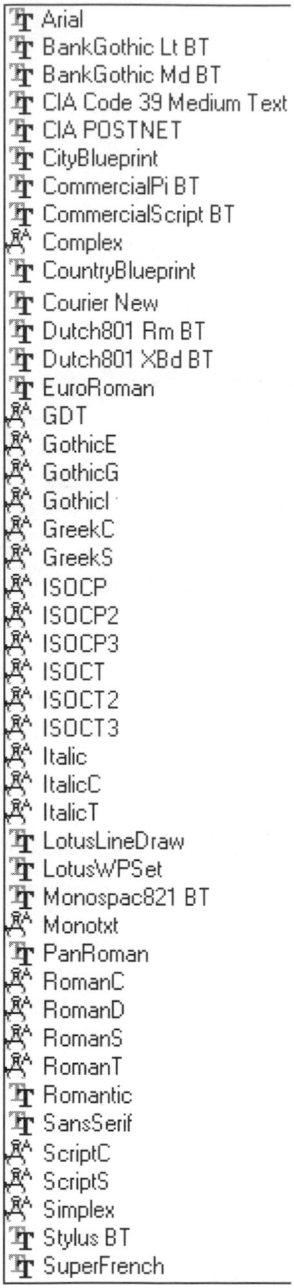

Arial
BankGothic Lt BT
BankGothic Md BT
CIA Code 39 Medium Text
CIA POSTNET
CityBlueprint
CommercialPi BT
CommercialScript BT
Complex
CountryBlueprint
Courier New
Dutch801 Rm BT
Dutch801 XBd BT
EuroRoman
GDT
GothicE
GothicG
GothicI
GreekC
GreekS
ISOCP
ISOCP2
ISOCP3
ISOCT
ISOCT2
ISOCT3
Italic
ItalicC
ItalicT
LotusLineDraw
LotusWPSet
Monospac821 BT
Monotxt
PanRoman
RomanC
RomanD
RomanS
RomanT
Romantic
SansSerif
ScriptC
ScriptS
Simplex
Stylus BT
SuperFrench

Fig. 6.13 The text fonts from AutoCAD 2000

Windows Truetype fonts: Those shown in Fig. 6.13 with a double **T** icon.

Windows Truetype text can be *entered* in **bold**, *italic* or <u>underlined</u>, or indeed in a mixture of all three – ***<u>bold, italic, underlined</u>*** text. The three buttons in the **Multiline Text Editor** as shown in Fig. 6.14 toggle these three features on/off to determine whether the text is **bold**, *italic* or <u>underlined</u>. Examples are given in Fig. 6.15.

Note

AutoCAD SHX fonts cannot be added in **bold** or *italic* but can be added in an <u>underlined</u> style.

Symbols

Left-click in the **Symbols** box of the **Multiline Text Editor** and using the tools shown in the popup list which is then brought down, a number of symbols – degrees (°), plus/minus symbol (±), diameter (Ø) can be added to text as shown in Fig. 6.16. If the **Other...** name is selected from the popup list the Windows **Character Map** appears from which symbols can be selected as needed.

Text Justification

Left-click on the **Properties** tab in the **Multiline Text Editor** dialogue box, and again in the **Justification** box which then appears and from a selection of the justification positions in the popup list which appears text can be placed in any justification position required. See Fig. 6.17. It is suggested that some experimentation with justification positions is attempted in order for an operator to familiarise him/herself with how the text justification feature works.

Notes

1. Attempt using other features in the **Multiline Text Editor**, such as those under **Line Spacing**, **Find/Replace**.
2. When **Mtext** is being used for *entering* text in a drawing, the **Style**, **Justification**, **Rotation** and other details associated with the text can be *entered* at the Command line by using the appropriate responses to the options appearing at the Command line.
3. The default font and its angle can always be amended either in the **Multiline Text Editor** or at the Command line.
4. The default font is that which has been selected from the **Text Style** dialogue box. See page 107.

Fig. 6.14 The three buttons in the **Multiline Text Editor** for toggling **bold**, *italic* or underline

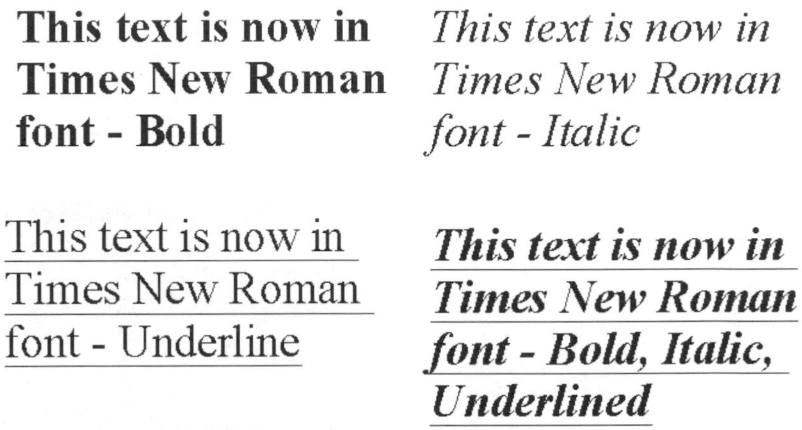

This text is now in Times New Roman font - Bold

This text is now in Times New Roman font - Italic

Fig. 6.15 A Windows Truetype text entered in a variety of **bold**, *italic* and underline

This text is now in Times New Roman font - Underline

This text is now in Times New Roman font - Bold, Italic, Underlined

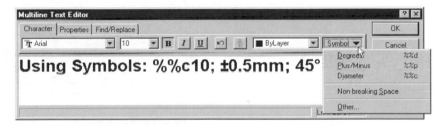

Fig. 6.16 Adding symbols to text in a drawing

Using Symbols: Ø10; ±0.5mm; 45°

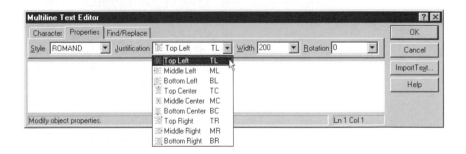

Fig. 6.17 The **Properties/ Justification** popup list in the **Multiline Text Editor**

Text Style

To call the **Text Style** dialogue box, either *left-click* on **Text Style...** in the **Format** pull-down menu, or *enter* **st** or **style** at the Command line (Fig. 6.18). When called the dialogue box appears on screen (Fig. 6.19).

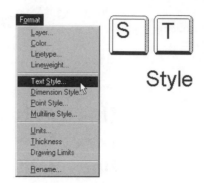

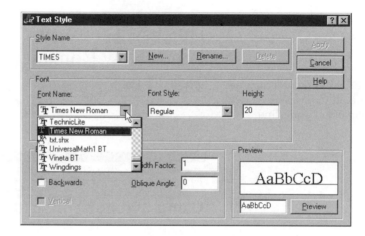

Fig. 6.18 Methods of calling the **Text Style** dialogue box on screen

Fig. 6.19 The **Text Style** dialogue box

To set a Text Style

1. Call the dialogue box on screen.
2. *Left-click* on the **New...** button. A small dialogue box **New Text Style** appears with the name **style1** in its **Style Name:** box (Fig. 6.20). *Left-click* on the **OK** button and the name **style1** appears in the **Style Name:** box of the main dialogue box.
3. *Left-click* on the **Rename...** button and another small dialogue appears – the **Rename Text Style** box (Fig. 6.21). *Enter* a new name in the **Style Name:** box, in the example given in Fig. 6.21 this is **romanc**. *Left-click* on the box's **OK** button and in the main dialogue box, the new name appears in its **Style Name:** box replacing **style1**.

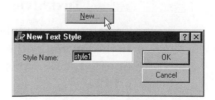

Fig. 6.20 Setting a **New Style**

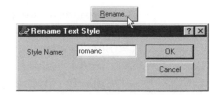

Fig. 6.21 Renaming a text style

4. *Enter* the required text height in the **Height:** box, in this example this is **10** and *left-click* on both the **Apply** and **Close** buttons of the **Text Style** dialogue box. The default style now set is **romanc** of height **10**. This is an AutoCAD SHX text font.

Adding text styles to a drawing template

In the case of the drawing template it is just as well now to add some text styles to the template. Call the template file saved in response as previously described onto screen. Set up new text styles one after the other as shown in Fig. 6.22. Save the drawing as **Yarwood.dwt**, or to your own name or initials. I prefer to have **romand** font set to a height of **5** as my default text style, mainly because as will be seen later I use that font and height for dimensioning.

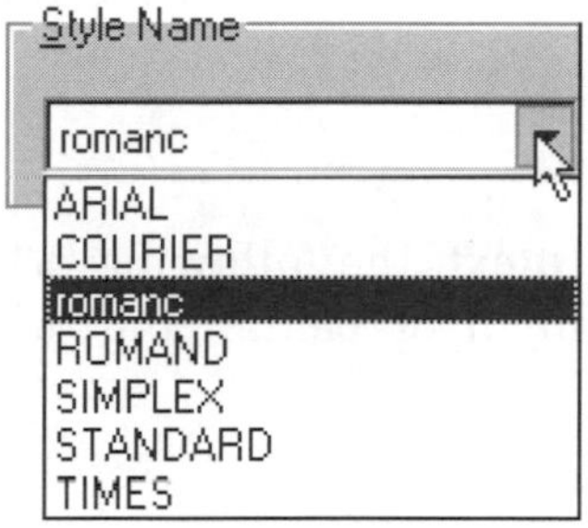

Fig. 6.22 Adding some text styles to a drawing template

Single Line Text or Dtext

To call **Single Line Text**, either *left-click* on **Single Line Text** in the **Draw** pull-down menu or *enter* **dt** at the Command line (Fig. 6.23).

Fig. 6.23 Calling **Single Line Text**

Command:_dtext
Current text style: 'ROMAND' Text height: 5
Specify start point of text or [Justify/Style]: *pick* (or *enter* coordinates
   and *right-click*)
Specify rotation angle of text <0>: *right-click*
Enter text: The text entered now is automatically seen on screen
   as it is entered at the keyboard. This is why it is dtext (or
   dynamic text)

In order to ensure the text *entered* as dtext remains on screen, press
the *Return* key (NOT a *right-click*). The prompt **Enter text:** reappears.
Another press of the *Return* key ends the text being *entered* but if
another line of text is required, continue *entering* text when the
prompt reappears, pressing *Return* at the end of each line of text.

Symbols when working with Dtext

When wishing to include symbols with **dtext**, the following **%%**
symbols must be *entered* either in front of or behind the text
pertaining to the symbol.

%%c20 will show as **Ø20**
%%p0.005 will show as **±0.005**
60%%d will show as **60°**
50%%% will show as **50%**

Some examples of AutoCAD SHX text fonts

Figure 6.24 shows a few examples of text using different heights and
oblique angles of AutoCAD SHX text fonts.

This is ROMAND text of a height of 8

This is SIMPLEX text at a height of 8

This is COURIER NEW text at a height of 12

*This is ROMANC text at a height of 15
and an Oblique angle of 10*

Fig. 6.24 Some examples of
text using AutoCAD SHX text
fonts

The set variable TEXTFILL

When printing or plotting drawings which include text in Windows
True Type fonts, they will print either as filled outlines or as
outlines only depending upon the setting of another set variable
TEXTFILL. When set on (**1**) True Type text prints with the text
outlines filled. When set off (**0**) the text prints outlines only. To set
the variable:

Command: *enter* textfill *right-click*
Enter new value for TEXTFILL <1>: either *right-click* to accept
   1 or *enter* 0 to turn textfill off
Command:

Checking text

There are several tools contained in AutoCAD 2000 which can be used for editing and/or amending text – **Find and Replace**; **Spelling**; **Text...** from the **Modify** pull-down menu.

Find and Replace

Find

Fig. 6.25 Methods of calling
Find and Replace

To call **Find and Replace** either *left-click* on the **Find and Replace** tool icon in the **Standard** toolbar or *enter* **find** at the Command line (Fig. 6.25). The **Find and Replace** dialogue box appears (Fig. 5.26).

In the example given in Fig. 6.26 the word **keyboard** has been wrongly spelled. *Enter the* wrongly spelt word in the **Find text string:** box and in the **Replace with:** box *enter* the correct spelling. Or a whole phrase can be change. A *left-click* on the **Find Next** button of the dialogue box, brings the word or phrase to be changed into the **Context:** area of the dialogue box with the word or phrase to be changed highlighted.

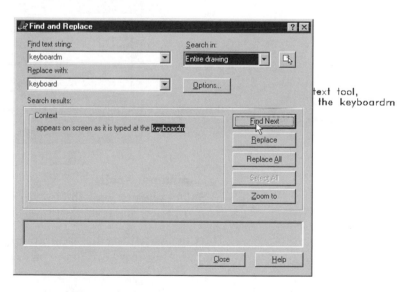

Fig. 6.26 The **Find and Replace** dialogue box

Spelling

To call the **Spelling** tool either *left-click* on **Spelling** in the **Tools** pull-down menu or *enter* **spell** at the Command line (Fig. 6.27). The Command line shows:

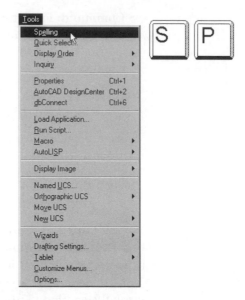

Fig. 6.27 Methods of calling
Spelling

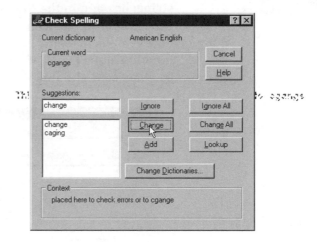

Fig. 6.28 The **Check Spelling**
dialogue box

Command:_spell
Select objects: *pick* the text in which a spelling error is thought
to have occurred and the *right-click*

The **Check Spelling** dialogue box appears (Fig. 6.28) with suggestions
for changing any word in the *picked* text, together with words in the

Fig. 6.29 The **Edit Text**
dialogue box

Fig. 6.30 Calling the **Edit Text** dialogue box

Suggestions: area of the dialogue box showing correct spellings. To accept the suggestions, *left-click* on the **Change** button.

Edit Text

To call the **Edit Text** dialogue box on screen (Fig. 6.29), *left-click* on **Text...** in the **Modify** pull-down menu (Fig. 6.30). The Command line shows:

> **Command:_ddedit**
> **Select an annotation object or [Undo]:** *pick* a line of text which requires to be edited.

The **Edit Text** dialogue box appears with the *picked* text showing in the **Text:** window of the dialogue box. The text can be edited as required and when satisfied a *left-click* on the **OK** button changes the text.

Questions

1. How many different forms of *right-click* menus can you describe?
2. Several set variables are described in this chapter. What is a set variable?
3. What are the differences between **Multiline Text** and **Single Line Text**?
4. Can text in Autodesk SHX fonts be placed on screen in a **bold** style?
5. Can text in Windows True Type fonts be placed on screen in an underlined style?
6. Have you attempted various justifications of text on screen?
7. What features can be set in the **Text Style** dialogue box?
8. What is the purpose of the **textfill** variable?
9. Can you name the tools used for editing text on screen?
10. What differences occur when editing **Mtext** when compared with editing **Dtext**?

Exercises

1. Using the **Mtext** tool, place some badly spelt text on screen and then edit its spelling with one of the text editing tools.
2. Do the same with some **Dtext** *entered* on screen.
3. *Enter t*he following on screen using both **Mtext** and **Dtext**:

   90°; Ø50 mm; ±0.005; 45%.

4. *Enter* the following on screen using the **Times New Romand** font of any suitable height:

This is bold; *This is italic*; <u>This is underlined</u>; This is ***text*** in bold, italic and underlined.

Chapter 7

Layers and other features

Layers

The concept of constructing drawings on layers is common in most CAD systems. Layers are similar to tracings when making technical drawings 'by hand'. In the same manner in which different features of a technical drawing can be drawn on tracing sheets laid over a master drawing, so features can be added on layers when working with a CAD system. In the same way in which tracings can be removed, replaced or edited, so layers can be:

Turned **on** – a selected layer is made visible.
Turned **off** – a selected layer is made invisible.
Frozen – a selected layer is turned off resulting in tool operations and any regenerations of the screen being speedier when working in other layers.
Thawed – a frozen layer is turned back on.
Locked – objects on a locked layer cannot be modified, although further objects can be added to a locked layer.
Unlocked – a locked layer can be unlocked.

Figure 7.1 is a simple technical drawing which has been constructed on six layers as shown in Fig. 7.2. Construction lines on which the outlines of the drawing were based were drawn on layer **CONSTRUCTION**; the outlines of the drawing views were constructed on layer **0**. Layer **CONSTRUCTION** was then frozen. Centre lines, hidden lines, dimensions and text were then added to their respective layers which were turned on as required.

The Layer Properties Manager dialogue box

To call the dialogue box, either *left-click* on **Layer...** in the **Format** pull-down menu or *left-click* on the **Layers** icon in the **Standard** toolbar (Fig. 7.3). The **Layer Properties Manager** appears showing the current layers, their linetypes and colours (Fig. 7.4).

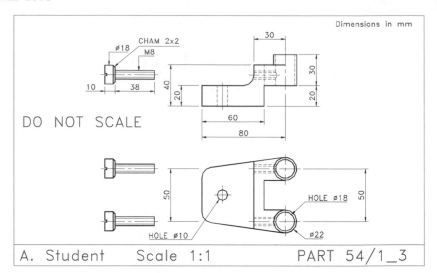

Fig. 7.1 A simple technical drawing constructed on six layers

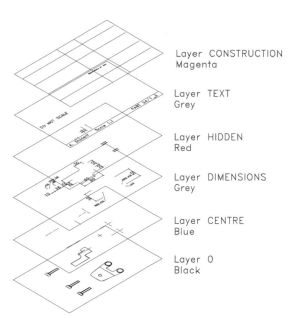

Fig. 7.2 The layers on which the drawing Fig. 7.1 was constructed

Fig. 7.3 Methods of calling the **Layer Properties Manager** dialogue box to screen

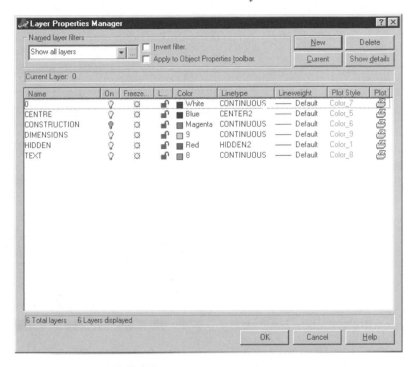

Fig. 7.4 The **Layer Properties Manager** dialogue box

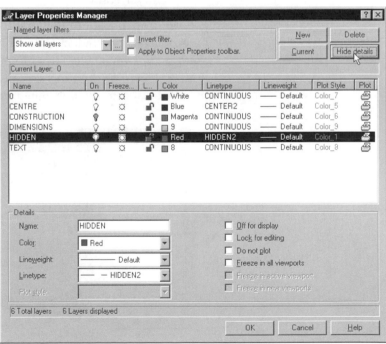

Fig. 7.5 The result of a *left-click* on the **Details...** button

Left-click on the name of any of the layers in the list of layers, the name highlights. *Left-click* on the **Show details...** button of the dialogue box and details of the selected layer appear at the bottom of the main dialogue box (Fig. 7.5).

To make a new layer

Left-click on the **New** button and another layer **Layer1** will be added to the layer list. Further *left-clicks* will bring **Layer2**, **Layer3** and so on into the list. *Enter* the required layer name over the word **Layer1**. In this example the layer was renamed **Insert**.

Fig. 7.6 Making a new layer

Layer colour

Left-click on the colour name or the colour icon in the line of details for any layer. The **Select Color** dialogue box appears, from which a *double-click* on a selected colour will set the colours for the layer (Fig. 7.7). Or *left-click* on a colour, followed by another *left-click* on the **OK** button of the dialogue box.

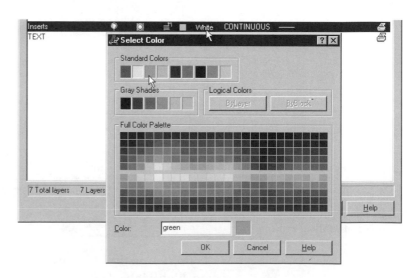

Fig. 7.7 Selecting a colour

Layer linetype

Left-click on a linetype name on any linetype name in the line of details for a layer. The **Select Linetype** dialogue box appears. *Left-click* on the **Load...** button and the **Load or Reload Linetypes** dialogue box appears from which a linetype can be selected with a *double-click* which brings that linetype into the **Select Linetype** dialogue, from where it can be selected for any layer (Fig. 7.8).

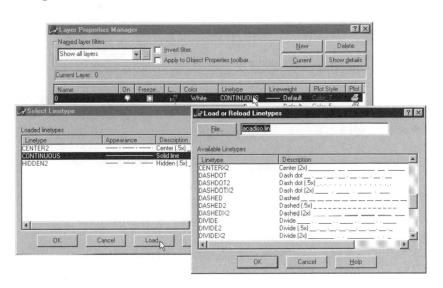

Fig. 7.8 Selecting a linetype for a layer

The Plot icon

A *left-click* on the **Plot** icon against any of the lines connected with layer names, causes a **Stop** icon to appear over the **Plot** icon (Fig. 7.9). When this occurs, the layer with the **Stop** icon will not print or plot (see Appendix B about plotting/printing).

Layer control icons

Left-click in the box to the right of the **Layers** icon, or *left-click* on the arrow to the right of the box and a popup list appears with all layers which have been set, with a set of icons against each layer name. Figure 7.10 shows, among other details, the tooltips associated with each of the icons:

Left-clicks on the **On** icon toggle a layer on/off, *left-click*.
Left-clicks on the **Freeze or Thaw** icon toggle between freeze and thaw
Left-clicks on the **Lock or Unlock** icon toggle the layer between lock and unlock. The lock icon opens or closes in response.
Left-clicks on the **Plot** icon toggle print/plot on/off for the layer.
A *left-click* on a layer name makes that layer the **Current** layer.

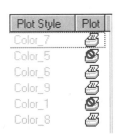

Fig. 7.9 The **Plot** stop icon in the **Layer Properties Manager** dialogue box

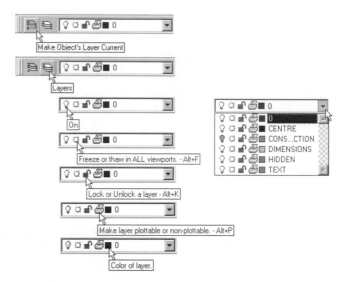

Fig. 7.10 The layer icons in the popup list

Lineweight

Left-click on the lineweight in any layer line and the **Lineweight** dialogue box appears (Fig. 7.10). Selecting any lineweight from this dialogue box makes that lineweight the current lineweight for the layer.

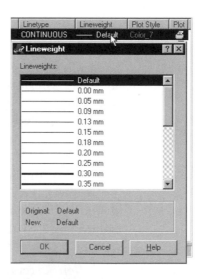

Fig. 7.11 The **Lineweight** dialogue box

Including layer setting in a drawing template

Open the drawing template described in pages 6–9 and when the template is on screen add layers to the template as shown in Fig. 7.2 on page 116. Then save the template to file in your selected template name. Mine has been be saved as **Yarwood.dwt**.

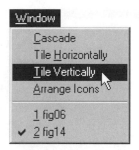

Fig. 7.12 Selecting **Tile Vertically** from the **Window** pull-down menu

The Multiple Document Environment

Load two (or more) drawings into the AutoCAD 2000 window from the **Select File** dialogue box and *left-click* on **Tile Vertically** in the **Windows** pull-down menu (Fig. 7.12). The two drawings appear together side by side in the AutoCAD 2000 window (Fig. 7.13). Each drawing will be in its own window.

A *left-click* in either drawing window will make that window current in which constructions can be made. It is easy to switch between drawings in this way. When blocks and/or xrefs have been inserted into any drawing in a multiple document environment, the inserts can be d*ragged and dropped* between drawings. In a similar manner any objects copied from the Windows clipboard can also be *dragged and dropped* between multiple documents in the AutoCAD 2000 window.

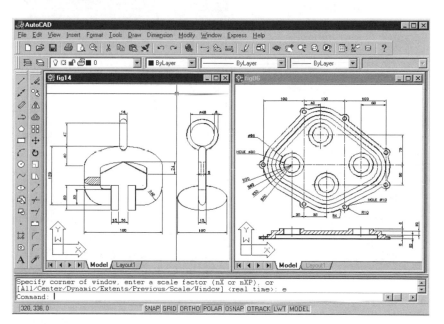

Fig. 7.13 Two drawings tiled vertically in the AutoCAD 2000 window

Any tool operations being performed at any one time can be effective in either drawing window by switching from one drawing to another with a *left-click* in the appropriate drawing window.

If required the drawing windows can be re-sized by *dragging* the Windows resizing cursors at the sides, top, bottom or corners of any of the drawing windows (Fig. 7.14). The drawing windows can also be *dragged* to new positions on screen with the cursor in the title bar of the window. In Fig. 7.14 all toolbars have been removed from the screen.

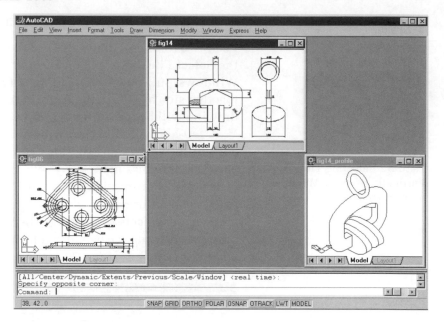

Fig. 7.14 Three drawing
windows in a multiple
document environment

Fig. 7.15 Calling
Customization... from the
Toolbar *right-click* menu

Customising a toolbar

Most operators will use a number of certain tools repeatedly. With
this is view it may be advisable to customise one's own toolbar,
selecting tools from existing toolbars and inserting them into a new
toolbar. The various stages needed to carry out this customisation
are:

1. *Right-click* in any toolbar on screen. The **Toolbars** right-click menu
   appears. From the menu select **Customize...** (Fig. 7.15).
2. The **Toolbars** dialogue box appears. *Left-click* on the **Customize...**
   button and the **Customize Toolbars** dialogue box appears.
3. In the **Categories** list, *left-click* on **Draw** and when the tool icons
   appear *drag* the **Line** tool icon into the AutoCAD 2000 drawing
   area. A toolbar **Toolbar1** starts to generate.
4. *Drag* another tool icon – **Polyline** into the new toolbar. It appears
   in the newly forming **Toolbar1**.
5. Repeat *dragging* tool icons from those toolbars carrying the required
   icons.
6. **Close** the **Customize Toobars** dialogue box. The new toolbar's
   name will appear in both the **Toolbars** dialogue box and in the
   Toolbars right-click menu.

   These operations are shown in Figures 7.15 and 7.16.

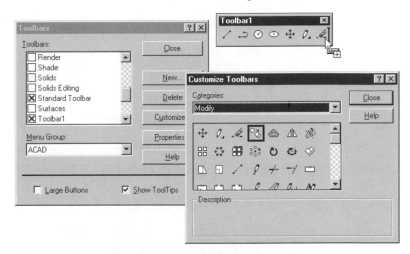

Fig. 7.16 Customising a new
toolbar

Fig. 7.17 The new toolbar
Toolbar1

The Options dialogue box

Some reference has already been made to settings in the **Options**
dialogue box. It is quite beyond the scope of a book the size of this
one to describe all the many option settings available in the dialogue
box.

When the dialogue box is called to screen (one method is as
shown in Fig. 7.18) it will be seen that within the dialogue box itself
are nine dialogues, each of which is called to screen with a *left-click*
on the respective tab at the top of the dialogue box. It is advisable to
look carefully at each of the nine dialogues in order to become
familiar with any settings one feels need to be changed. All constructions
in this book have been drawn with option settings in the two
dialogues **Display** and **Open and Save**, shown in Figures 7.19 and
7.20.

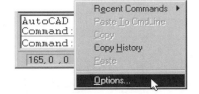

Fig. 7.18 Calling **Options...**
from the right-click menu in
the Command window

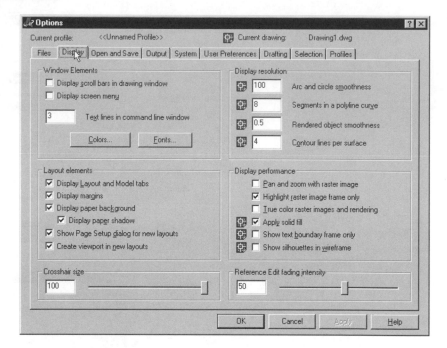

Fig. 7.19 The **Display** dialogue from the **Options** dialogue box

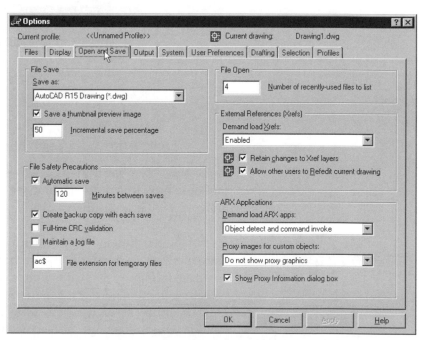

Fig. 7.20 The **Open and Save** dialogue from the **Options** dialogue box

Questions

1. Can you name two ways in which a layer can be turned off?
2. What is the purpose of locking a layer?

3. What advantage is there in freezing a layer as against turning the layer off?
4. How is a new layer added to the set of layers within a drawing?
5. What is the purpose of the **Plot** icon seen against layer names?
6. What advantages are there in the **Multiple Document Environment** system of AutoCAD 2000?
7. Can you describe how to set up your own toolbar?
8. If you set up your own toolbar, which tools would you wish to include in the toolbar?

Exercises

1. Load your answers to the two exercises **2** and **4** from Chapter 5 (Fig. 7.21) and experiment with drawing with tools in both AutoCAD 2000 windows while the tool sequences are showing in the Command line.

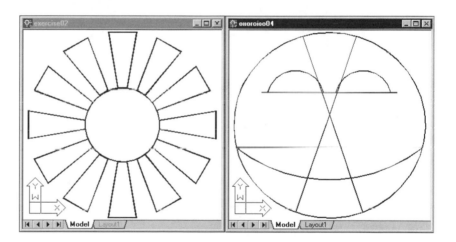

Fig. 7.21 Exercise 1

2. Call the **Options** dialogue box on screen and experiment with making different settings. *Note:* it is advisable to return the **Options** to the original settings as they were when the dialogue box was called to screen as a safeguard against other users becoming frustrated with what they would regard as incorrect settings.
3. Set up layers as shown in Fig. 7.2 in your own drawing template. Experiment with making different layers the current layer and making simple constructions while the selected layer is current.
4. Experiment with turning layers on and then back on; freezing layers and then thawing them; locking layers and attempting to use **Modify** tools on objects within the locked layer.

5. Add layers to those already set in your template and change the linetype in each of the new layers in order to determine which linetypes are available within AutoCAD 2000. When finished, do not save the template with its new layers.

6. Set the tool **Ltscale**, which determines the scale at which linetypes will appear on screen and when printed or plotted. The default scale is **1**. Try drawing lines on screen when the **Centre** layer is current and examine what happens to the lines when **ltscale** is set to **0.5** and again when set to **2**. To set the scale:

> **Command:** *enter* ltscale *right-click*
> **Enter new linetype scale factor <1.0000>:** *enter* 2 *right-click*
> **Command:**

Chapter 8

Zooms and Pans. The AutoCAD Design Center

The Zoom tools

The **Zoom** tools are among those very frequently used by operators using CAD systems. With their aid, the most minute portion of a drawing can be inspected, modified or added to with accuracy. There are several ways in which the **Zoom** tools can be called into action:

From the Standard toolbar: Three **Zoom** and a **Pan** tool can be selected from icons in the **Standard** toolbar (usually docked at the top of the AutoCAD 2000 window below the **Object Properties** toolbar). These are shown in Fig. 8.1.

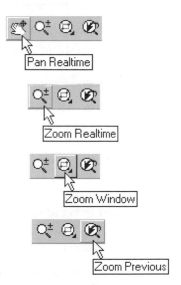

Fig. 8.1 The three **Zoom** tool icons and a **Pan** tool icon in the **Standard** toolbar

From the Zoom toolbar: *Right-click* in any toolbar and from the **Toolbar** menu *left-click* on **Zoom**. The **Zoom** toolbar appears (Fig. 8.2).

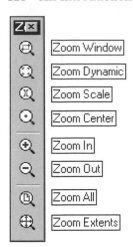

Fig. 8.2 The **Zoom** toolbar

Fig. 8.3 Methods of calling
Zoom

From the View pull-down menu: Fig. 8.3.

Entering Z: At the Command line (Fig. 8.3). The Command line then shows:

Command: *enter z right-click*
ZOOM Specify corner of window, enter a scale factor (nX or nPX), or
[All/Center/Dynamic/Extents/Previous/Scale/Window] <real time>:

Entering the capital letter of any of the prompts brings that method of zooming into action.

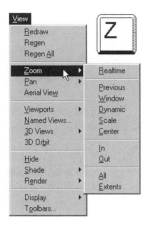

Examples of Zooms

In the examples shown in Figs 8.4 to 8.6, any method of calling the required zoom produces a similar result. If however, **Zoom** is called by *entering* **z** at the Command line, the correct prompt letter must be *entered* to obtain the required zoom.

Zoom All: Fig. 8.4 shows an example of calling **Zoom All**. The AutoCAD 2000 window zooms to the limits as set for the window in which it was drawn.

Zoom Extents: Fig. 8.5 shows an example of calling **Zoom Extents**. The drawing zooms to enlarge as big as possible within the drawing area of the AutoCAD 2000 window.

Zoom Window: Fig. 8.6 shows an example of calling **Zoom Window**. No matter how this method of zooming is called, the following appears at the Command line:

Command:_zoom
ZOOM Specify corner of window, enter a scale factor (nX or nPX), or
[All/Center/Dynamic/Extents/Previous/Scale/Window] <real time>:
  _w

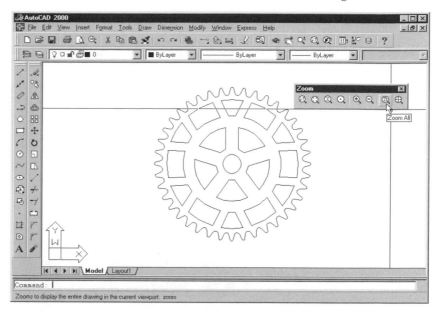

Fig. 8.4 An example of **Zoom All**

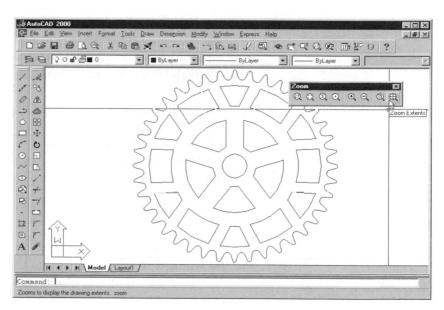

Fig. 8.5 An example of **Zoom Extents**

Specify first corner: *pick* (or *enter* coordinates and *right-click*)
Specify opposite corner: *pick*
Command:

Experiment with other zooms:

Zoom real time: Requires the *picking* on the corners of a window, producing the same result as **Zoom Window**.

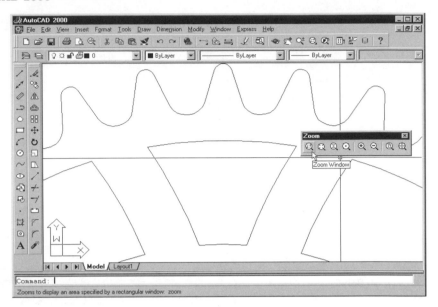

Fig. 8.6 An example of **Zoom Window**

Zoom Dynamic: Produces a window which can be *dragged* and resized under the action of the left button of the mouse. *Right-click* and the portion of drawing within the dynamic window appears.

Zoom Scale: Requires *entering* a scale as a decimal figure – e.g. 0.5 for half scale or $\frac{1}{2}$ for half scale.

Zoom Center: *pick* a point on a drawing and right-click and the drawing repositions with the *picked* point at the centre of the AutoCAD 2000 drawing area.

Zoom Out: The drawing enlarges in scale (default 2).

Zoom In: The drawing reduces in scale (default 0.5).

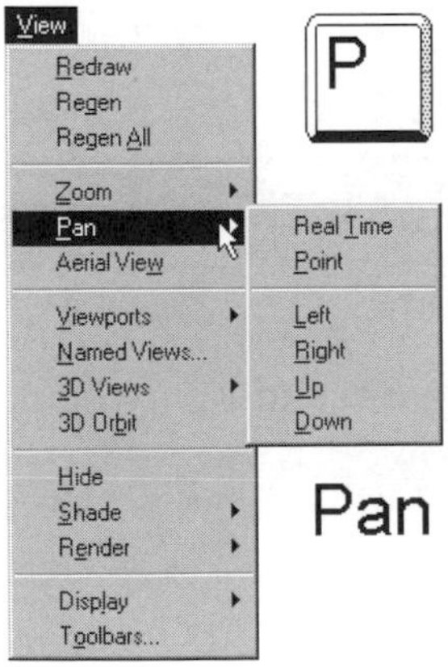

The Pan tools

The **Pan** tool allows the movement of a drawing within the AutoCAD 2000 window to allow any part to be examined, modified or added to. The tool is particularly useful when a drawing within large limits is being constructed.

The tool can be called either with a *left-click* on the tool icon in the **Standard** toolbar (Fig. 8.1 on page 127), or with a *left-click* on **Pan** in the **View** pull-down menu, or by *entering* **p** or **pan** at the Command line (Fig. 8.7). If the tool icon is selected or a **p** *entered* at the Command line, then **real time** panning occurs:

Fig. 8.7 Methods of calling **Pan**

Command:_pan
Press ESC or ENTER to exit, or right-click to display shortcut
   menu

And an icon resembling a hand appears. *Dragging* the icon (by holding down the left mouse button) in any direction pans the drawing. To get out of panning either press the **Esc** or **Enter** keys or *right-click* to display the shortcut menu. See Figures 8.8 and 8.9. Figure 8.8 shows part of a large drawing before panning and Fig. 8.9 the same drawing after being panned in order to display another part of the drawing.

If other types of panning are selected from the **View** pull-down menu, the panning takes place in stages left (**Left**), or right (**Right**), up (**Up**) or down (**Down**) or from a selected point (**Point**).

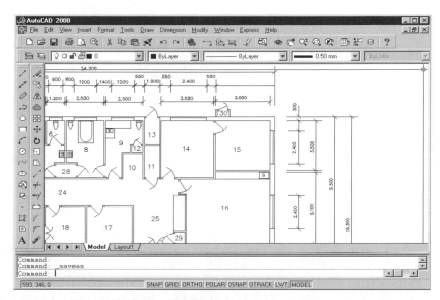

Fig. 8.8 A large drawing before panning

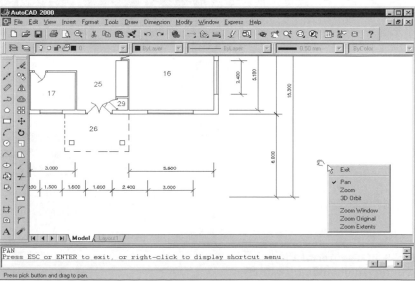

Fig. 8.9 The same drawing as in Fig. 8.8 after panning

The Aerial View window

Left-click on **Aerial View** in the **View** pull-down menu and the
Aerial View window appears (Fig. 8.10). The whole of the drawing
loaded in AutoCAD 2000 appears in the **Aerial View** window and
that portion of the drawing seen in the AutoCAD 2000 drawing area
is bounded by a thick line in the **Aerial View** window. This gives the
operator an exact idea of where the portion of a drawing on screen
relates to the whole drawing. Figure 8.11 gives an example of the
same drawing as in Fig. 8.10 after using the **Pan** tool.

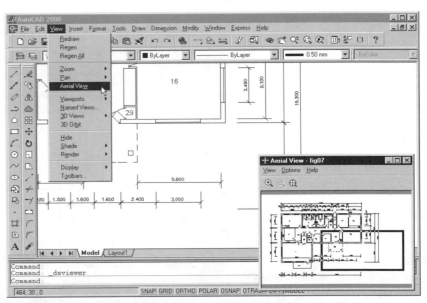

Fig. 8.10 The **Aerial View**
window

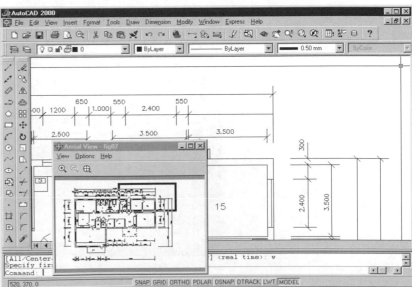

Fig. 8.11 The **Aerial View**
window after a **Pan** operation

The **Aerial View** window is a true Windows window – it can be resized if necessary in the same way as can any other window.

The AutoCAD Design Center

Left-click on the **AutoCAD Design Center** icon in the **Standard** toolbar (Fig. 8.12) and the **AutoCAD Design Center** appears (Fig. 8.13). The **Design Center** is a Windows **Explorer** type of window in which files from any directory and disk can be identified. It is a true window as can be seen by *dragging* the **Design Center** away from the position in which it appears (Fig. 8.14).

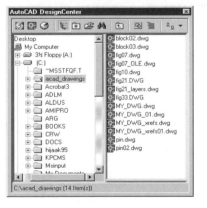

Fig. 8.12 Selecting the **AutoCAD Design Center** tool icon from the **Standard** toolbar

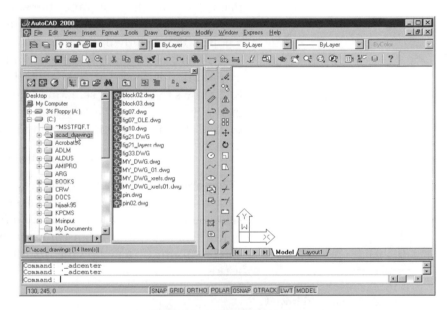

Fig. 8.13 The **AutoCAD Design Center**

Fig. 8.14 The **AutoCAD Design Center** is a true Windows window

At the top of the **Design Center** is a line of buttons, the names of which are shown in Fig. 8.15. It must be noted that a *left-click* on the

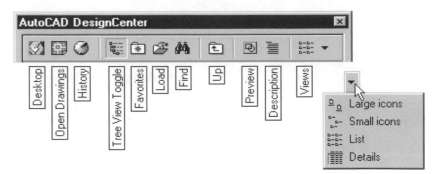

Fig. 8.15 The tool tips of the line of icons at the top of the **Design Center**

Tree Top Toggle button, changes the line of icons in such a manner that the button itself becomes the left-hand button of the row.

A *left-click* on the far right button (an arrow) in the row brings up a popup list as shown in Fig. 8.15.

There is insufficient space in an introductory book of this type to explain in details the actions of all the buttons in the row, but Fig. 8.16 shows the result of selecting a file name followed by a *left-click* on the **Preview** icon. It is advisable to experiment with *left-clicks* on each of the buttons to understand their actions.

The two columns of the Design Center

There are two main parts of the **Design Center**. A left-hand column lists directories and a right-hand column lists the files from a selected directory (Fig. 8.17). A *left-click* on the **Tree View Toggle** button changes the **Design center** from a two-column listing to a single column – that showing the files in a selected directory (Fig. 8.18).

Fig. 8.16 The result of selecting a file name followed by a *left-click* on the **Preview** button

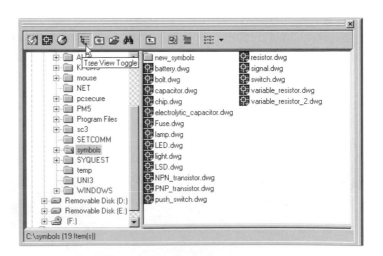

Fig. 8.17 The two columns of the **Design Center**

Fig. 8.18 The column showing
file names from a selected
directory after a *left-click* on
the **Tree View Toggle** button

Fig. 8.19 *Dragging* a drawing
file from a **AutoCAD Design
Center** list

Dragging files from the Design Center

Drawings (and some other types of graphics) can speedily be loaded
into the AutoCAD 2000 drawing area by selecting the file name of the
required graphic and *dragging* from the file name of the drawing into
the drawing area. The drawing is *dragged* as a small rectangle (Fig.
8.19). As the rectangle is *dropped* so the Command line shows:

> **Command: Specify insertion point or [Scale/X/Y/Z/Rotate/PScale/
> PX/PY/PZ/PRotate]:** *pick* (or enter coordinates) of an insertion
> point
> **'C:\symbols\battery drawing'**
> **Enter X scale factor, specify opposite corner, or [Corner XYZ]
> <1>:** *right-click*
> **Enter Y scale factor <Use X scale factor>:** *right-click*
> **Command:**

And the drawing (in this case a battery symbol) is inserted into the
drawing area at the *picked* insertion point.

Any drawing (or some forms of graphics) can be dragged from the
Design Center into the R15 drawing area in this manner.

An electronics circuit

Figure 8.20 shows a number of electrical/electronics symbols which
have been *dragged* and *dropped* into the AutoCAD 2000 in this
manner. The symbols are inserted at suitable points for the construction
of a circuit diagram and any details not *dragged* and *dropped* from
the **Design Center** are added when all symbol drawings have been
inserted.

Figure 8.21 shows the resulting simple circuit drawing constructed
from the symbols.

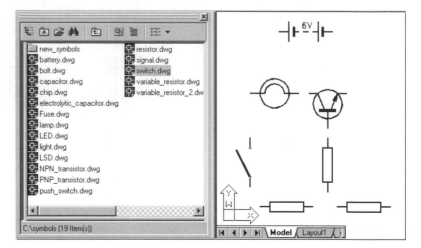

Fig. 8.20 A number of symbols *dragged* and *dropped* from the **design Center**

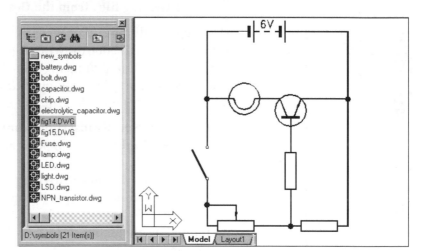

Fig. 8.21 The circuit diagram formed from the symbols shown in Fig. 8.20

Other graphics from the Design Center

Other forms of graphic files can be *dragged* and *dropped* from the **Design Center** into the R15 window. Figure 8.22 shows a drawing which has been taken from its file name in the **Design Center** and Fig. 8.23 a graphics in the form of a **PCX** file, also *dragged* from the **Design Center**. Graphics files such as those with extensions ***bmp**; ***.pcx**; ***.eps**; ***.wmp** among others can be *dragged* from the **Design Center** as well as drawings.

File details

Details of the Blocks (page 193), Dimension Styles (page 169), Layers, Layouts, Linetypes, Text Styles and Xrefs (page 200) can be shown in the **Design Center**. *Left-click* on the **Tree View Toggle**

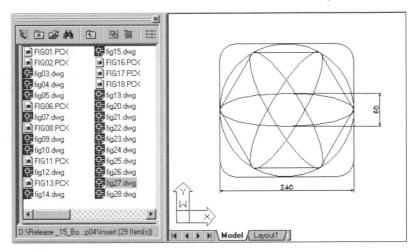

Fig. 8.22 A drawing from the
Design Center

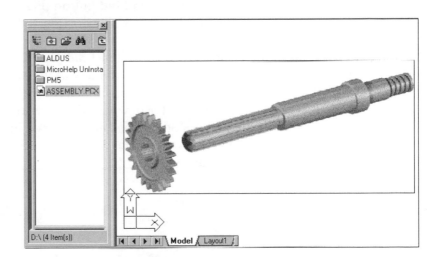

Fig. 8.23 A PCX graphics from
the **Design Center**

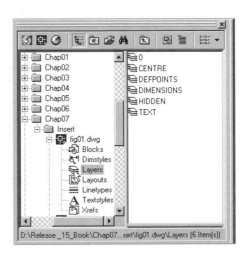

Fig. 8.24 Details of the
contents of a drawing file in
the **Design Center**

button to ensure both columns are showing. *Double-click* on a directory name or *left-click* on the + sign to its left, which brings all file names into the left-hand column. Then *double-click* on a drawing file name (or *left-click* on its + sign) and a list of icons and names appears below the file name. Then *left-click* on the required icon in the list (or on its name) and details of that item appears in the right-hand column. Figure 8.24 shows the layers in the drawing of file name d:\Chap07\insert\fig01.dwg. It is worthwhile experimenting with this facility.

If blocks or xrefs are contained within a drawing, they may be *dragged* and *dropped* from the **Design Center** into the AutoCAD 2000 drawing area with the aid of this facility.

The Find dialogue box

Left-click on the **Find** button (Fig. 8.25) in the **Design Center**. The **Find** dialogue box appears (Fig. 8.26). In the dialogue box *enter* the name of the file to be found in the **Search for the word(s)** box, and then *left-click* on the **Find Now** button. The files of the name so *entered* appear in the box at the lower end of the dialogue box. A *double-click* on the file names which appear takes one back to the **Design Center** in which the file name is highlighted. The found file can then be *dragged* and *dropped* into the AutoCAD 2000 drawing area. Make sure the file is *dragged* from the right-hand column of the **Design Center**.

Fig. 8.25 Select the **Find** icon in the **Design Center**

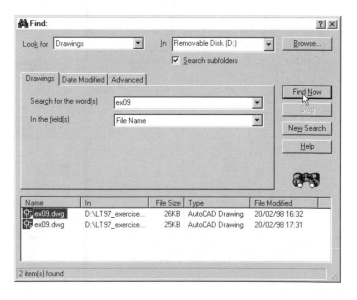

Fig. 8.26 The **Find** dialogue box

Fig. 8.27 The **Load** button in the **Design Center**

The Load Design Center Palette

Left-click on the **Load** button of the **Design Center** (Fig. 8.27) and the **Load DesignCenter Palette** dialogue box appears (Fig. 8.28). When a file is selected from this dialogue, the file name becomes automatically highlighted in the **Design Center**, together with the icons showing the various parts of the drawing file. This enables *drag* and *drop* of the selected file (or its parts) from the **Design Center**.

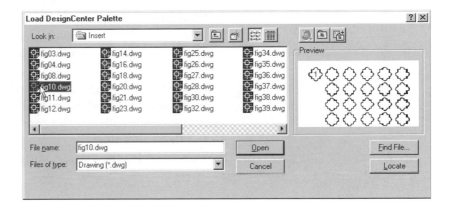

Fig. 8.28 The **Load DesignCenter Palette** dialogue box

Questions

1. What happens on screen when the **Zoom Dynamic** tool is in operation?
2. Can you explain the difference between the use of **Zoom All** and **Zoom Extents**?
3. How does one exit from using the **Pan** tool?
4. What is the purpose of the **Aerial View** window?
5. When the **AutoCAD Design Center** window first appears on screen it is likely to contain two columns. How can the two columns be replaced by a single column?
6. The **Design Center** is held in a window. Can the window be resized?
7. What is the purpose of the **Preview** button in the **Design Center**?
8. How is the **Find** dialogue box of the **Design Center** brought on screen?
9. What is the purpose of the **Find** dialogue box?
10. What is the purpose of the **Load** button of the **Design Center**?

Exercises

1. Load any drawing into the AutoCAD 2000 window. Use the following **Zoom** tools in the loaded drawing:

   Zoom Window; Zoom All; Zoom Extents; Zoom Dynamic; Zoom Scale; Zoom Previous; Zoom real time.

2. Load a large drawing on screen and experiment with the various **Pan** tools from the **View** pull-down menu.

3. Call the **Aerial View** window on screen with a drawing loaded. Experiment with the buttons in the **Aerial View** window. Note that some are not active, depending upon which **Zooms** are active in the AutoCAD 2000 window.

4. Experiment with *dragging* the **Aerial View** window to new sizes.

5. Call the **AutoCAD Design Center** into the AutoCAD 2000 window and experiment with *dragging* and *dropping* various types of files for the **Design Center**.

6. Experiment with the various buttons at top of the **Design Center**.

Chapter 9

Types of technical drawing

Isometric drawing

AutoCAD 2000 includes features constructing the 2D pictorial form
of drawing known as isometric drawing. This form of drawing must
not be confused with 3D (three-dimensional) drawing which will be
described in Chapters 15–17. The pictorial views produced in
isometric drawing are based upon three axes – vertical axis (90°), at
the angle of 30° and at 150° (Fig. 9.1).

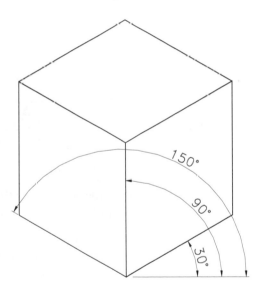

Fig. 9.1 The three isometric
axes in isometric drawing

Setting up for isometric drawing

Left-click on **Drafting Settings…** in the **Tools** pull-down menu (Fig.
9.2) and in the **Drafting Settings** dialogue which appears (Fig. 9.3)
left-click on the **Snap and Grid** tab, followed by another in the check
circle against **Isometric Snap**. Then *left-click* on the **OK** button of the
dialogue box. The AutoCAD 2000 window changes as shown in Fig.
9.4.

Fig. 9.2 Calling the **Drafting Settings** dialogue box to screen

Fig. 9.3 Setting **Isometric Snap** in the **Drafting Settings** dialogue box

Setting Isometric style from the Command line

An alternative method is to *enter* **sn** or **snap** at the Command line:

> **Command:** *enter* sn (snap) *right-click*
> **Specify grid spacing or [ON/OFF/Rotate/Style/Type] <10>:** *enter* s (Style) *right-click*
> **Enter snap grid style [Standard/Isometric] <S>:** *enter* i (Isometric) *right-click*
> **Specify vertical spacing <10>:** *right-click*
> **Command:**

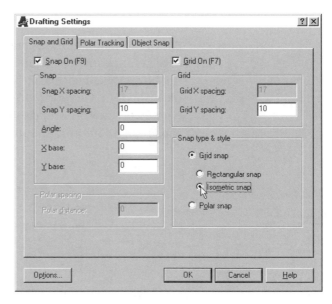

Isoplanes

Either press the function key **F5** repeatedly, or press **Ctrl+E** keys repeatedly. The Command line shows:

> **Command: <Isoplane Top>**
> **Command: <Isoplane Right>**
> **Command: <Isoplane Left>**

As the keys are pressed.

Figure 9.4 shows the AutoCAD 2000 window with **Isoplane Left** set. Watch the cursor hairs change as the key **F5** is pressed. Figure 9.5 shows isometric squares drawn in the three **Isoplane** positions.

Isocircles

When a circular part is included in an isometric drawing, the circle becomes elliptical (an isocircle). The slope of the major axis depends upon the isoplane on which it is drawn. To draw an isocircle:

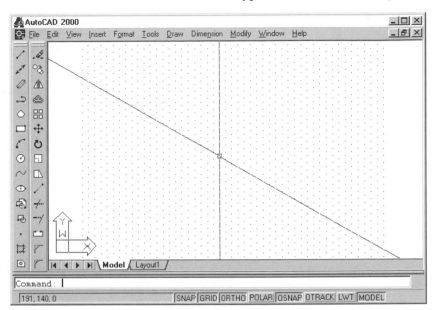

Fig. 9.4 The AutoCAD 2000 window after setting **Isometric Snap**

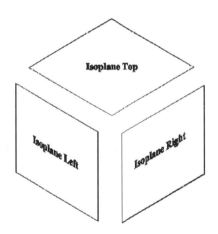

Fig. 9.5 The three **Isoplane** positions

Command: *enter* el (for ellipse) *right-click*
Specify axis endpoint of ellipse or [Arc/Center/Isocircle]: *enter* i (Isocircle) *right-click*
Specify center of isocircle: *pick* (or *enter* coordinates)
Specify radius of isocircle or [Diameter]: *enter* a figure *right-click*
Command:

Figure 9.6 shows three isocircles on their respective Isoplanes.

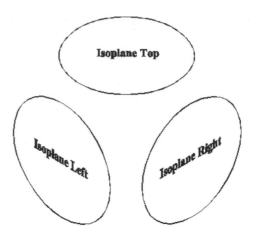

Fig. 9.6 Isocircles on the three isoplanes

Worked example 1 – isometric drawing (Fig. 9.7)

1. Set up the AutoCAD 2000 window in **Isometric Snap** style.
2. Press **F5** until **Isoplane Right** is current.
3. Make sure **Sap** is set on (Press **F9** if necessary).
4. Call the **Line** tool.
5. *Pick* coordinate point 303,5 as the **Line** start point.
6. *Drag* the cursor along the vertical cursor and *enter* 70 *right-click*
7. *Drag* the cursor along the 30° cursor and *enter* 100 *right-click*
8. *Drag* the cursor along the vertical cursor and *enter* 70 *right-click*
9. Continue in this manner until the outline numbered 1 to 8 is drawn.
10. Press **F5** to set **Isoplane Top**
11. Call **Line** again and starting at point 6 of the outline complete the top – a rhombus of depth from to back of 60.

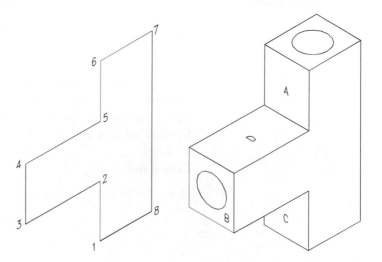

Fig. 9.7 Worked example 1 – isometric drawing

Plate I Front view of a house showing hatching

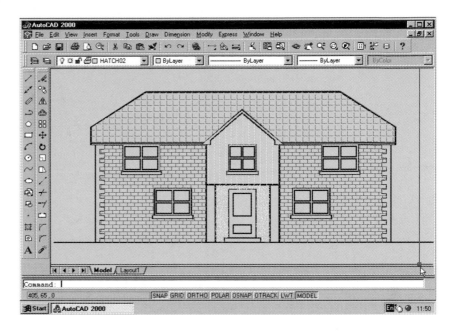

Plate II The **Boundary Hatch** dialogue box and **Hatch Pattern Palette**

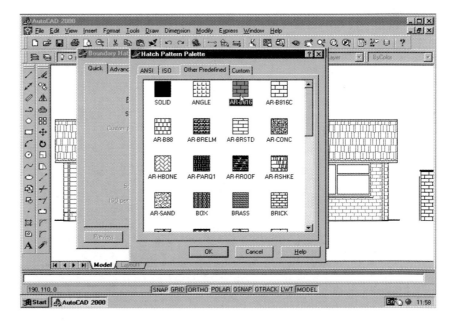

Plate III Two-view drawing
with a bitmap image of the
component

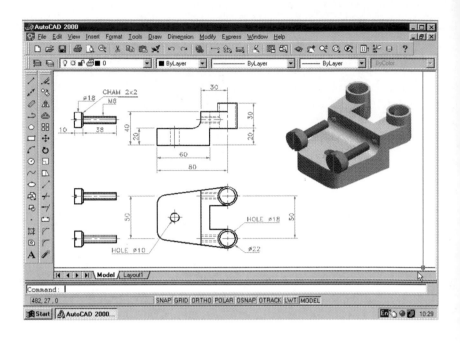

Plate IV Use of the **Multiple
Document Environment**

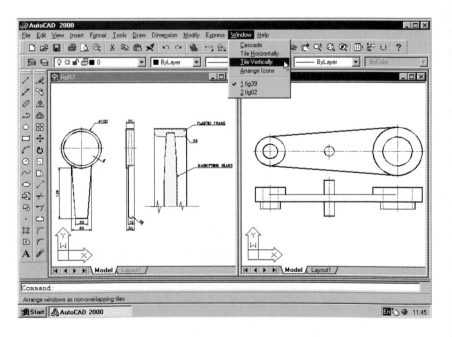

Plate V Constructing a 3D model in a four-viewport window

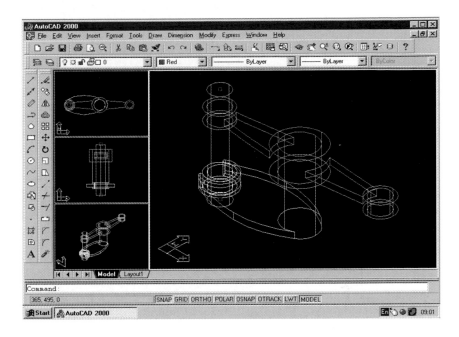

Plate VI Two-view orthographic projection in a **Layout** window

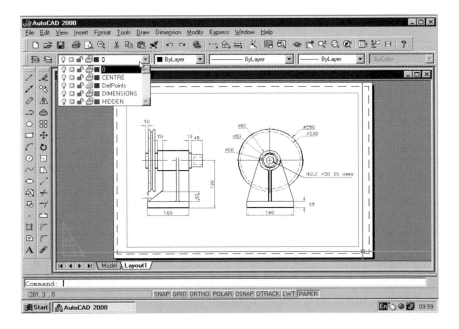

Plate VII Dragging and *dropping* a symbol from the **Design Center**

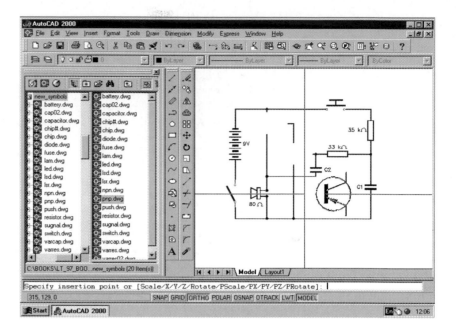

Plate VIII 3D model drawings constructed and rendered in AutoCAD 2000 and pasted into a PageMaker document

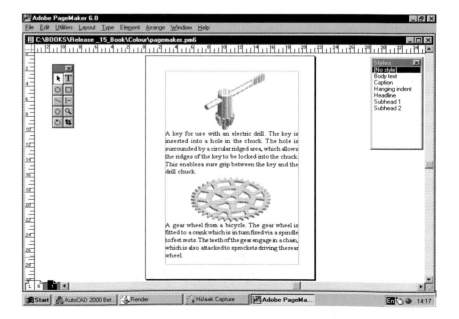

Plate IX 3D model
constructed and rendered in
AutoCAD 2000

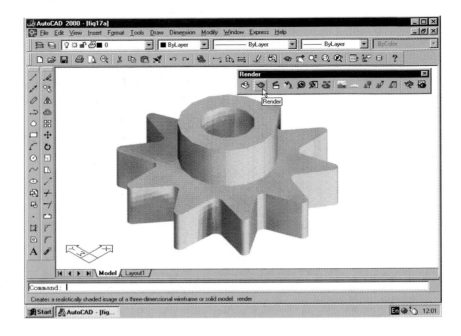

Plate X 3D model constructed
and rendered in AutoCAD
2000

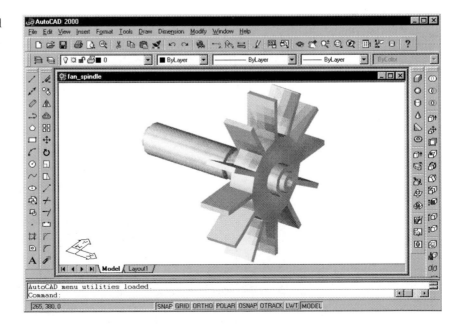

Plate XI 3D model assembly constructed and rendered in a variety of materials

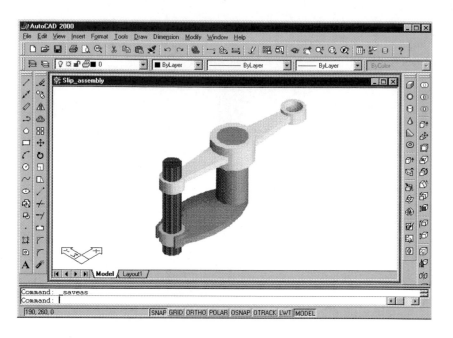

Plate XII 3D model assembly constructed and rendered in two materials

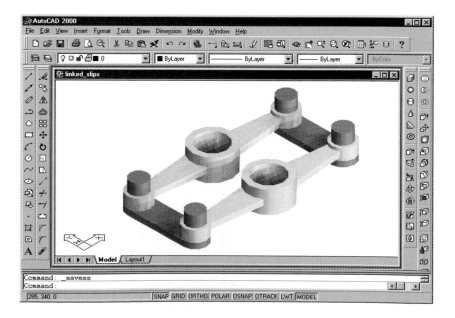

Plate XIII 3D model assembly constructed and rendered in a variety of materials

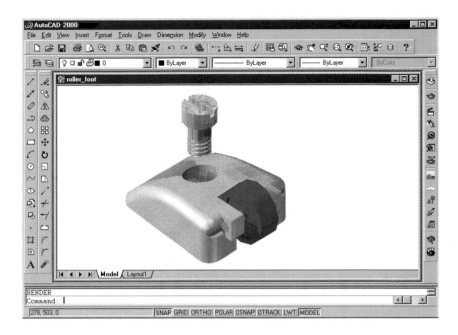

Plate XIV The rendered model shown in Plate XIII set against a background

Plate XV Four 3D models constructed and rendered in AutoCAD 2000

Plate XVI Four renderings shown in another example of the use of the Multiple Document Environment

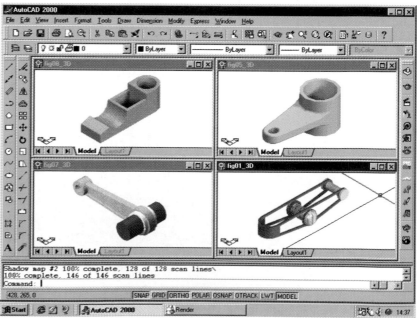

12. Set **Isoplane Left** and add the three faces **A**, **B** and **C**.
13. Set **Isoplane Top** and draw last line to give face **D**.
14. Set **Snap** to 5 from the Command line.
15. **Isoplane** is at **Top**. Call the **Ellipse** tool in its **isocircle** mode. *Pick* the isocircle centre at 307,248 and draw the isocircle of radius 20.
16. Set **Isoplane** to **Left** and with centre 191,75 construct another isocircle of radius 20.

Worked example 2 – isometric drawing (Fig. 9.9)

1. Set **Isoplane Top** current.
2. Draw an isocircle of centre 165,205 and radius 50.
3. With the **Copy** tool copy the isocircle 20 below the original.
4. With the **Line** tool draw lines along the 30° axis 90 long tangential to the ellipses and complete drawing **1**.
5. With the **Trim** tool trim parts of the isocircles and lines. With **Line** and with the osnap **near** to complete drawing **2**.

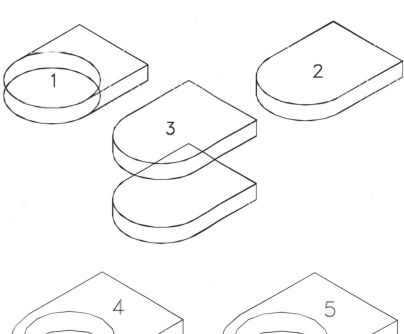

Fig. 9.8 First stages of worked example 2 – isometric drawing

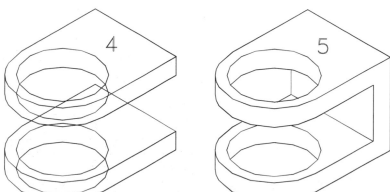

Fig. 9.9 Final stages of worked example 2 – isometric drawing

6.   With the **Copy** tool copy the drawing so far (drawing **2**) 80 units vertically down to produce drawing **3**.
7.   Draw an isocircle of centre 165,205 and radius 50.
8.   **Copy** the circle to produce drawing **4**.
9.   Add lines for the back of the drawing.
10. With the **Trim** tool trim unwanted lines and parts of isocircles to produce drawing **5**.

Orthographic projection

Orthographic projection is probably the most widely used method of technical drawing. This method relies upon looking at the object being drawn from front, from above, from left, from right, or from any other viewing position. What is seen is imagined as being projected via parallel rays onto planes parallel to the face being viewed, or perpendicular to the viewing direction.

Figure 9.10 shows the basis of orthographic projection:

FRONT VIEW: The object to be drawn is imagined as being looked at from the front and what is seen is projected onto a vertical plane.

END VIEW: The object is then viewed from one side and what is seen projected onto another vertical plane.

PLAN: The object is then viewed from above and what is seen projected onto a horizontal plane.

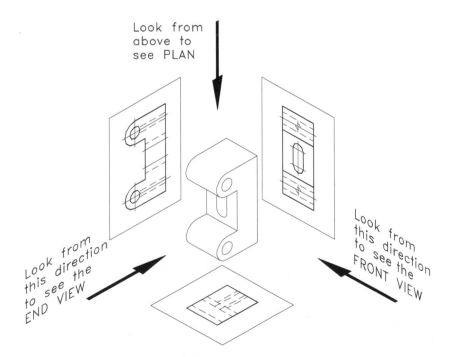

Fig. 9.10 The basis of orthographic projection

The three views are then placed side by side onto a 2D plane (a flat surface). This is what is known as the orthographic projection (Fig. 9.11). In this projection hidden and centre lines have been included.

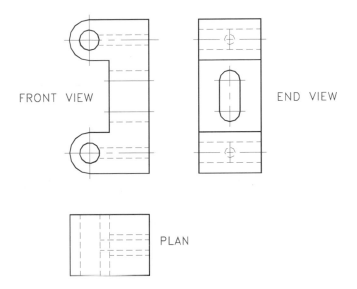

Fig. 9.11 Front and end views and plan rearranged as an orthographic projection

Notes

1. Any number of views can be given in an orthographic projection. The principle of determining the number of view is the need to obtain the best possible description of the object(s) appearing in the projection.
2. There are two major forms of orthographic projection – **FIRST ANGLE** – an example is given in Fig. 9.11, and **THIRD ANGLE** – as shown in Fig. 9.12.
3. The basis of third angle projection is different from that of first angle. In third angle projection the imaginary planes are placed between the viewer and the object and what is seen is, as it were, drawn onto the planes between the viewer and the object.
4. Names of the views are not usually included in an orthographic projection, unless it is thought labels will make for easier interpretation.

Some rules for orthographic projection

1. In first angle projection end views and plans face outwards from the front view.
2. In third angle projection end views and plans face inwards from the front view.
3. Centre lines are normally drawn through all circular parts in all three directions.

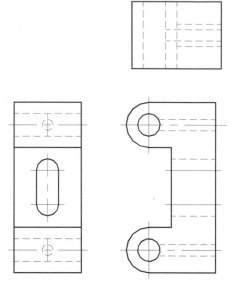

Fig. 9.12 A third angle
projection

4. Lines in the views which cannot be seen from the outside are
   indicated by hidden lines.
5. Where necessary, in order to make the meaning of a drawing clear,
   sectional views may be included with orthographic views. Examples
   of sectional views are given in Chapter 10.

Drawing sheet layout

Drawings to which students in colleges and people in industry work
are often referred to as 'working drawings' and are frequently based
upon orthographic projection. Depending on the reason for which
the drawings are being constructed, different forms of drawing
layout may be employed. Two examples are given – Fig. 9.13, which

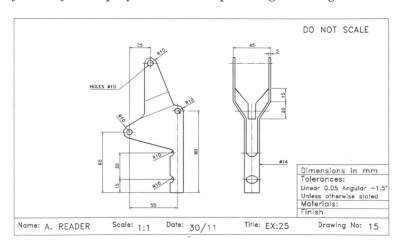

Fig. 9.13 A simple form of
drawing layout

would be a suitable layout for students constructing drawings in response to exercises and Fig. 9.14, a form of layout suitable for drawings from a small engineering firm.

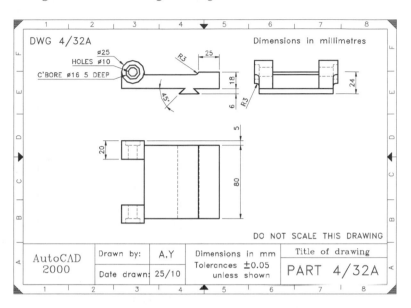

Fig. 9.14 A more complicated form of drawing layout

Questions

1. How is the AutoCAD 2000 window set up ready for the construction of an isometric drawing?
2. Isometric drawing is a form of pictorial drawing. Can it be said to be a three-dimensional form of drawing?
3. How many ways can the **Isoplanes** be set?
4. What are the differences between an ellipse and an isocircle?
5. What are the differences between first and third angle orthographic projections?

Exercises

The exercise below should be regarded partly as exercises to practise isometric drawing and orthographic projections, but should also form a useful revision of work from previous chapters.

1. Figure 9.15 is an isometric drawing of the part shown in the first angle projection Fig. 9.16. Construct the isometric drawing to the details given in Fig. 9.15.

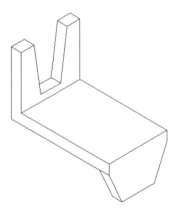

Fig. 9.15 The isometric drawing for exercise 1

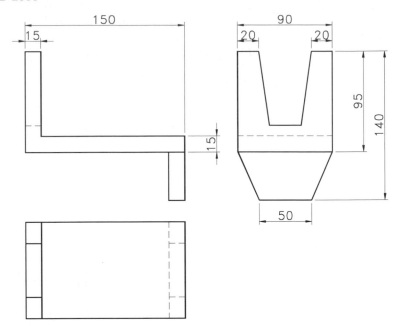

Fig. 9.16 The first angle
orthographic projection for
exercise 1

2. Figure 9.17 is an isometric drawing of the fork coupling shown in
    a two-view orthographic drawing Fig. 9.18. Figure 9.18 could be
    in either first or third angle.

    Construct a three-view third angle projection of the fork which
    includes an end view to the details given in the two drawings.

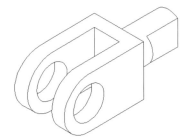

Fig. 9.17 The isometric
drawing for exercise 2

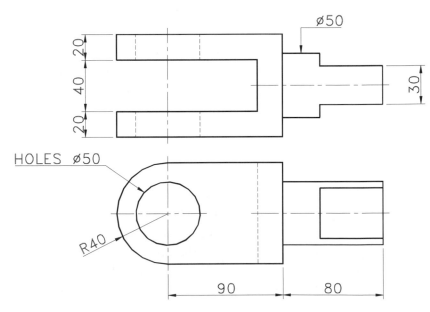

Fig. 9.18 The orthographic
projection for exercise 2

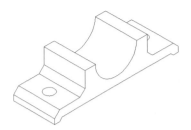

Fig. 9.19 The isometric
drawing for exercise 3

3. Figure 9.19 is an isometric projection of a half bearing. Figure 9.20
    is a two-view third angle projection of the bearing.
       Construct a three-view first angle orthographic projection of the
    bearing, to include an end view.

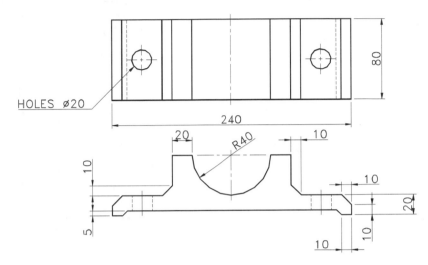

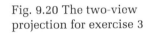

Fig. 9.20 The two-view
projection for exercise 3

4. Construct a third angle three-view orthographic projection of the
    part shown in Figures 9.21 and 9.22
5. Construct an isometric drawing of the part shown in Figures 9.21
    and 9.22 to the sizes given with Fig. 9.22

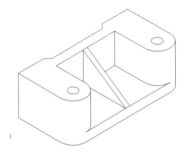

Fig. 9.21 The isometric
drawing for exercises 4 and 5

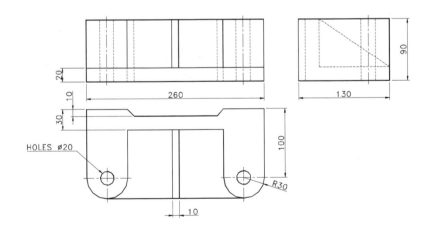

Fig. 9.22 The three-view first
angle projection for exercise 4

6. Construct an isometric drawing of the post support shown in
    Figures 9.23 and 9.24 to the sizes given in Fig. 9.24.
7. Construct a two-view first angle orthographic projection to the
    details given in Fig. 9.24.

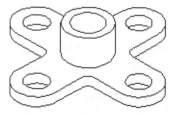

Fig. 9.23 The isometric drawing for exercises 6 and 7

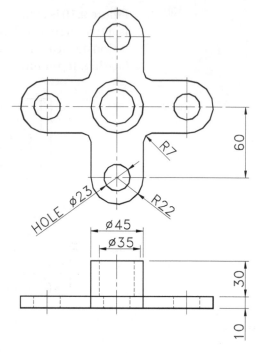

Fig. 9.24 Two-view orthographic pojection for exercises 6 and 7

8.   A two-view orthographic projection of another support stand is shown in Figures 9.25 and 9.26.
     Construct a three-view first angle orthographic projection of the stand.

9.   Construct an isometric drawing of the stand shown in Fig. 9.25.

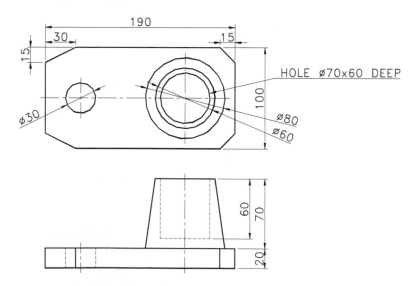

Fig. 9.25 Exercises 8 and 9

10. Construct the three-view orthographic projection shown in Fig. 9.26 in third angle projection,

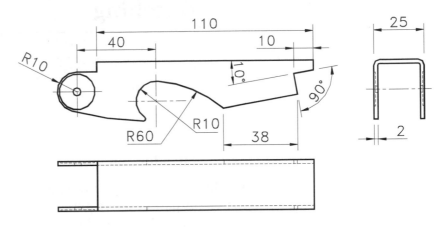

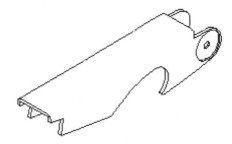

Fig. 9.26 Exercise 10

Fig. 9.17 Isometric drawing for exercise 10

Chapter 10

Hatching

Introduction

Hatching, which is the filling of outlines with line patterns, is an important part of the features of most CAD systems. In AutoCAD 2000 hatching is initiated by calling the **Boundary Hatch** dialogue box by either selecting **Hatch...** from the **Draw** pull-down menu, with a *left-click* on the **Hatch** tool icon in the **Draw** toolbar, or by *entering* **h**, **bh** or **bhatch** at the Command line (Fig. 10.1). It should be noted here that if **hatch** is *entered*, the **Boundary Hatch** dialogue box does not appear and hatching is initiated through *entries* in response to prompts at the Command line.

When the tool is called, the **Boundary Hatch** dialogue box appears (Fig. 10.2).

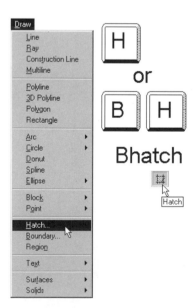

Fig. 10.1 Methods of calling the **Boundary Hatch** dialogue box to screen

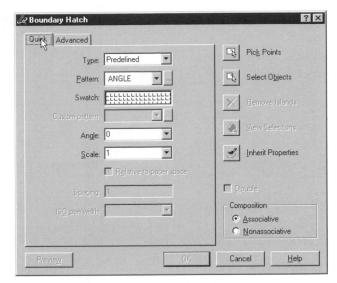

Fig. 10.2 The **Boundary Hatch** dialogue box

The Boundary Hatch dialogue box

There are two parts of the dialogue box – The **Quick** dialogue (Fig. 10.2) and the **Advanced** dialogue (Fig. 10.3).

In the **Quick** dialogue, *left-click* on the **Swatch:** box and the **hatch Pattern** dialogue box appears showing a group of **ANSI** patterns (Fig. 10.4), In the dialogue box, *left-click* on the **Other Predefined** tab and a group of various hatch patterns appear (Fig. 10.5). Spool through the patterns to examine the fairly large variety of hatch patterns available in AutoCAD 2000.

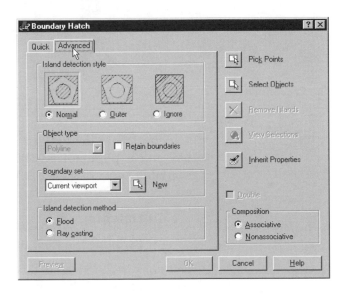

Fig. 10.3 The **Advanced** dialogue of the **Boundary Hatch** dialogue box

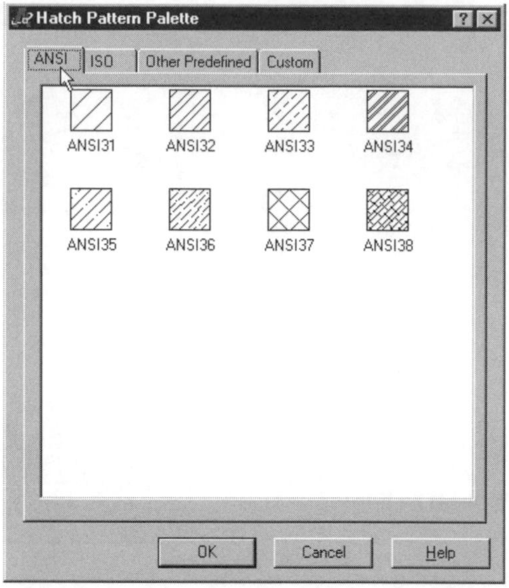

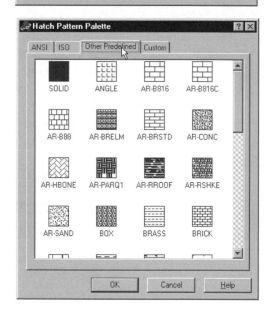

Fig. 10.4 The **ANSI** hatch
pattern palette

Fig. 10.5 The **Predefined**
dialog

Left-click in the **Pattern:** box, or on the arrow to the right of the
box and a popup list with the names of all the hatch patterns
available appears (Fig. 10.6).

Hatching

By using the Pick Points button

Left-click in the **Swatch:** box, followed by a *double-click* on a hatch
pattern in one of the **Hatch Pattern Palettes**. The selected pattern
appears in the **Swatch:** box. To apply the selected pattern within a

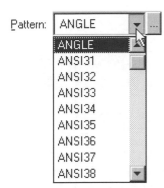

Fig. 10.6 The popup list showing all available hatch patterns by name

drawing outline *left-click* on the **Pick points** button. The Command line shows:

> **Command: BHATCH** The **Boundary hatch** dialogue box appears
> **Select internal point:** *pick* inside the outline to be hatched
> **Selecting everything. Selecting everything visible...**
> **Analyzing the selected data...**
> **Analyzing internal islands...**
> **Select the internal point:** *right-click* dialogue box reappears

Left-click on the **Preview** button and the outline reappears with the hatching in place.

> **<Hit enter or right-click to return to the dialog> :**

Examine the hatching and *right-click*. The dialogue box reappears. If the hatching was OK, *left-click* on the **OK** button of the dialogue box to complete the hatching. If the hatching requires adjustment – for example adjustment of scale or a different hatch pattern, make the adjustment and **Preview** again.

By using the Select Objects button

Left-click in the **Swatch:** box, followed by a *double-click* on a hatch pattern in one of the **Hatch Pattern Palettes**. The selected pattern appears in the **Swatch:** box. To apply the selected pattern within a drawing outline *left-click* on the **Select Objects** button. The Command line shows:

> **Command: BHATCH** The **Boundary hatch** dialogue box appears
> **Select objects:** *pick* one of the objects in the outline **1 found**
> **Select objects:** *pick* another **1 found, 2 total**
> **Select objects:** *pick* another **1 found, 3 total**
> **Select objects:** *pick* another **1 found, 4 total**
> **Select objects:** *right-click* – the dialogue box reappears

Left-click on the **Preview** button and the outline reappears with the hatching in place.

> **<Hit enter or right-click to return to the dialog> :**

Examine the hatching and *right-click*. The dialogue box reappears. If the hatching was OK, *left-click* on the **OK** button of the dialogue box to complete the hatching. If the hatching requires adjustment – for example adjustment of scale or a different hatch pattern, make the adjustment and **Preview** again.

Figure 10.7 shows four outlines hatched using either of these two methods. The hatch pattern from the palette is shown alongside each of the outlines.

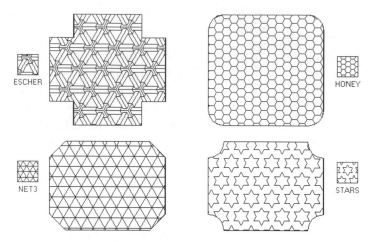

Fig. 10.7 Examples of outlines after hatching

The Advanced options

The three **Island detection styles** in the **Advanced** dialogue of the **Boundary Hatch** dialogue box determine which parts of series of outlines within an outline. Figure 10.8 shows part of the **Advanced** dialogue and Fig. 10.9 the results of selecting each of the three options.

In the examples given in Fig. 10.9 the hatch pattern used was **ANSI37** and the **Scale** was *entered* at **2**.

Fig. 10.8 The three **Island detection styles** in the **Advanced** dialogue

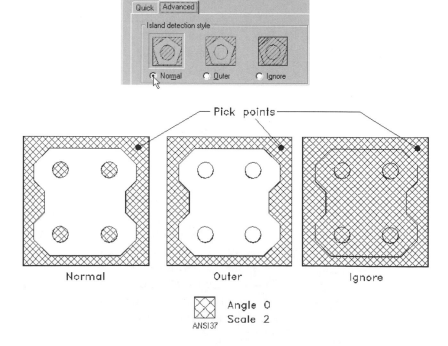

Fig. 10.9 The results of selecting the three **Island detection styles**

Select Objects

Fig. 10.10 The **Select Objects** button of the **Boundary Hatch** dialogue box

Hatching boundaries which are not closed

Figure 10.12 shows three outlines, in the boundaries of which a break has occurred. In order that the areas within the outlines could be hatched, a *left-click* on the **Select Objects** button (Fig. 10.10) was required because an internal point within a broken boundary brings the **Boundary Detection Error** warning box on screen, with the message **Valid hatch boundary not found** (Fig. 10.11)

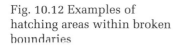

Fig. 10.11 The **Boundary Detection** warning box

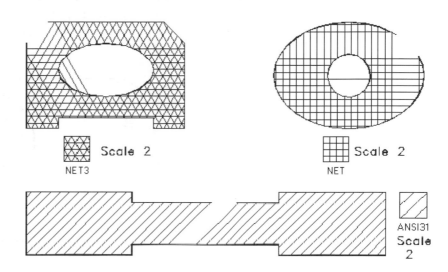

Fig. 10.12 Examples of hatching areas within broken boundaries

Associative hatching

If the check circle against the name **Associative** in the **Composition** area of the **Boundary Hatch** dialogue box is set on (dot in check circle), then if any outlines within a hatched area are either moved, rotated or scaled, the hatching in outline accommodates to the new position of the inner outline. Examples of moving and rotating inner outlines are given in Fig. 10.14.

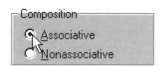

Fig. 10.13 Setting **Associative** on in the **Boundary hatch** dialogue box

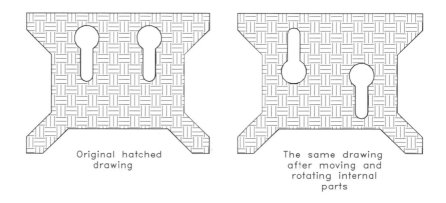

Fig. 10.14 Examples of Associative hatching

Examples of hatching in sectional views

Example 1

Figure 10.15 shows a front view and a sectional end view of a post stand in third angle projection. Again the sectional plane has been taken. Figure 10.16 shows a pictorial view of the stand showing that a sectional plane has cut through the component, the front half has been discarded and the cut surface hatched with the hatch pattern ANSI31. Included with the pictorial view is the resulting sectional front view and plan based upon details given in Fig. 10.15 and in the pictorial view. Note the following in Fig. 10.16:

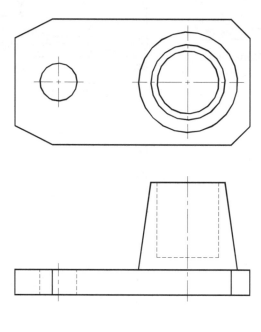

Fig. 10.15 Third angle orthographic projection of example 1

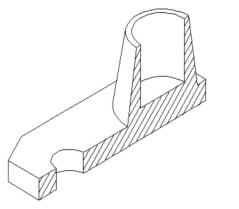

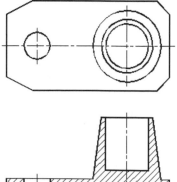

Fig. 10.16 Sectional front view of example 1

1. When no indication is given of where a section plane has made its cut, it is assumed it has been taken along the centre line of the view from which the sectional view is derived.
2. The hatch pattern in general use when hatching sections in engineering drawings is **ANSI31**. Other hatch patterns can be used as indicated in the **AutoCAD Text Window** (Fig. 10.17) showing the names and uses of some of the hatch patterns. This text window appears when:

> **Command:** *enter* hatch *right-click*
> **Enter a pattern name or [?/Solid/User defined] <ANSI31>:** *enter* ? *right-click*
> **Enter pattern(s) to list <*>:** *right-click*

And the text window (Fig. 10.17) appears.

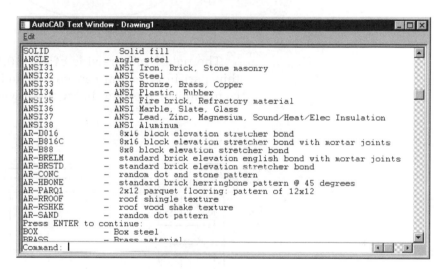

Fig. 10.17 The **AutoCAD Text Window** showing the hatch pattern names

Example 2

Figure 10.18 shows a front view and a sectional end view of a pulley wheel. Again the section plane has been taken along the vertical line of the front view.

Example 3

The two views to the left of Fig. 10.19 show a front view and a sectional end view. In the sectional view the hatching pattern of the insets is at right angles to that of the outer casing. This is the general form taken when alternate hatch is necessary in order to avoid confusion between two parts in a sectional view.

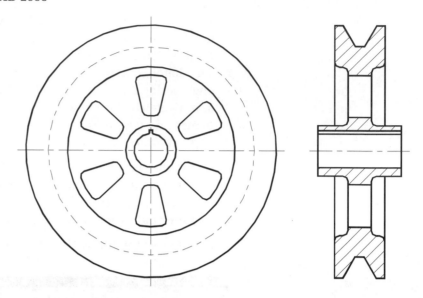

Fig. 10.18 Example 2

The right-hand drawing of Fig. 10.19 shows how hatching of a thin part in a section can be hatched at an alternate angle to its companion in the view, but with a lower scale setting for the pattern.

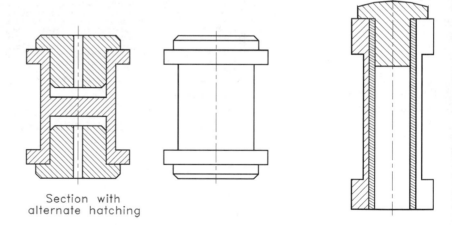

Fig. 10.19 Example 3

Section with
alternate hatching

Example 4

Several different types of sectional views are shown in Fig. 10.20. A label with each view states the type of projection displayed.

Example 5

Figure 10.21 shows some of the rules governing how sectional views should be hatched:

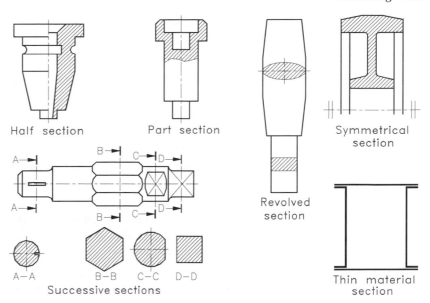

Half section   Part section   Symmetrical
                                          section

Revolved
section

A—A   B—B   C—C   D—D   Thin material
                                              section

Successive sections

Fig. 10.20 Example 4

1. If necessary the edge of a section plane should be shown by a thin centre line ending in two thick lines, against which lettered (or numbered) arrows indicate the direction in which the sectional view should be viewed.
2. Features such as bolts, screws, nuts, webs, ribs and similar parts are shown as outside views.

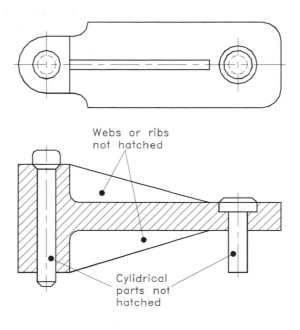

Webs or ribs
not hatched

Cylidrical
parts not
hatched

Fig. 10.21 Example 5. Exceptions to standard sectioning rules

Questions

1. What are the various ways of calling the **Boundary hatch** dialogue box to screen?
2. What happens when **hatch** is *entered* at the Command line?
3. What is the difference between using the **Pick Points** and the **Select Objects** buttons of the **Boundary hatch** dialogue box?
4. What happens when an attempt is made to hatch the area within a boundary which is not closed?
5. What is meant by **Associative** hatching?
6. How can one find out which of the ANSI hatch patterns should be used to represent a particular material?
7. What is meant by 'alternate hatching'?
8. What is a 'revolved section'?
9. What type of feature is shown by outside views within a sectional view in a mechanical engineering drawing?
10. How is a sectional view through an object made from sheet material shown?

Exercises

1. Figure 10.22 is a two-view orthographic projection of a hand lens, together with a separate drawing of an enlargement showing how the lens is held in the holder.

    Working to full scale, construct a two-view orthographic projection of the hand lens with the end view (the right-hand view in Fig. 10.22) showing a sectional view taken along the centre line of the front view.

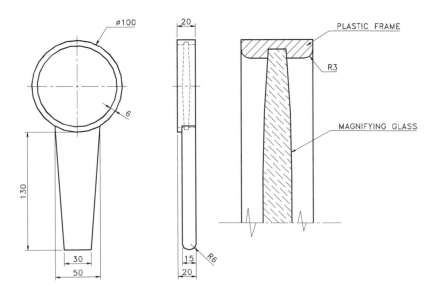

Fig. 10.22 Exercise 1

2. Figure 10.23 shows a pictorial view of a rail holder, together with an end view of the part. The holder is 150 mm long.

Construct the given end view as a sectional view with the cutting plane of the section taken through the web. Add a front view in third angle projection to your drawing.

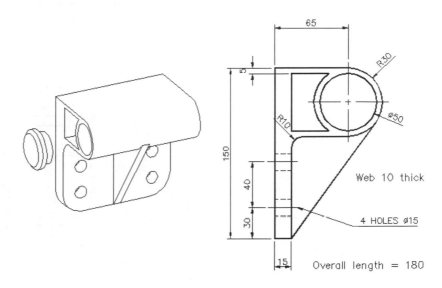

Fig. 10.23 Exercise 2

3. Figure 10.24 shows a pictorial view, together with a two-view first angle orthographic projection of a slider.

Construct the following two views in third angle projection, with both screws in place within their screw holes:

The given front view (upper view of Fig. 10.24);

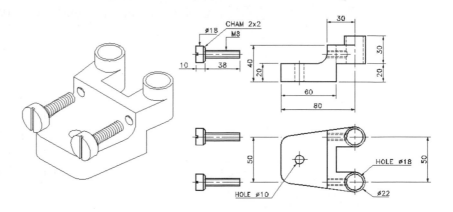

Fig. 10.24 Exercise 3

A sectional plan with the section plane taken through the screws in the front view.

4. Figure 10.25 shows a pictorial view, together with an exploded three-view first angle projection of a guide from a machine. Working in third angle projection, construct the following views with the roller and its pin in their correct positions:

The given front view and plan;

A sectional end view with the section plane cutting through the pin and roller.

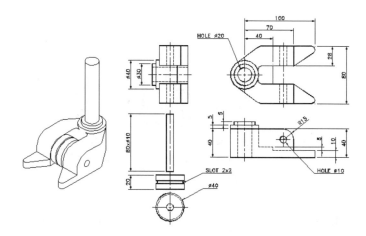

Fig. 10.25 Exercise 4

5. A two-view third angle orthographic projection, together with a pictorial view of a component from a machine is given in Fig. 10.26.

With the pin shown in the pictorial view fully in position, construct the following orthographic views of the component in first angle projection:

The two given views;

A sectional end view with the cutting plane taken through the pin.

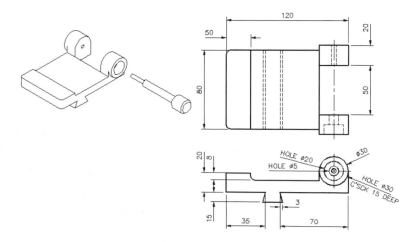

Fig. 10.26 Exercise 5

6. Figure 10.27 is a first angle projection showing the front view and sectional plan of the cover of a small gear box.

   Copy the two given views and add a sectional end view in line with the front view (upper view in Fig. 10.27) working in third angle projection.

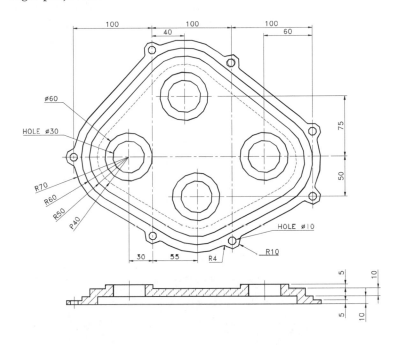

Fig. 10.27 Exercise 6

7. Figure 10.28 shows a pictorial view together with a two view orthographic projection of a hanging device.

   Taking the right-hand view as the end view, construct the following two views:

   The given end view;

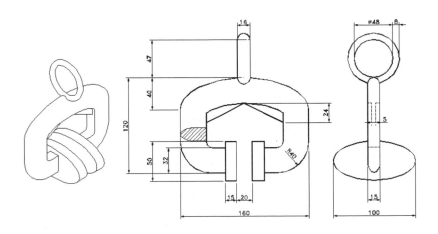

Fig. 10.28 Exercise 7

A sectional front view with the section cutting plane taken vertically through the centre of the end view.

Note

Do not include any dimensions with your answers. The dimensioning of drawings will be dealt with in the next chapter. It is advisable to save your answers to the above questions to disk in order they can be reloaded and have dimensions added at a later date.

Chapter 11

Dimensions

The Dimension tools

Right-click in any toolbar on screen and in the **Toolbar** menu which appears, *left-click* on **Dimension**. The **Dimension** toolbar (Fig. 11.1) appears. Tools for dimensioning can be selected as required from the toolbar.

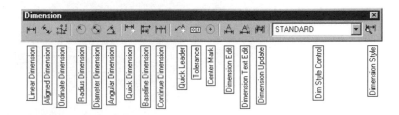

Fig. 11.1 The **Dimension** toolbar with its tool tips

Tools for dimensioning can also be selected from the **Dimension** pull-down menu (Fig. 11.2).

Dimension Styles

Either *left-click* on the **Dimension Style** tool icon in the **Dimension** toolbar, *left-click* on **Style...** in the **Dimension** pull-down menu, or *enter* **d** at the Command line. The **Dimension Style Manager** dialogue box appears (Fig. 11.3).

The dialogue box really consists of a series of dialogues. *Left-click* on the **Modify...** button of the dialogue box and the **Modify Dimension Style** dialogue appears. Aligned near the top of the dialogue are a series of tabs, *left-clicks* on which produce different dialogues.

Setting up MY_STYLE dimension style

Fig. 11.2 The **Dimension** pull-down menu

1. When the **Modify Dimension Style** dialogue box appears the **Lines and Arrows** dialogue will be on screen. Amend the entries in the various parts of this dialogue as shown in Fig. 11.4.

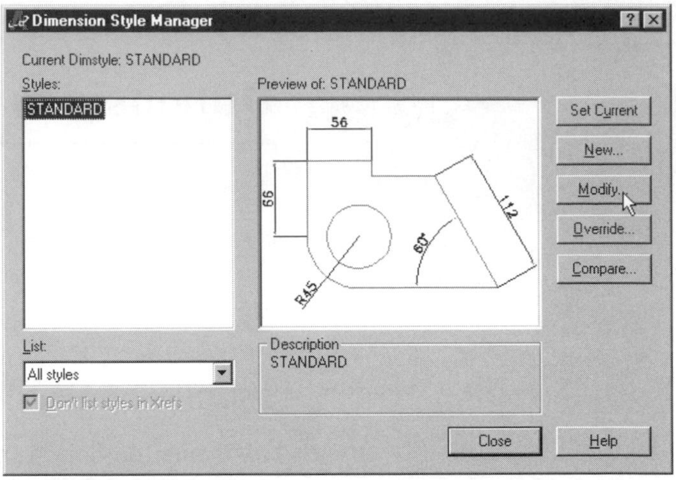

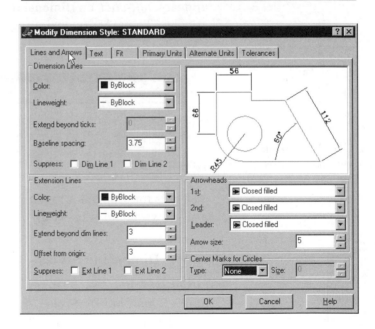

Fig.11.3 The **Dimension Style Manager** dialogue box

Fig. 11.4 The entries in the **Lines and Arrows** dialogue

2. *Left-click* on the **Text** tab and amend the entries in the various parts of the dialogue as shown in Fig. 11.5.
3. *Left-click* on the **Primary Units** tabs and make entries in the dialogue as shown in Fig. 11.6.
4. *Left-click* on the **OK** button of the **Modify Dimension Style** dialogue box to return to the **Dimension Style Manager**.
5. *Left-click* on the **New...** button and the **New Dimension Style** dialogue appears. In its **New Style Name:** box *enter* a suitable name such as that shown **MY_STYLE** (Fig. 11.7).
6. *Left-click* on the **Continue** button and the name **MY_STYLE** appears in the **Styles** list of the **Dimension Style Manager**.

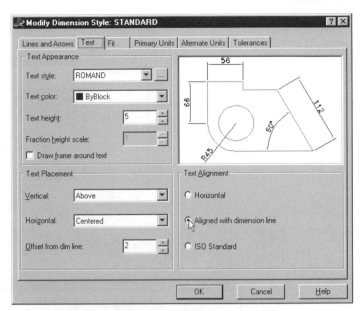

Fig. 11.5 The entries in the
Text dialogue

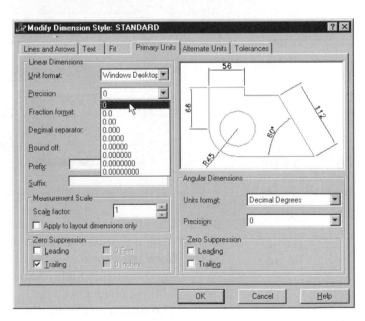

Fig. 11.6 The entries in the
Primary Units dialogue

7. *Left-click* in the **List** box and from the popup list select **All Styles**. The **Styles** list then appears as in Fig. 11.8.
8. *Left-click* on the name **MY_STYLE** in the **Styles** list and again in the **Set Current** button to make this style the dimension style in current use.

   Notes

1. *Left-click* on each style name in the **Styles** list and examine each style as it appears in the **Preview** box.

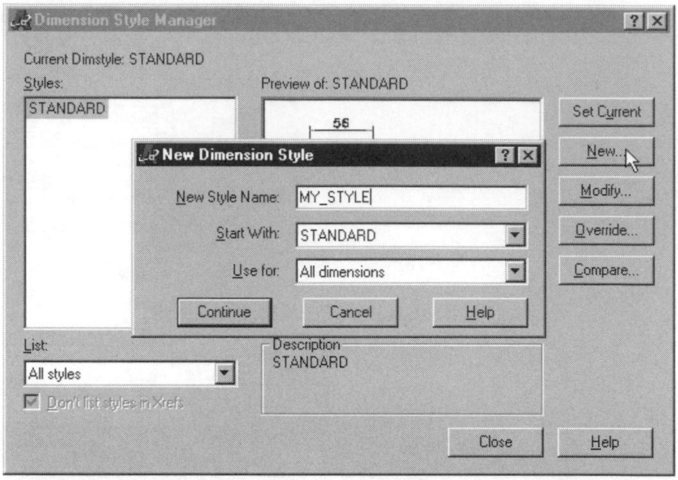

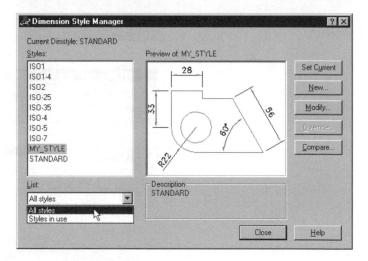

Fig. 11.7 *Entering* a new style name

Fig. 11.8 The style name **MY_STYLES** appearing with all styles in the **Styles** list

2. The dimension style as set above should now be saved to your personal drawing template.
3. Each operator may wish to set his/her own entries for each part of the **Dimension Style Manager**, or to select one of the existing styles as the chosen style.
4. The dimension style as set out above is the style used throughout all drawings in this book.

Methods of adding dimensions to drawings

There are two ways in which dimensions may be added to a drawing:

1. By selecting dimension tools either from the **Dimension** toolbar or from the **Dimension** pull-down menu.
2. By making entries at the Command line.

The results will be the same no matter which method is used. Some operators may wish to use methods **1**, others method **2**, while others may wish to operate using a mixture of both methods.

Examples of dimensioning using tools from the toolbar

Example – Linear Dimension (Fig. 11.9)

Select **Dim Linear** (toolbar) or **Linear** (pull-down menu)

Command:_dimlinear
Specify first extension line origin or <select object>: *pick*
Specify second extension line origin: *pick*
Specify dimension line location or [Mtext/Text/Angle/Horizontal/
  Vertical/Rotated]: *pick*
Dimension text = 140
Command:

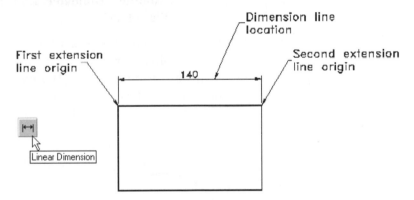

Fig. 11.9 Example – **Linear Dimension**

Example – Aligned Dimension (Fig. 11.10)

The Command line prompts and responses when adding an aligned dimension to a drawing are the same as for **Linear Dimension**, but an alternative method (shown here) can be used for either, by *picking* the object being dimensioned, rather than its ends.

Call **Aligned Dimension** (toolbar) or **Aligned** (pull-down menu):

Command:_dimaligned
Specify first extension line origin or <select object>: *right-click*
Select object to dimension: *pick*
Specify second extension line origin: *pick*
Specify dimension line location or [Mtext/Text/Angle]: *right-click*
Dimension text = 98
Command:

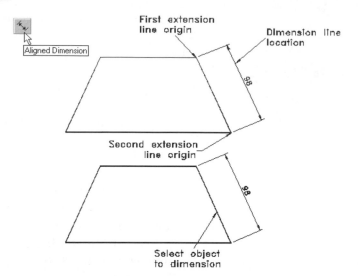

Fig. 11.10 Example **Aligned Dimension**

Example – Diameter, Radius and Angle dimensions (Fig. 11.11)

Figure 11.11 shows the results of calling these three tools to dimension suitable objects from either the toolbar or from the pull-down menu.

In the examples of the **Diameter** and **Radius** dimensions in this illustration, the examples include the selection of a dimension line location both inside and outside the objects.

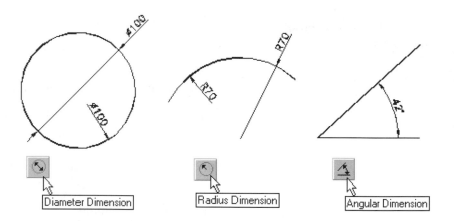

Fig. 11.11 Example – **Circle**, **Radius** and **Angle** dimensions

Example – Quick Dimension (Fig. 11.12)

Quick Dimension allows the dimensioning of several parts of an outline in a single operation.

Fig. 11.12 Example – **Quick Dimension**

Example – Baseline Dimension (Fig. 11.13)

When using this tool, a linear, or other dimension should first be added to the drawing from which baseline dimensions can be added. A warning to this effect is given if an attempt is made to use the tool without a previous dimension being in position.

The set variable **dimdli** controls the spacing between the baseline dimensions. The default setting of **dimdli** is **4**. To rest the variable:

Command: *enter* dimdli *right-click*
Enter ncw value for DIMDLI <4>: *enter* 10 *right-click*
Command:

And now the baseline dimensions will now be 10 units apart.

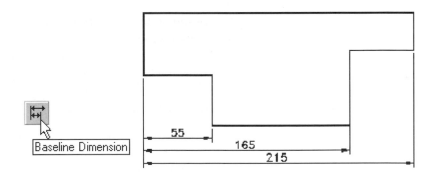

Fig. 11.13 Example – **Baseline Dimension**

Example – Continue Dimension (Fig. 11.14)

As with **Baseline Dimension** a previously placed dimension must be in place for **Continue Dimension** to function.

Geometric tolerances

1. *Left-click* on the **Tolerance** tool icon in the **Dimension** toolbar and the **Geometric Tolerance** dialogue box appears on screen (11.15).
2. A *left-click* in one of the **Sym** boxes and the **Symbols** dialogue appears.

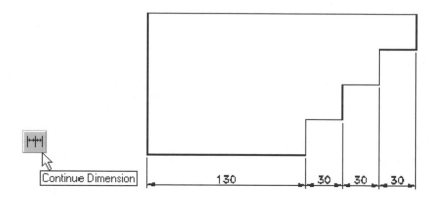

Fig. 11.14 Example – **Continue Dimension**

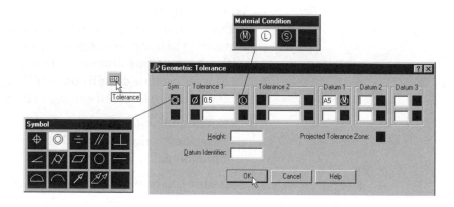

Fig. 11.15 Geometric Tolerances

3. *Left-click* on one of the symbols in the dialogue and the selected symbol appears in the selected **Sym** box.
4. *Left-click* in one of the boxes to the right of the **Tolerance 1** area and the **Material Condition** dialogue appears.
5. *Left-click* on any one of the material symbols and the symbol appears in the selected box.

When satisfied that the required symbols have been added to the various boxes and that *entries* have been made in other parts of the dialogue box, *left-click* on the box's **OK** button. The required geometric tolerance can then be inserted in any required position on screen.

Figure 11.15 shows the dialogue boxes involved in this operation. Figure 11.16 shows the geometric symbol resulting from the entries made as shown in Fig. 11.15.

Figure 11.17 shows a number of simple drawings dimensioned with geometric tolerances. The meaning of the various geometric tolerance symbols in given in Fig. 11.18.

Fig. 11.16 An example of a geometric tolerance symbol

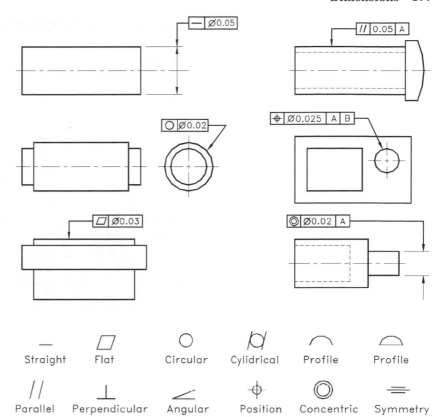

Fig. 11.17 Some examples of geometric tolerance symbols in place in drawings

Fig. 11.18 Geometric tolerance symbols

Linear tolerances

Left-click on **Modify...** in the **Dimension Style Manager** and in the **Modify Dimension Style** dialogue *left-click* on the **Tolerance** tab and set up the dialogue as shown in Fig. 11.19.

Example – Linear tolerances (Fig. 11.20)

Figure 11.20 shows an example of linear dimensioning with tolerances set as shown in Fig. 11.19.

Dimensions from the Command line

At the Command line:

Command: *enter* dim *right-click*
Dim: *enter* hor *right-click*
Specify first extension line origin or <select object>: *pick*
Specify second extension line origin: *pick*
Specify dimension line location or [Mtext/Text/Angle]:

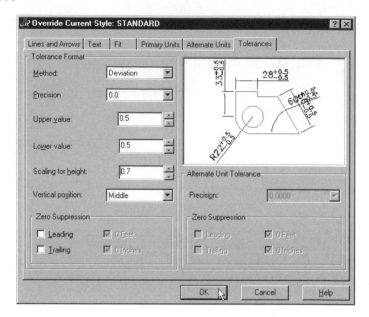

Fig. 11.19 Setting up linear tolerances in the **Tolerance** dialogue

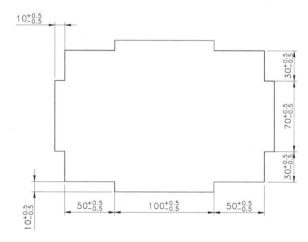

Fig. 11.20 Example – **Linear tolerances**

Enter dimension text <140>: either *right-click* to accept this figure, or enter another figure, followed by a *right-click*
Command:

And the dimension appears with the drawing. Other dimensions can be added in this manner using the following abbreviations:

ve –   vertical
l –   leader
ra –   radius
d –   diameter
al –   aligned
te –   tedit – same as **Dimension Text Edit**

an – angular

cen – center mark

Dimensions and the Properties (Fig. 11.21)

With a dimensioned drawing on screen, *left-click* on the **Properties** tool in the **Standard** toolbar as indicated in Fig. 11.21. The **Properties** dialogue box appears on screen. *Pick* the dimension one wishes to be changed and in the **Properties**, select the item to be changed – in this case changing text height from 5 to 8. When the item has been changed a *right-click* completes the change in the dimensions in the drawing.

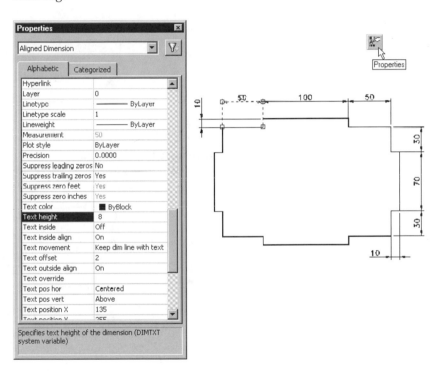

Fig. 11.21 Using the **Properties** dialogue on dimensions

Dimensions are associative

If either of the two tools **Stretch** or **Scale** are used upon a dimensioned drawing, the dimensions included with the drawing change to accept the new shapes, sizes and scales. The series of figures Fig. 11.22 to Fig. 11.24 show the effect of these two tools on a dimensioned outline. Note that in each case the dimensions adjust to the stretched or scaled drawings.

Notes

1. In Fig. 11.22 drawing **1** is the original and drawing **2** the stretched drawing.

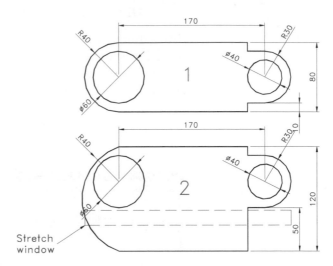

Fig. 11.22 The action of **Stretch** on a dimensioned drawing

2. In Fig. 11.23 drawings **3** and **4** show the results of using **Stretch** on drawing **1** in Fig. 11.22.

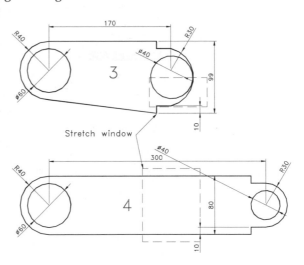

Fig. 11.23 The action of **Stretch** on a dimensioned drawing

3. Note the effect of **Stretch** on circles in drawing **3** of Fig. 11.23.
4. Figure 11.23 The action of **Stretch** on a dimensioned drawing Fig. 11.24 shows the effects of **Scale** on a dimensioned drawing. The drawing being scaled is drawing **1**.

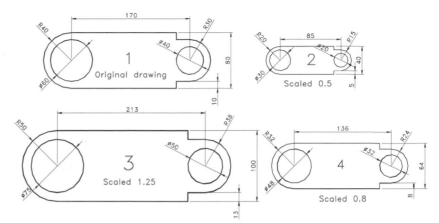

Fig. 11.24 The action of **Scale** on a dimensioned drawing

Questions

1. In how many ways can the **Dimension Style Manager** dialogue be called to screen?
2. Can you enumerate the stages required to set up arrow style, text style, units and tolerance from the **Dimension Style Manager**?
3. Have you saved dimension styles to your own personal template file yet?
4. The **Linear Dimension** tool can be effectively used in two ways. What are they?
5. Have you looked at the popup list which is brought down with a *left-click* in the **Dim Style Control** box?
6. Try using the **Dimension Update** tool. What happens when you do?
7. What are the differences between dimensions added with the aid of **Baseline Dimension** and those added with the aid of **Continue Dimension**?
8. Before using either of the tools mentioned in question **7**, what must be included in your drawing?
9. Can you list the abbreviations for dimension tools used when working from the Command line?
10. What is the difference between a linear tolerance and a geometric tolerance?

Exercises

1. Reload any drawings you may have constructed in answer to exercises in previous chapters and dimension each one as fully as possible.

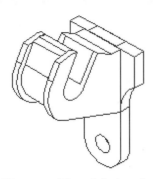

Fig. 11.25 Pictorial view for exercise 4

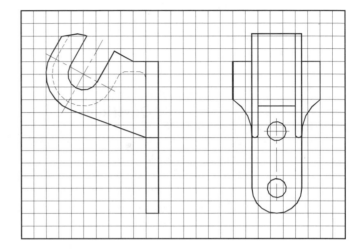

Fig. 11.26 Exercise 4

2. Text can be edited and moved by using either **tedit** from the Command line or **Dimension Text Edit** from the **Dimension** toolbar. Practise using these two tools.

3. Figure 11.25 is a pictorial view of the two-view orthographic projection of a bracket shown in Fig. 11.26.

   Fig. 11.26 shows the two views in a grid of 10 mm squares. Using the grid as a guide construct the two views and add all necessary dimensions.

5. Figure 11.27 is a pictorial view of the clutch device shown in two orthographic views of Fig. 11.28.

   In Fig. 11.28, the two views are drawn in a 10 mm square grid. Using the grid as an indication of the sizes of the device, construct and fully dimension the two views.

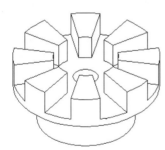

Fig. 11.27 Pictorial view for exercise 5

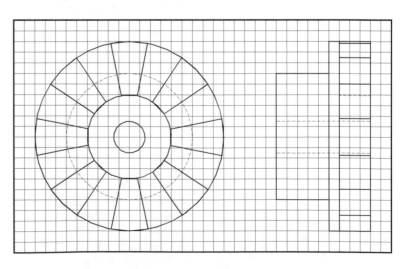

Fig. 11.28 Exercise 5

Fig. 11.29 Pictorial view for
exercise 6

6. Figure 11.29 is a pictorial view of a gear wheel from a bicycle.
   Figure 11.30 is a front view of the gear wheel, together with details
   of the method of obtaining the polar array representing the gear
   teeth. Many dimensions are not included with this view. The
   reader is advised to estimate how to draw each of the holes in the
   wheel and then using **Array** array each part around the wheel
   centre. Construct and dimension the wheel.

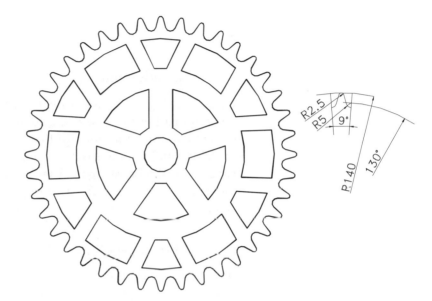

Fig. 11.30 Exercise 6

Chapter 12

OLE and DXF

Introduction

Object linking and embedding (OLE) allows text or graphics from one application to be linked into and with another application, or embedded into another application. For example an AutoCAD drawing can be linked with or embedded into, other applications such as word processing packages desktop publishing packages and the like. It also means that text or graphics from other applications can be linked or embedded into AutoCAD 2000.

Linked graphics

When objects are linked from one application to another, changes made in the original object automatically update in the linked graphic. Thus, if an AutoCAD 2000 drawing is linked to a document form a desktop publishing application, any subsequent changes made to the AutoCAD 2000 drawing also takes place in the linked object.

Embedded graphics

When text or graphics are embedded from one application to another, with the **Paste** command, there is no link between the embedded object(s) in the application from which it originated and the text or graphics into which it has been pasted. Changes subsequently made in the original objects are not taken into the embedded objects.

Examples of OLE

First example (Fig. 12.1 to Fig. 12.3)

1. Figure 12.1 shows a drawing of a front view of a four-bedroomed house opened in AutoCAD 2000 (Fig. 12.1).

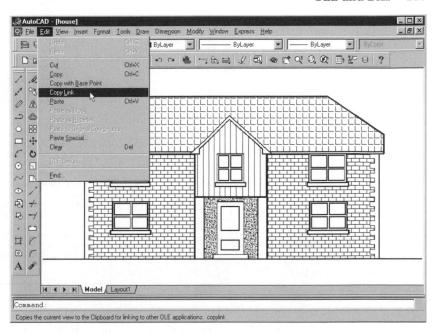

Fig. 12.1 A drawing opened in
AutoCAD 2000

2. *Left-click* on **Edit** in the menu bar and again on **Copy Link** in the
   pull-down menu.
3. Open a new document in a word processing package or as shown
   in Figs 12.2 and 12.3 in a desktop publishing package.

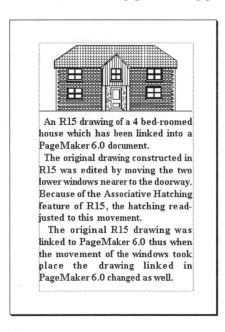

Fig. 12.2 The drawing inserted
into a document in a desktop
publishing program, together
with added text

4. Using the **Paste** command in the desktop publishing program,
   paste the drawing from R15 into the document.

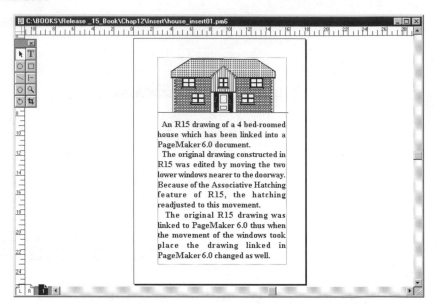

Fig. 12.3 Changes made in the AutoCAD 2000 inserted drawing reflected in the desktop publishing document

5. Add text as required. Figure 12.2 shows the document with the inserted drawing and added text.
6. Go back to the drawing in AutoCAD 2000 and with the **Move** tool, move the lower two windows. Because the hatching is associative, the hatch pattern adjusts to the movement. Save the drawing.
7. In the desktop publishing document, the inserted drawing has changed (Fig. 12.3).

Second example (Fig. 12.4 and Fig. 12.5)

1. In AutoCAD 2000, construct the drawing shown in Fig. 12.4.
2. *Left-click* on **Edit** in the menu bar and again on **Copy** in the pull-down menu. In response to prompts at the Command line, window the drawing (Fig. 12.4).
3. Open a new document in a desktop publishing program and with the **Paste** command, paste the AutoCAD 2000 drawing into the document (Fig. 12.5).
4. Any changes made in the AutoCAD 2000 drawing will not be reflected in the document. The drawing is embedded, but not linked.

Note

The drawing shown in Fig. 12.4 demonstrates a feature concerning text within hatch patterns. Text is surrounded by an invisible boundary when added to a drawing in AutoCAD 2000. If the text is hatched, the hatching respects this invisible boundary.

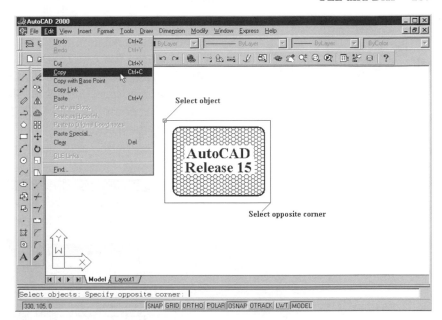

Fig. 12.4 A drawing constructed in AutoCAD 2000 and being copied for embedding elsewhere

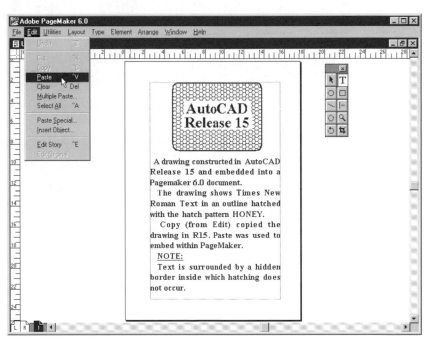

Fig. 12.5 The drawing from Fig. 12.4 embedded in a desktop publisher document

Third example (Fig. 12.6 to Fig. 12.9)

1. Figure 12.6 shows a rendering of a 3D solid model made in AutoCAD 2000 (see Chapter 18). A screen dump program (Hijaak 95) was used to save the rendering as a bitmap file (extension *.bmp).

Fig. 12.6 The rendering of a gear wheel, constructed as a 3D drawing and rendered in AutoCAD 2000

2. Open the bitmap in Windows **Paint** program (Fig. 12.7). With the aid of the **Select All** command, followed by **Copy**, copy the bitmap for pasting into the AutoCAD 2000 window.
3. **Paste** the bitmap copy into AutoCAD 2000 (Fig. 12.8). The windowed bitmap can be *dragged* to a suitable position on screen.
4. The resulting complete AutoCAD 2000 drawing with a front view of the gear wheel and an embedded rendering of the gear wheel is shown in Fig. 12.9.

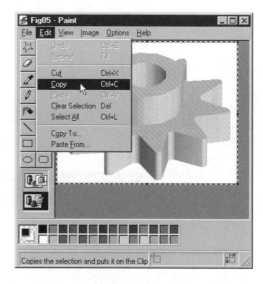

Fig. 12.7 The bitmap of the rendering opened in **Paint** and copied for pasting into AutoCAD 2000

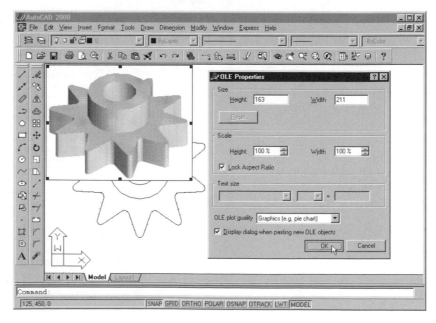

Fig. 12.8 The bitmap of the rendering pasted into AutoCAD 2000

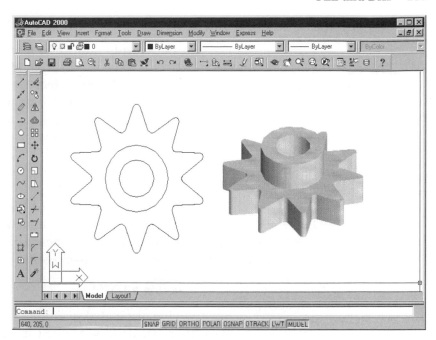

Fig. 12.9 The bitmap *dragged* into its required position

Note

1. As shown in Fig. 12.8, when an object is pasted into AutoCAD 2000, the **OLE Properties** dialogue box appears, in which the type of graphics being pasted can be selected from the popup list appearing with a *left-click* in the **OLE plot quality** box. See Fig. 12.10. The **Scale** of the size of the pasted object can also be amended in this dialogue box.
2. If text is pasted into an AutoCAD 2000 window, the text takes on the font style which is currently the default font selected for the **Text Style** dialogue box.

Fig. 12.10 The **OLE Properties** dialogue box

Fig. 12.11 The **Edit** pull-down menu

Other tools in the Edit pull-down menu

The two tools **Undo** and **Redo** have been dealt with earlier. If a pasted object is to be erased from the screen, select the object and *left-click* on the **Cut** or the **Clear** tool name.

It is advised that some experimentation be carried out using other tools in the menu. It should be noted that **Space Special...** and **Find...** bring up dialogue boxes.

DXF files

The file type ***.dxf** is a form of file originated by Autodesk (the publisher of AutoCAD software), but which is now used by practically all other CAD systems as a means of saving and opening drawings between different CAD packages.

Saving a DXF file

Any drawing originated in AutoCAD 2000 can be saved as a ***.dxf** file which can then be opened in other CAD systems. To save a drawing as a DXF file:

1. Open a drawing and:
2. Either *left-click* on the **Save As** name from the **File** pull-down menu and when the **Save Drawing As** dialogue box appears, select **AutoCAD 2000 DXF (*.dxf) from the** File of type: popup list (Fig. 12.12).

    Or, at the Command line

    Command: *enter* dxfout *right-click*

    And the **Save Drawing As** dialogue box appears with **AutoCAD 2000 DXF (*.dxf)** showing in the **Save as type:** box.

Fig. 12.12 The **Save Drawing As** dialogue box

3. *Enter* the desired file name in the **File name:** box, followed by a *left-click* on the **Save** button.

Opening a DXF file

To open an existing DXF file:

Either, *left-click* on **Open...** in the **File** pull-down menu. The **Select File** dialogue box appears. Select **DXF (*.dxf)** from the **Files of type:** popup list.

Or, at the Command line:

Command: *enter* dxfin *right-click*

And the **Select File** dialogue box appears with **DXF (*.dxf)** already appearing in the **Files of type:** box.

From the list of files appearing in a selected directory, *left-click* on the DXF file name followed by another *left-click* on the **Open** button, or *double-click* on the file name and the drawing is saved as a DXF file.

Fig. 12.13 The **Select File** dialogue box

Questions

1. What is the difference between the uses for **Copy** and **Copy Link** from the **Edit** pull-down menu?
2. What is the difference between linking a drawing or text and embedding an object or text?
3. If a drawing from AutoCAD 2000 is embedded into a document from a word processing package, what happens if the AutoCAD 2000 drawing is changed by some form of modification?
4. If a bitmap object is pasted into an R14 drawing, can the drawing be printed with the bitmap appearing in the printout?
5. Have you tried the **Raster Image...** command from the **Insert** pull-down menu?

6.   Why are DXF files important?
7.   DXF files used to be known as Data eXchange Files. Why is the new name Drawing Interchange files a better description of the file type?
8.   How is a DXF file opened in AutoCAD 2000?
9.   Have you tried the **Export...** command from the **File** pull-down menu?
10. What is the purpose of the command **Cut** from the **Edit** pull-down menu? Is there a difference between the **Cut** and **Clear tools**?

Exercises

If you have saved any of your drawings in answer to exercises set in earlier chapters, practise saving them as DXF files and then reloading them into AutoCAD 2000. Better still, if you have access to another CAD system, try loading the DXF files from AutoCAD 2000 into this CAD system.

Chapter 13

Blocks and Inserts

Introduction

Any AutoCAD drawing can be inserted into any other AutoCAD drawing. In addition, any part of an AutoCAD drawing can be saved as a separate drawing file and if necessary inserted into another AutoCAD drawing. The two tools which make these tasks possible are **Make Block** and **Insert Block**. In addition, another tool, **wblock** can be used to create a drawing file from an AutoCAD drawing or part of a drawing.

Methods of inserting drawings

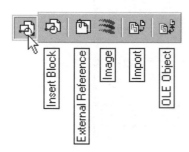

Several methods of inserting AutoCAD 2000 drawings into other AutoCAD 2000 drawings are available:

1. Using the **AutoCAD Design Center** system (see pages 133–8).
2. Using the **Insert** tool to insert blocks (Fig. 13.1).
3. Using the **External Reference** tool to add xrefs to a drawing (Fig. 13.1).

Because reference has already been made to the **AutoCAD Design Center**, details of its use will not be included in this chapter.

Fig. 13.1 The **Insert Block** tool icon from the **Draw** toolbar together with its flyout

Blocks and Xrefs

The difference between a block and an xref (external reference) is that when an xref is added to a drawing, if the drawing of the xref is modified in any way, the drawing which includes the xref automatically updates to include the modifications. When a block is inserted into a drawing, the block becomes part of the drawing and editing of the original block is not reflected in the drawing into which it has been inserted.

Two types of block – wblock and block

Blocks can only be saved and re-inserted within the drawing in which they were saved. If part of a drawing or a symbol is to be inserted into another drawing it must be saved independently of the drawing of which it was part. To do this use the **wblock** (written block) command.

The Wblock tool

To create a written block, which is really another drawing file:

Command: *enter* wblock (or w) *right-click*

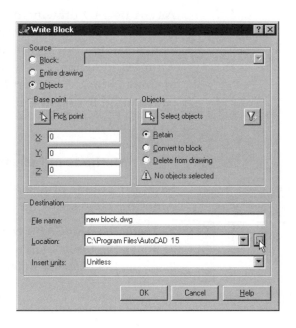

Fig. 13.2 The **Write Block** dialogue box

Fig. 13.3 The **Select Objects** button

The **Write Block** dialogue box appears (Fig. 13.2). In the dialogue box, *left-click* on the **Select Objects** button (Fig. 13.3). The drawing from which the wblock is to be saved reappears and the Command line shows:

Select objects: *pick* a points above and to the left of the drawing
Specify opposite corner: *pick* bottom right (Fig. 13.4)

The dialogue box reappears. *Left-click* on the **Pick Insertion Base Point** button (Fig. 13.5). The drawing reappears. *Pick* a suitable insertion base point in the drawing. The dialogue box reappears. In the dialogue box *left-click* on the button to the right of the **Location:** box, which brings up the **Browse for Folder** dialogue box (Fig. 13.6).

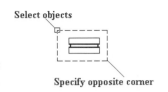

Fig. 13.4 Selecting the objects forming the wblock

In the dialogue box select a suitable directory. The **Write Block** dialogue box reappears. In the **File name:** box *enter* a suitable filename, followed by a *left-click* on the **OK** button of the dialogue box. The drawing will be saved as an AutoCAD 2000 file with the drawing extension ***.dwg**, which means it is an AutoCAD drawing file.

Fig. 13.5 The **Insertion Base Point** button

Fig. 13.6 The **Browse for Folder** dialogue box

Notes

1. When the **OK** button of the dialogue box is selected, the dialogue box disappears and, for a short time, the **WBLOCK Preview** box appears at the top left-hand corner of the AutoCAD 2000 window. This confirms the saving of the wblock as desired. See Fig. 13.7.
2. This may seem a long process as described above but, in fact, The whole process takes very little time, once the sequence of events is practised and skill gained with such practising.

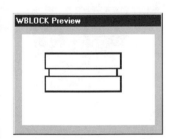

Fig. 13.7 The **WBLOCK Preview** box

Including a wblock in a drawing

Figure 13.8 is a three-view orthographic projection of a component from a machine. Several wblocks are to be added to the drawing from previously saved wblocks. In this example, when the wblocks have been inserted, some details in each of the views will require modifying, mainly to replace outlines with hidden detail. The three wblocks are **roller.dwg**, **pin.dwg** and **roller_end.dwg**. To add the blocks:

Either *left-click* on the **Insert Block** tool icon in the **Draw** toolbar, or *enter* **i** at the Command line. The **Insert** dialogue box appears. To select the required wblock, *left-click* on the **Browse...** button, which

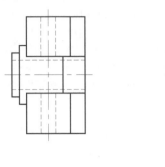

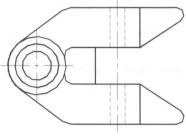

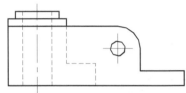

Fig. 13.8 An AutoCAD 2000AutoCAD 2000 drawing into which wblocks are to be inserted

brings up the **Select Drawing File** dialogue box. From the dialogue box, select the required file, in the example given in Fig. 13.9 this is **roller_end.dwg**. *Left-click* on the **Open** button and the name of the drawing appears in the **Name:** box of the **Insert** dialogue. *Left-click* on the **OK** button of the dialogue box and the drawing appears ready to be *dragged* around the screen by its previously selected **Base Insertion Point**. *Drop* the wblock at its required position in the drawing.

Fig. 13.9 Selecting a drawing for insertion

Repeat this operation for the other two wblocks (**pin.dwg** and **roller.dwg**) and the original drawing will appear as in Fig. 13.10.

The drawing will now require some modification because the inserts have covered parts of the drawing which should be shown in hidden detail lines. Figure 13.11 shows the drawing after these modifications have taken place.

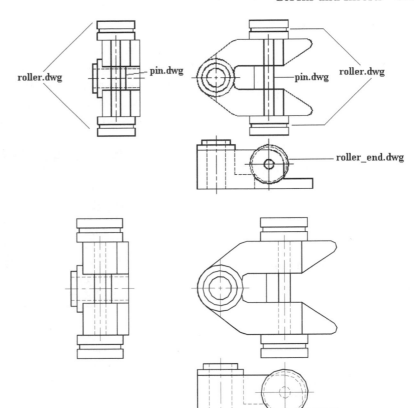

Fig. 13.10 The drawing with
inserted wblocks

Fig. 13.11 The completed
drawing after modifications

Notes

1. If modification of inserted wblocks is needed, make sure the
   Explode check box of the **Insert** dialogue box is set on (tick in box).
   See Fig. 13.9. If this suggestion is forgotten, inserted wblocks can
   be exploded using the **Explode** tool, either by selection for the
   Draw toolbar or by *entering* **x** at the Command line.
2. Before objects are selected when writing a block, the **Objects** area
   of the **Write Block** dialogue box shows an icon labelled **No objects
   selected** (Fig. 13.12). This changes to a note stating the number of
   objects selected after selection has taken place.

Fig. 13.12 The **No objects
selected** icon

The Make Block tool

When a block is made, it becomes part of the data of the AutoCAD
2000 window in which it was made, unlike wblocks, which become
independent drawings in their own right. In the examples of the use
of blocks, they are being constructed for the construction of a circuit
diagram.

Fig. 13.13 The drawing for the block

To make a block

1. Construct the drawing of the feature to be made into a block – in this example an electronic symbol for an npn transistor (Fig. 13.13).
2. Call the **Make Block** tool – either *left-click* on the tool icon from the **Draw** toolbar (Fig. 13.14) or *enter* **bmake** at the Command line. The **Block Definition** dialogue box appears (Fig. 13.15).

Fig. 13.14 Call **Make Block**

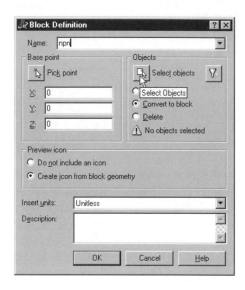

Fig. 13.15 The **Block Definition** dialogue box

3. *Enter* a name for the block in the **Name:** box.
4. *Left-click* on the **Select objects** button and the dialogue box disappears. Select the npn drawing within a window (Fig. 13.16).

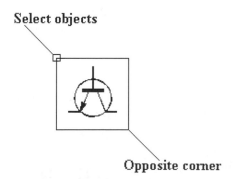

Fig. 13.16 Selecting the objects within the block drawing

5. When the dialogue box reappears, *left-click* on the **Pick Insertion Base Point** button (Fig. 13.17).
6. The dialogue box disappears. *Pick* a suitable insertion base point on the drawing (Fig. 13.18).

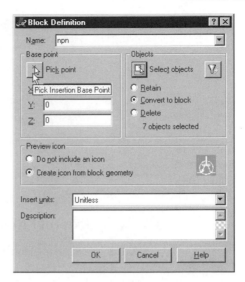

Fig. 13.17 *Left-click* on the
Pick Insertion Base Point
button

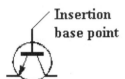

Fig. 13.18 *Pick* a suitable
insertion base point

Constructing a circuit drawing from blocks

The simple electronics circuit diagram Fig. 13.19 was made up from
a number of blocks constructed as described above and then copied
and moved to form the circuit. Lines for conductors and donuts for
intersections were added to complete the circuit.

Figure 13.20 shows the **Insert** dialogue box with the popup list
from the **Name:** box displayed showing the blocks within the circuit.
The circuit could equally as well have been constructed from
wblocks or from previously saved drawings *dragged* and *dropped*
from the **Design Center**.

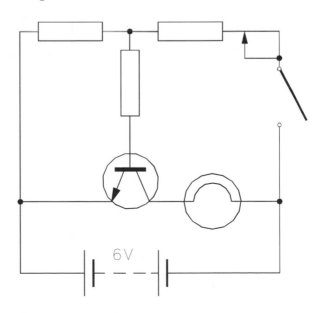

Fig. 13.19 A simple
electronics circuit made up
from blocks or wblocks

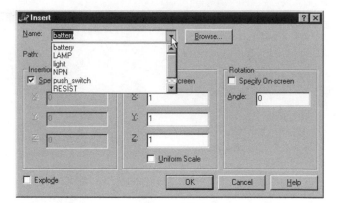

Fig. 13.20 The popup list
showing blocks within the
circuit Fig. 13.19

External References (Xrefs)

Xrefs are similar to blocks except that when an xref is inserted into
an existing drawing, any later modifications made to the xref
drawing is reflected in the insertion.

An example of an xref in a drawing

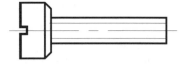

Fig. 13.21 A drawing of a
screw

1. The drawing Fig. 13.21 was constructed and saved to file.
2. The drawing Fig. 13.22 shows a two-view orthographic projection
    into which the drawing Fig. 13.21 is to be added three times as an
    xref.

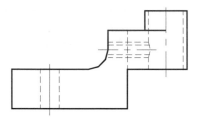

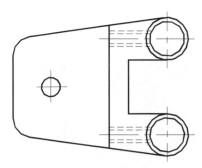

Fig. 13.22 The drawing to
which an xref is to be added

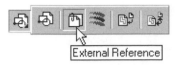

Fig. 13.23 Calling the **External Reference** tool

3. To add the xref either *enter* **xref** at the Command line or *left-click* on the **External Reference** tool icon in the **Draw** toolbar (Fig. 13.23).
4. The **Xref Manager** dialogue box appears (Fig. 13.24). *Left-click* on the **Attach...** button which brings up the **Select Reference File** dialogue box (Fig. 13.25).

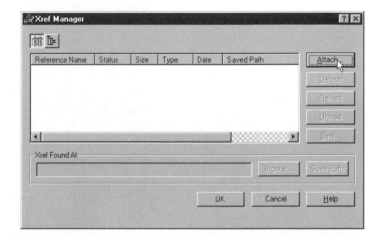

Fig. 13.24 The **Xref Manager** dialogue box

Fig. 13.25 The **Select Reference File** dialogue box

5. In this dialogue box select the drawing file to be used as an xref, in this example **bolt.dwg**. The **External Reference** dialogue box appears with the name of the selected file in its **Name:** box (Fig. 13.26).
6. *Left-click* on the **OK** button of the dialogue box and the xref appears in the AutoCAD 2000 window for *dragging* into position.
7. Repeat three times and the three identical xrefs show as in Fig. 13.27.
8. Save the drawing with its xrefs.
9. Reload the **bolt.dwg** (the xref) and modify the drawing as in Fig. 13.28. Save the modified drawing.

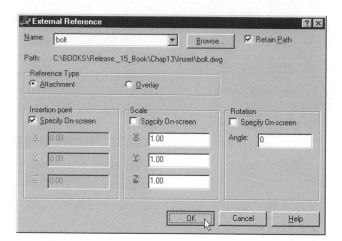

Fig. 13.26 The **External Reference** dialogue box

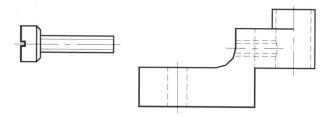

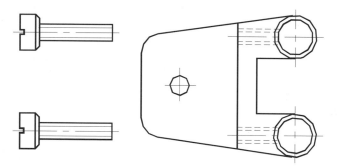

Fig. 13.27 The three xrefs in position in the drawing

10. Now load back the drawing to which the xrefs have been added and it will be seen that the modifications to the xref drawing are now reflected in the main drawing (Fig. 13.29).

Questions

1. What is the difference between making a block and making a wblock?

Fig. 13.28 The modified xref drawing

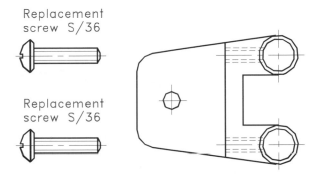

Fig. 13.29 The xrefs as they now appear in the drawing

2. What is the major difference between a drawing inserted as a block into another drawing and an xref added to a drawing?

3. Why is the **AutoCAD Design Center** a valuable tool for the construction of circuit diagrams?

4. What is the purpose of the **WBLOCK Preview** box?

5. In the **Write Block** dialogue box, a small icon is labelled as **No objects selected**. What happens to this icon when objects are selected?

6. Why is it important to be careful when selecting an insertion point for a block?

7. Can a complete drawing be *dragged* into the R15 window from the **Design Center**?

8. There are at least two methods of calling the **Insert** dialogue box to screen. Can you name them?

9. There are two methods of calling the **Xref Manager** dialogue box to screen. What are they?

10. Can you describe the stages by which a block for a symbol is created?

Exercises

1. Figure 13.30 is a pictorial view of an assembly linking four parts to each other in such a manner that as any one of the four members is rotated through small angles, the other will rotate in sympathy.

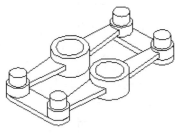

Fig. 13.30 Exercise 1 – pictorial drawing

Figure 3.31 is a partial front view and plan of the assembly showing one of the larger links with the left-hand of the smaller links in place.

Complete the two-view drawing given in Fig. 13.31 showing all four links together in front view and plan views.

As a separate drawing design and draw a similar link to link into the two holes in the two larger links. Then insert your design into the remainder of the two-view drawing as a block.

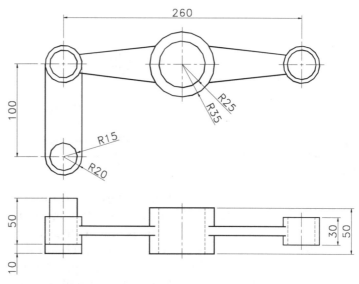

Fig. 13.31 Exercise 1

2. Figure 13.32 is a pictorial drawing of a circular plate. Figure 13.33 is a two-view orthographic projection of the plate.

Construct the given drawing Fig. 13.33. Save your drawing to a suitable file name.

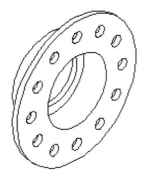

Fig. 13.32 Exercise 2 – pictorial drawing

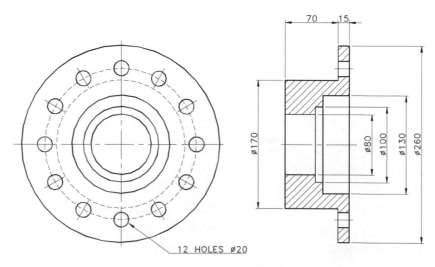

Fig. 13.33 Exercise 2

As a separate drawing construct the left-hand view of Fig. 13.34. Save this new drawing to file. Reload the two-view drawing and insert the second drawing in a suitable position in the first as an xref. Save the drawing with the xref.

Reload the xref drawing and modify it to the shape given in the right-hand drawing of Fig. 13.34. Save the modified drawing.

Now reload the original drawing and note the changes in the xref.

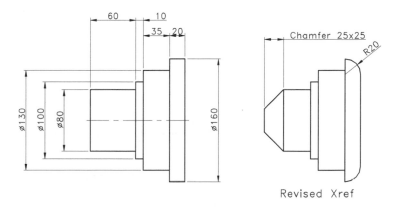

Fig. 13.34 Xrefs for exercise 2

Revised Xref

3. Figure 13.35 shows a small library of symbols for the drawing of plans for building drawings.

Construct each of the symbols in turn and save each as a wblock to the file name given with each symbol.

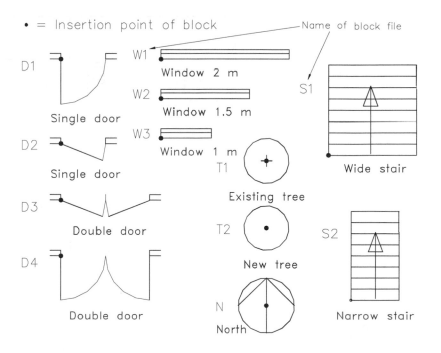

Fig. 13.35 A small 'library' of building drawing symbols

Inserting symbols from this small library you have compiled, construct the given plan view of a single storey house given in Fig. 13.36, working to a scale you consider suitable.

Fig. 13.36 Exercise 3

4. Figure 13.37 shows an outline plan drawing of the two storeys of a house. Using a suitable scale and inserting the symbols from your drawing of those shown in Fig.13.35, construct building drawing plans of the two storeys.

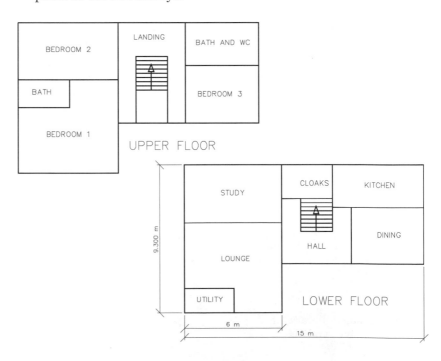

Fig. 13.37 Exerrcise 4

5. Figure 13.38 is a site plan of a bungalow. Working to a suitable scale and using the symbols from Fig. 13.35, construct the given site plan.

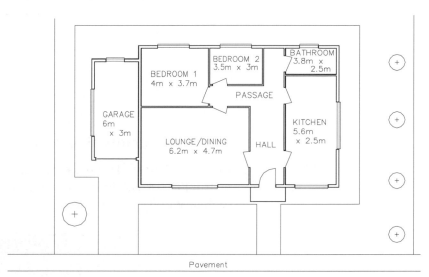

Fig. 13.38 Exercise 5

Chapter 14

Modify II tools and attributes

The Modify II toolbar

Bring the **Modify II** toolbar on screen from the toolbars *right-click* menu (Fig. 14.1). Figure 14.2 shows the names of those tools in this toolbar which will be shown in use in this chapter.

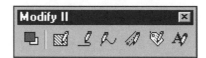

Fig. 14.1 The **Modify II** toolbar

The Polyline Edit tool

Either *left-click* on the **Polyline Edit** tool icon in the **Modify II** toolbar, or on **Polyline** in the **Modify** pull-down menu, or *enter* **pe** at the Command line:

> **Command_pedit Select polyline:** *pick* the pline to be edited
> **Enter an option [Open/Join/Width/Edit vertex/Fit/Spline/Decurve/**
> **Ltytpe gen/Undo]:** *enter* an option

Figure 14. 3 shows the results of using the options **Width**, **Spline**, **Fit** and **Close** on the rectangular pline in the top left drawing of Fig. 14.3.

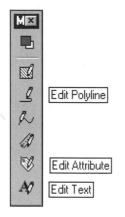

Fig. 14.2 The **Modify II** toolbar showing the names of the tools used in this chapter

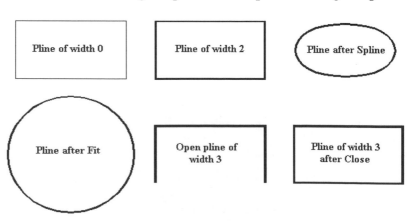

Fig. 14.3 The effect of some of the options from the **Polyline Edit** sequence

It is advisable to experiment with the **pedit** tool options because they allow the operator to edit plines to good advantage in some constructions. These options will be found to be of particular value when using plines for the purpose of constructing 3D solid drawings as described in the following three chapters.

Attributes

Attributes allow the naming of blocks which have been inserted into drawings with attribute tags and prompts which can be included with a block via the **Attribute Definition** and **Attribute Edit** dialogue boxes.

An example of attributes

Figure 14.4 shows the sequence involved in adding an attribute to an inserted block. The procedure can be followed for any number of

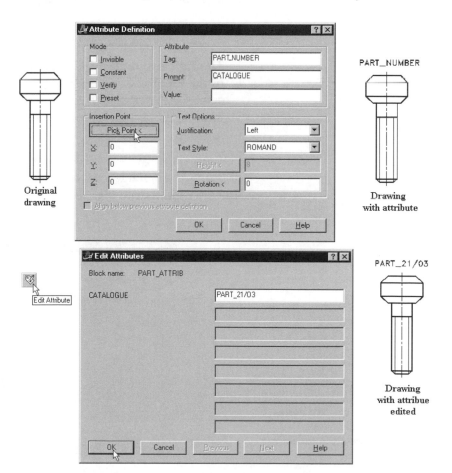

Fig. 14.4 An example of including an attribute with a block

attributes within a drawing, following the appropriate prompts and tags.

1. Construct the drawing for the block to be inserted into another drawing.
2. Call the **Attribute Definition** dialogue box:

     Command: *enter* ddattdef *right-click*

   The **Attribute Definition** dialogue box appears.
3. In the dialogue box *enter* a suitable name in the **Attribute Tag:** box – in this example **PART_NUMBER**. In the **Attribute Prompt:** box *enter* a suitable prompt – in this example **CATALOGUE**.
4. *Left-click* on the **Pick Point <** button. The dialogue box disappears. *Pick* a suitable point for the positioning of the attribute – in this example this was above the drawing.
5. Save the drawing with its attribute to a suitable file name.
6. **Insert** the drawing with its attribute tag into another drawing.
7. *Left-click* on the **Edit Attribute** tool icon:

     Command:_ddattedit
     Select block reference: *pick* the block which has been inserted

   The **Edit Attributes** dialogue box appears
8. In the **Catalogue** box *enter* the required attribute prompt – in this example **PART_21/03**. followed by a *left-click* on the **OK** button. The attribute appears in position in the block which has been inserted.

Figure 14.5 shows the **Edit Attributes** dialogue box with a number of prompts associated with a block which have been inserted four times within a drawing.

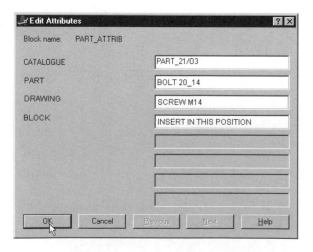

Fig. 14.5 The **Edit Attributes** dialogue box showing attributes to be added to four blocks

The Edit Text tool

Left-click on the **Edit Text** tool icon in the **Modify II** toolbar, or *enter* **ddedit** at the Command line, or select **Text...** from the **Modify** pull-down menu. The Command line shows:

Command:_ddedit
Select an annotation object or [Undo]: *pick* the text to be edited

The **Edit Text** dialogue box appears. In this box, the text can be edited as required. When the editing is complete, a *left-click* on the **OK** button takes the edited text back to the text to be edited. Figure 14.6 shows an example of the use of this tool.

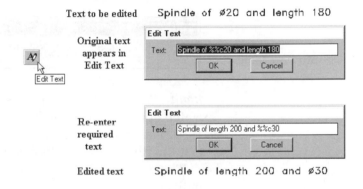

Fig. 14.6 An example of the use of **Edit Text**

Questions

1. What is the tool abbreviation for the **Edit Polyline** tool?
2. Which would you prefer to use – selection from the **Lineweights** popup list or using **Edit Polyline** to change the width of lines?
3. Can an attribute be edited with the aid of the **Edit Text** tool?
4. If several different blocks with attributes are included in a drawing, can all the attributes with the blocks be changed from a single Edit Attributes dialogue box?

Chapter 15

The Surfaces tools

The Surface toolbar

Fig. 15.1 The **Surfaces** toolbar

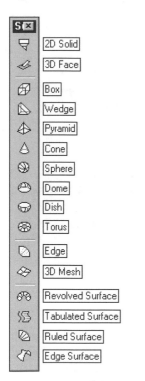

Fig. 15.2 The tools in the **Surfaces** toolbar

Fig. 15.3 The **Surfaces** tools from the **Draw** pull-down menu

Right-click in any toolbar on screen and from the toolbar menu which appears, select **Surfaces**. The **Surfaces** toolbar appears (Fig. 15.1). The names of the tools in the toolbar as given in Fig. 15.2. Note that the first tool in the toolbar (**2D Solid**) is not a 3D tool.

The tools can also be selected from the **Draw** pull-down menu as indicated in Fig. 15.3.

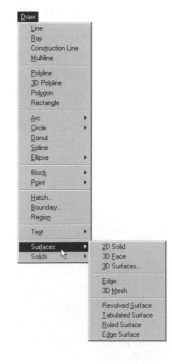

3D (three-dimensional) drawing

So far in this book we have been dealing with drawings constructed in a 2D (two-dimensional) screen. Attention has been drawn to the 3D coordinates showing in the Status bar at the bottom of the AutoCAD 2000 window. 3D solid model drawings can be constructed in AutoCAD 2000 because, in addition to the ability to construct in two dimensions the software allows drawing in three dimensions. In 2D work we are working in terms of x,y coordinate points on screen.

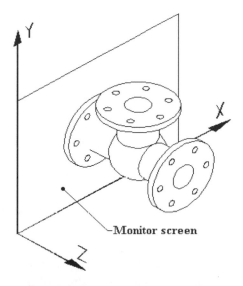

Fig. 15.4 A 3D solid model drawing on screen showing the directions of the three coordinate axes x,y,z

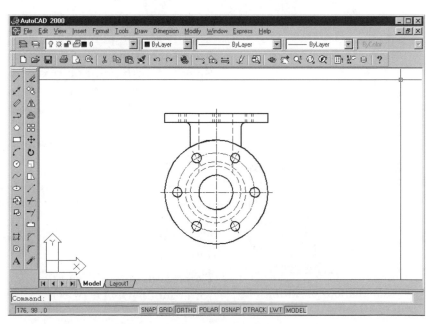

Fig. 15.5 A front view of the 3D solid model drawing shown in Fig. 15.4

In 3D work a third coordinate **Z** allows the third axis essential to 3D constructions, to be effective. Figure 15.4 shows a pictorial view of a 3D model on screen based on the 2D drawing of Fig. 15.5. Figure 15.4 also indicates the directions of the three coordinates axes **X**, **Y** and **Z**. The additional **Z** axis allows any point in space to be determined in terms of *x,y,z* coordinates.

Notes

1. The **Z** axis is vertical to the AutoCAD 2000 window, with positive **Z** axis direction towards the operator. This means that the negative **Z** axis direction is away from the operator.
2. Usually the coordinate point *x,y,z* = 0,0,0 is at the bottom left-hand corner of the AutoCAD 2000 drawing area – but not always.

The 2D Solid tool

Before going on to deal with the 3D surfaces tools, a short description of the **2D Solid** tool is appropriate. To call the tool, either *left-click* on its tool icon in the **Surfaces** toolbar, *left-click* on the name in the sub-menu of **Surfaces** in the **Draw** toolbar, or *enter* **so** at the Command line (Fig. 15.6).

Three examples of the use of the **2D Solid** tool are given in Fig. 15.7. The upper line of drawings show the order in which points in the solid filling prompts sequence are selected take place to produce the drawings in the middle row of drawings.

When the tool is called, the Command line shows:

Command: _solid **Specify first point:** *pick* or *enter* coordinates
Specify second point: *pick* or *enter* coordinates
Specify third point: *pick* or *enter* coordinates
Specify fourth point or <exit>: *pick* or *enter* coordinates
Specify third point: *pick* or *enter* coordinates
Specify fourth point or <exit>: *pick* or *enter* coordinates
Specify third point: *pick* or *enter* coordinates
Specify fourth point or <exit>: *right-click*
Command:

The first, third and fourth points are requested repeatedly until the required area is solid filled at the **Specify fourth point or <exit>:** prompt.

The filling only takes place if the set variable **Fill** is ON. To set the variable:

Command: *enter* fill *right-click*
Enter mode [ON/OFF] <OFF>: *enter* on *right-click*
Command:

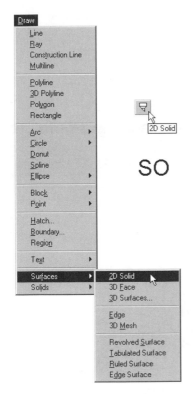

Fig. 15.6 Methods of calling the tool **2D Solid**

The lower line of drawings in Fig. 15.7 show the same solid filled areas with the variable **Fill** set **OFF**.

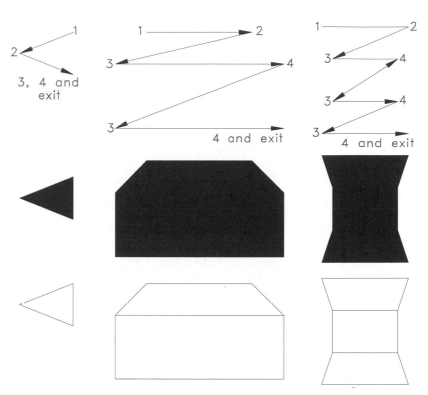

Fig. 15.7 Examples of the use of **2D Solid**

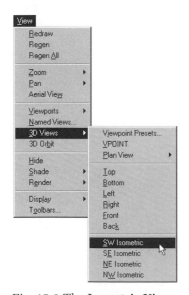

Fig. 15.8 The **Isometric Views** from the **View** pull-down menu

The Isometric 3D viewpoints

Left-click on **View** in the menu bar and again on **3D Views** in the pull-down menu. In the sub-menu which appears, the four lower commands allow 3D solid model drawings to be placed in one of four isometric views. See Fig. 15.8. Figure 15.9 shows a 3D solid model drawing in each of the four isometric viewpoints.

X,Y,Z filters

When constructing 3D drawings the 3D filters **.x**, **.y**, **.z**, **xy**, **.xz** and **.yz** are of value for determining **x,y,z** coordinate points in some drawings. As an example the line from **x,y,z** = 50,100 to 100,150,100 could be determined as follows:

Command: *enter* l (Line) *right-click*
Specify first point: *enter* 50,100 *right-click*
Specify next point or [Undo}: *enter* .xy *right-click*
of *enter* 100,150 *right-click* **(need Z)** *enter* 100 *right-click*
Specify next point or [Undo]:

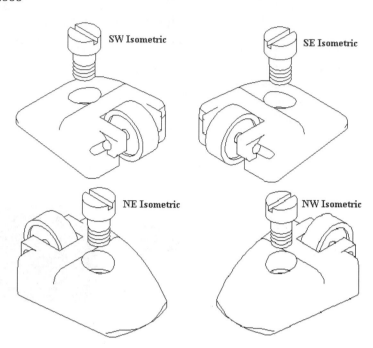

Fig. 15.9 The four isometric viewpoints

Figure 15.10 shows an isometric view of several lines drawn in this manner in a 3D setting.

If the computer being worked at is using an Intellimouse mouse, pressing the central wheel of the mouse during the operation of a tool, brings up a menu from which the 3D filters can be selected (Fig. 15.11).

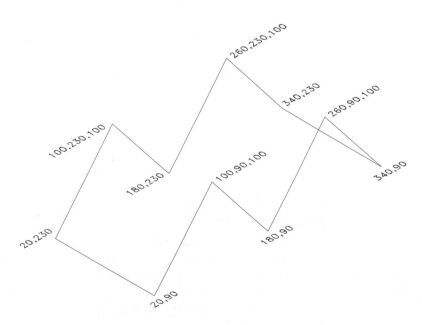

Fig. 15.10 An example of line drawing with the aid of the **.XY** filter

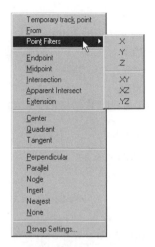

Fig. 15.11 the menu which appears when the wheel of an Intellimouse is pressed

Fig. 15.12 Methods of calling the **Hide** tool

The Hide tool

The **Hide** tool is of value when constructing 3D solid model drawings because when called it can be used to hide all lines behind the front 3dfaces of 3D solid model drawings.

To call the tool, either select **Hide** from the **View** pull-down menu, or bring the **Render** toolbar on screen (*right-click* in any toolbar on screen and select **Render** from the menu which appears), or *enter* **hi** or **hide** at the Command line (Fig. 15.12). All that is needed is to call the tool, and *right-click*.

Tools from the Surfaces toolbar

The 3dface tool

Either *pick* **3D Face** from the toolbar, or *enter* **3dface** at the Command line:

> **Command:_3dface**
> **Specify first point or [Invisible]:** *pick* 120,230
> **Specify second point or [Invisible]:** *pick* 120,90
> **Specify third point or [Invisible] <exit>:** *enter* .xy *right-click*
> **of** *pick* 120,190 **(need Z):** *enter* 100 *right-click*
> **Specify fourth point or [Invisible] <create 3-sided face>:** *enter* .xy *right-click*
> **of** *enter* 120,230 **(need Z):** *enter* 100 *right-click*
> **Specify third point or [Invisible] <exit>:** *right-click*
> **Command:_3dface**
> **Specify first point or [Invisible]:** *enter* .xy *right-click*

of *pick* 120,230 **(need Z)** *enter* 100 *right-click*
Specify second point or [Invisible]: *enter .xy right-click*
of *pick* 170,230 **(need Z)** *enter* 150 *right-click*
Specify third point or [Invisible] <exit>: *enter .xy right-click*
of *pick* 170,190 **(need Z):** *enter* 150 *right-click*
Specify fourth point or [Invisible] <create 3-sided face>: *enter*
   .xy right-click
of *enter* 120,190 **(need Z):** *enter* 100 *right-click*
Specify third point or [Invisible] <exit>: *right-click*
Command:

Now mirror the two 3D faces to set up a second pair of 3D faces 300 units apart.

Now construct a fifth 3D face at 150 units above the x,y plane to form a 'roof' connecting the mirrored 3D faces. The result is shown in a SW isometric view in Fig. 15.13.

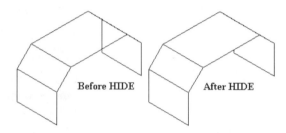

Before HIDE   After HIDE

Fig. 15.13 An example of the 3use of the **3D Face** tool

Figure 15.14 shows three additional 3D faces applied to the front of the drawing, followed by **Hide**.

Note

1. If the **Invisible** prompt is used, the line of the 3D Face being drawn will be invisible. However the face is still there as can be seen if 3D Faces are applied using the **Invisible** response and then using **Hide** on the resulting face.

2. All 3D models constructed using the **Surfaces** tools are a series of mesh surfaces, behind which any constructional lines or other surfaces can be hidden with **Hide**.

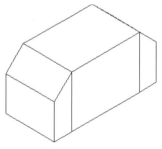

Fig. 15.14 The same example as in Fig. 15.12 with 3D faces at the front

The 3D Objects tools

In the **Draw** pull-down menu, *left-click* on **3D Surfaces…** in the **Surfaces** sub-menu of the pull-down (Fig. 15.15). The **3D Objects** dialogue box appears (Fig. 15.16).

In this dialogue box, note that the 3D Objects are the same as the tools in the second groups showing in the **Surfaces** toolbar.

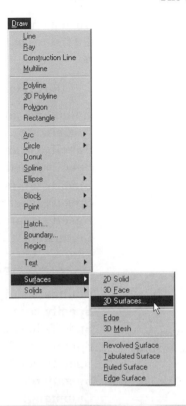

Fig. 15.15 Selecting **3D Surfaces...** from the **View** pull-down menu

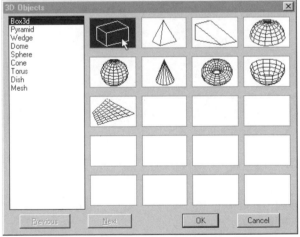

Fig. 15.16 The **3D Objects** dialogue box

Figure 15.19 shows a number of the 3D objects which have been constructed in the AutoCAD 2000 drawing area. The following, rather long sequence of Command line prompts and responses describes how the objects shown in Fig. 15.19 were constructed.

The tools for the following examples can either be selected from the **3D Objects** dialogue box (*double-click* in the icon of the tool) or from the **Surfaces** toolbar. In the examples which follow, only the coordinate figures are given – these may either be *picked* on screen or the figures *entered* at the Command line and followed by a *right-click*

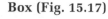

Fig. 15.17 Select the **Box** tool from the **Surfaces** toolbar

Box (Fig. 15.17)

Command:_ai_box
Initializing ... 3D Objects Loaded
Specify corner point of box: 60,130
Specify length of box: 100
Specify width of box: 80
Specify height of box: 120
Specify rotation angle of box about the Z axis or [Reference]: 0
Command:

Fig. 15.18 Select the **Wedge** tool from the **Surfaces** toolbar

Wedge (Fig. 15.18)

Command:_ai_wedge
Specify corner point of wedge: 205,130
Specify length of wedge: 120
Specify width of wedge: 60
Specify height of wedge: 45
Specify rotation angle of box about the Z axis or [Reference]: 0
Command:

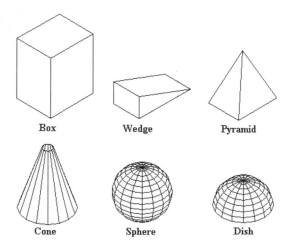

Fig. 15.19 Examples of drawings constructed with the **3D Objects** tools from **Surfaces**

Fig. 15.20 Select the **Pyramid** tool from the **Surfaces** toolbar

Pyramid (Fig. 15.20)

Command:_ai_pyramid
Specify first corner point for base of pyramid: 360,130
Specify second corner point for base of pyramid: 450,130
Specify third corner point for base of pyramid: 450,200

Specify fourth corner point for base of pyramid: 360,200
Specify apex point of pyramid or [Ridge/Top]: 405,165,100
Command:

Cone (Fig. 15.21)

Command:_ai_pyramid
Specify center point for base of cone: 100,50
Specify radius for base of cone or [Diameter]: 50
Specify radius for top of cone or [Diameter]: 10
Specify height of cone: 120
Enter number of segments for surface of cone >16>: *right-click*
Command:

Fig. 15.21 Select the **Cone** tool from the **Surfaces** toolbar

Sphere (Fig. 15.22)

Command:_ai_sphere
Specify center point of sphere: 260,50
Specify radius of sphere or [Diameter]: 50
**Enter number of longitudinal segments for surface of sphere
      <16>:** *right-click*
Enter number of latitudinal segments for surface of sphere <16>:
      right-click
Command:

Fig. 15.22 Select the **Sphere** tool from the **Surfaces** toolbar

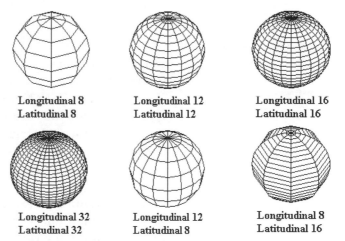

Longitudinal 8
Latitudinal 8

Longitudinal 12
Latitudinal 12

Longitudinal 16
Latitudinal 16

Longitudinal 32
Latitudinal 32

Longitudinal 12
Latitudinal 8

Longitudinal 8
Latitudinal 16

Fig. 15.23 Spheres of different longitudinal and latitudinal segments

Dome (Fig. 15.24)

Command:_ai_dome
Specify center point of dome: 405,50
Specify radius of sphere or [Diameter]: 50
Enter number of longitudinal segments for surface of sphere

Fig. 15.24 Select the **Dome** tool from the **Surfaces** toolbar

<16>: *right-click*
Enter number of latitudinal segments for surface of sphere <16>:
  right-click
Command:

Note

1. In the next chapter (Chapter 16) the use of tools from the **Solids** toolbar will be described for the construction of true solid model drawings. Although some of the names of the tools in the **Solids** toolbar are similar to those in the **Surfaces** toolbar, the tools have different actions. The **Surfaces** tools showing in the **3D Objects** dialogue box are used to construct surfaces. The **Solids** tools are used to construct true 3D solid drawings.

2. When, say the **Box** tool is called from **Surfaces** the Command line shows **Command:ai_box**. When the **Box** tools is called from **Solids** the Command line shows **Command:_box**.

3. The number of segments shown in the **Cone**, **Sphere** and **Dome** prompts sequences can be changed if thought necessary. Figure 15.23 shows the differences between a number of spheres of different segment numbers.

Fig. 15.25 Select the **Box** tool from the **Surfaces** toolbar

The 3D Mesh tool (Fig. 15.25)

An example of a drawing constructed with the aid of this tool is given in Fig. 15.26. Call the tool from the **Surfaces** toolbar or from the **Draw** pull-down menu. The Command line shows:

Command:_3d mesh
Enter size of mesh in M direction: 4
Enter size of mesh in N direction: 4
Specify location for vertex (0, 0): *enter* 70,260 *right-click*
Specify location for vertex (0, 1): 70,140
Specify location for vertex (0, 2): 120,165,50
Specify location for vertex (0, 3): 120,245,50
Specify location for vertex (1, 0): 170,260
Specify location for vertex (1, 1): 70,140
Specify location for vertex (1, 2): 220,165,50
Specify location for vertex (1, 3): 220,245,50
Specify location for vertex (2, 0): 270,140
Specify location for vertex (2, 1): 265,260
Specify location for vertex (2, 2): 310,245,50
Specify location for vertex (2, 3): 310,165,50
Specify location for vertex (3, 0): 365,140
Specify location for vertex (3, 1): 365,260
Specify location for vertex (3, 2): 405,245,50

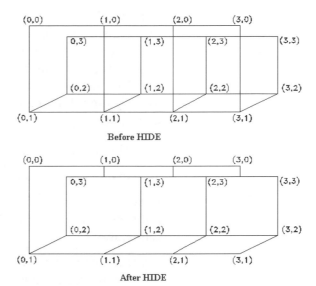

Fig. 15.26 An example of the use of the tool **3D Mesh**

Specify location for vertex (3, 3): 405,165,50
Command:

Other tools from the Surfaces toolbar

The Edge tool (Fig. 15.27)

Fig. 15.27 Select the **Edge** tool from the **Surfaces** toolbar

This tool can be used to make lines of a 3D Face invisible. All that is required is to call the tool and when the prompt line appears, *pick* the edge of a 3D face that is to be made invisible. The edge line disappears. Figure 15.28 shows the drawing of Fig. 15.14 after the action of the **Edge** tool on the two lines joining the three 3D faces of the front of the drawing.

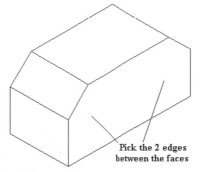

Fig. 15.28 After **Edge** has been used on the drawing of Fig. 15.14

Pick the 2 edges between the faces

The Revolved Surface tool (Fig. 15.29)

Left-click on the **Revolved Surface** tool from the **Surfaces** toolbar (Fig. 15.29). The Command line shows:

Fig. 15.29 the **Revolved
Surface** tool from **Surfaces**

Command:_revsurf
Current wire frame density: SURFTAB1=6 SURFTAB2=6
Pick object to revolve: *pick*
Select object that defines the axis of revolution: *pick*
Specify start angle <0>: *right-click*
Specify included angle (+=ccw, −=cw) <360>: *right-click*
Command:

The Surftab variables

To set **Surftab1** and **Surftab2**:

Command: *enter* surftab1
Enter new value for SURFTAB1 <6>: *enter* 16 *right-click*
Command:

The settings of these two variables will vary according to the surface of revolution being constructed. The set of four illustrations Figs 15.30 to 15.33 show the effects of different settings of the two surftabs.

> Figure 15.30 – The object to be revolved is a closed polyline. The axis of revolution is a line. The two drawings on the right show the effects of revolving the polyline around the axis with different settings of the two surftab variables.

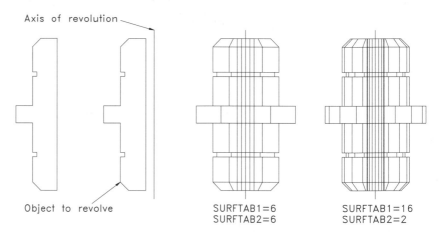

Fig. 15.30 Examples of the use
of the **Revolved Surface** tool

> Figure 15.31 – Shows the two revolved surfaces in a **NW Isometric** view after using the **Hide** tool.
> Figure 15.32 – A **Pline** consisting of arcs and lines is **Offset** by 2 and the ends of the original pline and the offset are joined. The drawing was then made into a closed polyline with the aid of **Polyline Edit** (pedit). An axis of revolution was added and the surface of revolution formed from the closed pline.

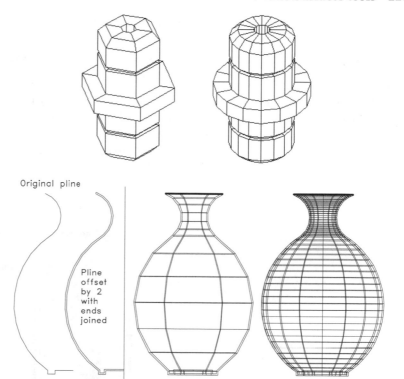

Fig. 15.31 Isometric views of the two revolved surfaces shown in Fig. 15.30

Fig. 15.32 Further examples of the use of the **Revolved Surface** tool

Figure 15.33 – Two versions of the revolved surface of Fig. 15.24 with different settings of the two surftab variables.

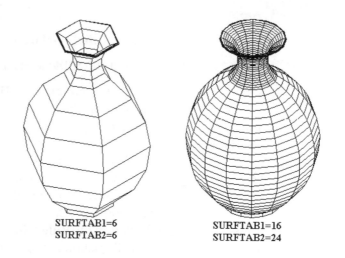

SURFTAB1=6
SURFTAB2=6

SURFTAB1=16
SURFTAB2=24

Fig. 15.33 Two versions of the revolved surface of Fig. 15.32 with different settings of surftabs

The Tabulated Surface tool (Fig. 15.34)

Left-click on the **Tabulated Surface** tool from the **Surfaces** toolbar (Fig. 15.34). The Command line shows:

Fig. 15.34 Select the
Tabulated Surface tool from
the **Surfaces** toolbar

Command:_tabsurf
Select object for path curve: *pick*
Select object for direction vector: *pick*
Command:

Figure 15.35 shows in the upper drawing a path curve – a closed polyline, together with a direction vector (a line) and in the lower drawing pictorial views of two versions of the tabulated surface formed from the path curve and direction vector. Note the difference between the two versions in the settings of the **Surftab** variables.

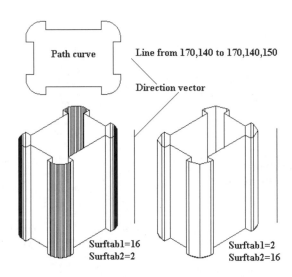

Fig. 15.35 Examples of the use
of the **Tabulated Surface** tool

The Ruled Surface tool (Fig. 15.36)

To construct the ruled surface shown in Fig. 15.38:

Fig. 15.36 Select the **Ruled
Surface** tool from the **Surfaces**
toolbar

1. Place the screen into the **3D Views/Right** view (Fig. 15.37).
2. With the **Polyline** tool construct the object shown in the upper drawing of Fig. 15.38.
3. Change the view to **3D Views/Top**.
4. With **Copy**, copy the pline object 300 units to the right. The two plines are shown in the upper drawing of Fig. 15.38.
5. Place the screen in the **3DViews/SW Isometric** view.
6. Set **Surftab1** to 32.
7. *Left-click* on the **Ruled Surface** tool from the **Surfaces** toolbar (Fig. 15.36). The Command line shows:

Command:_rulesurf
Current wire frame density: SURFTAB1=32
Select first defining curve: *pick* one of the plines
Select second defining curve: *pick* the other pline
Command:

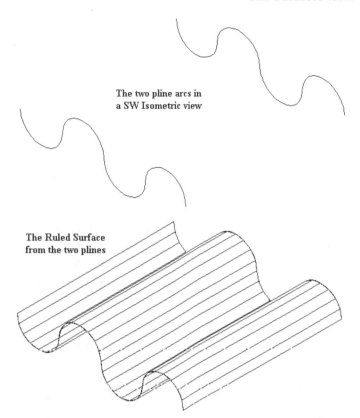

The two pline arcs in
a SW Isometric view

The Ruled Surface
from the two plines

Fig. 15.37 Select **Right** from
the **3D Views** sub-menu of the
View pull-down menu

Fig. 15.38 An example of a
ruled surface

And the ruled surface forms as shown in the lower drawing of Fig.
15.38.

The Edge Surface tool (Fig. 15.39)

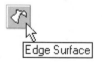

Fig. 15.39 Select the **Edge
Surface** tool from the **Surfaces**
toolbar

1. Place the screen in **3D Views/Right**.
2. Draw plines as shown in Fig. 15.40.
3. Place the screen in **3D Vies/Top**.
4. Move the straight pline 300 units to the right.
5. Place the screen in **3D Views/Top**.
6. Join the ends of the two pline as shown in Fig. 15.41.
7. Place the screen in **3D Views/SE Isometric**.
8. Set both surftabs to 24
9. Call the **Edge Surface** tool:

Fig. 15.40 Plines drawn in **3D
Views/Right** for the **Edge
Surface** example

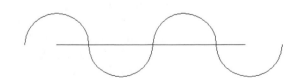

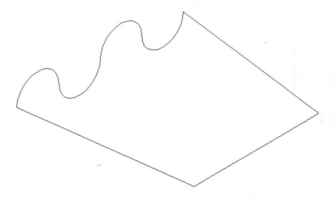

Fig. 15.41 The four edges for the **Edge Surface** example

Command:_edgesurf
Select object 1 for surface edge: *pick* one of the objects
Select object 2 for surface edge: *pick* another of the objects
Select object 3 for surface edge: *pick* another of the objects
Select object 4 for surface edge: *pick* the last of the objects
Command:

And the surface forms as shown in Fig. 15.42.

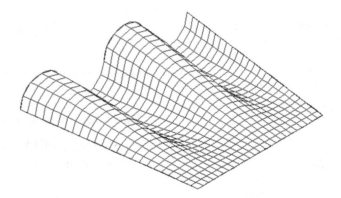

Fig. 15.42 The resulting **Edge Surface**

Questions

1. Have you tried using the **Torus** tool form the **Surfaces** toolbar?
2. One of the tools in the **Surfaces** toolbar is not a 3D tool. What is the name of this tool?
3. What is the major difference in coordinate axes when constructing a drawing using any of the **Surfaces** tools?
4. In which menu are the **Isometric Viewpoints** found?
5. What is the purpose of the **Hide** tool?
6. What is meant by the term '3D filters'?
7. There is no **Surfaces** tool for cylinders. How then are surface cylinders constructed?

8. When constructing a surface with many faces, the **3D Face** tool can be used. However, many lines may occur in the resulting surface. How are such lines erased, without affecting the 3D Face as a mesh surface behind which other constructions can be hidden?

9. One problem when using the **Tabulated Surface** tool is that, when the **Hide** tool is used, there is no upper surface to the resulting solid. How could this be remedied?

10. What is the major difference between obtaining a surface using **Ruled Surface** and one obtained by using **Edge Surface**?

Exercises

1. Figure 15.43 shows the outline of a shed constructed with the aid of the **3D Face** tool. Construct the given drawing to the sizes shown using the **3D Face** tool.

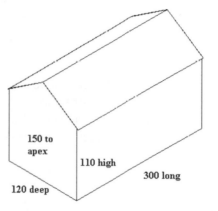

150 to apex

110 high

300 long

120 deep

Fig. 15.43 Exercise 1

2. Construct the surfaces 3D drawing shown in Fig. 15.44 to the sizes indicated with the drawing.

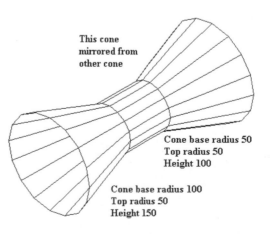

This cone mirrored from other cone

Cone base radius 50
Top radius 50
Height 100

Cone base radius 100
Top radius 50
Height 150

Fig. 15.44 Exercise 2

3. Figure 15.45 shows a surfaces 3D drawing formed from a cone, a dish, a dome and a torus.

Working to sizes of your own choice construct a surfaces model similar to that shown in the illustration.

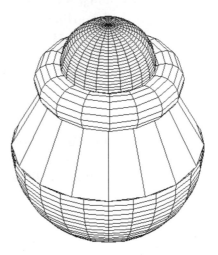

Fig. 15.45 Exercise 3

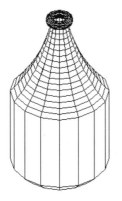

Fig. 15.46 3D drawing for exercise 4

4. Figure 15.46 shows a pictorial view of a surface of revolution constructed from the polyline shown in Fig. 15.47.

Construct the model to the information given in the two illustrations working to sizes of your own choice.

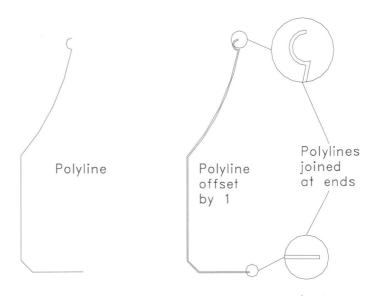

Fig. 15.47 Exercise 4

5. Figure 15.48 shows a surface formed with the aid of the tool
   Rulesurf. The two semicircles are 250 units apart.
   Construct the given surface.

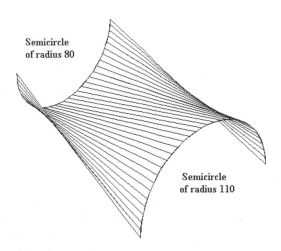

Semicircle
of radius 80

Semicircle
of radius 110

Fig. 15.48 Exercise 5

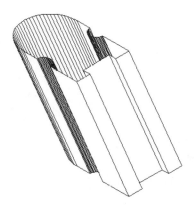

Fig. 15.49 Exercise 6

Fig. 15.50 Path curve and
direction vector for exercise 6

6. Figure 15.49 shows a surface produced with the aid of the tool
   Tabulated Surface. Figure 15.50 shows the dimensions of the two
   parts of the tabulated surface.

   Working to the dimensions given in Fig. 15.50 construct the
   tabulated surface.

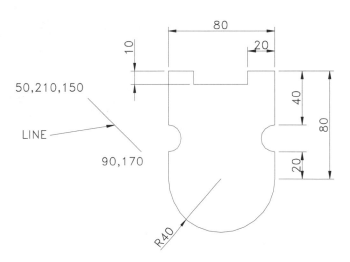

50,210,150

LINE

90,170

80

20

10

40

80

20

R40

7. Construct the surfaces 3D model drawing to the information given with the Fig. 15.51, working to sizes of your own choice.

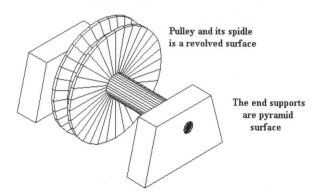

Pulley and its spidle
is a revolved surface

The end supports
are pyramid
surface

Fig. 15.51 Exercise 7

8. Figure 15.52 shows a 3D surface model constructed from three tools from the **Surfaces** toolbar.

Working to sizes of your own choice construct a 3D surface drawing similar to that given

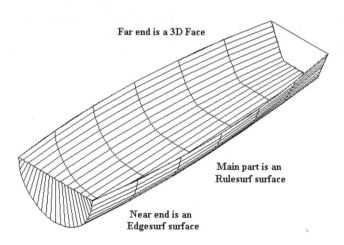

Far end is a 3D Face

Main part is an
Rulesurf surface

Near end is an
Edgesurf surface

Fig. 15.52 Exercise 8

Chapter 16

The UCS and the Solids tools

The User Coordinate System (UCS)

We have so far used the AutoCAD 2000 window with the coordinate system in what is known as the **WORLD** coordinate system, in which the Z axis is perpendicular to the screen. With the aid of the **UCS** the operator can set the X,Y,Z coordinate system at any angle he/she desires to facilitate the construction and viewing of 3D drawings. The tools for the UCS are held in two toolbars – the **UCS** and the **UCS II** (Fig. 16.1). As can be seen from Fig. 16.2 the **UCS II** toolbar includes a popup list from which orthographic views of a 3D solid model drawing can be selected.

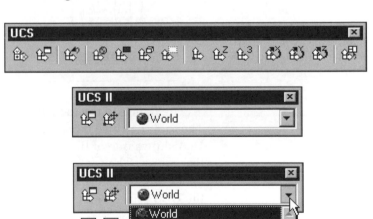

Fig. 16.1 The two UCS toolbars – **UCS** and **UCS II**

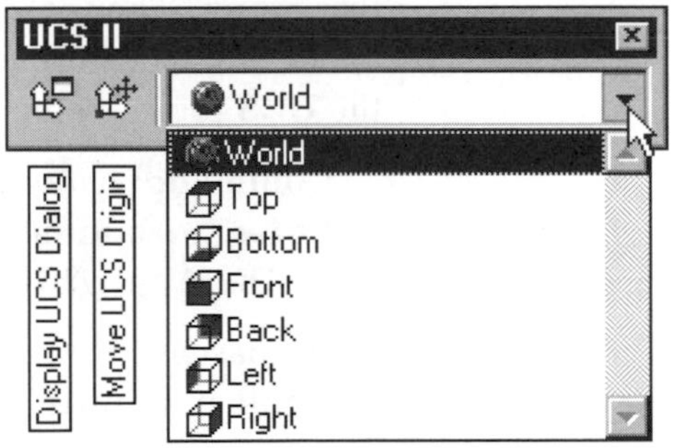

Fig. 16.2 The names of the two tools in the **UCS II** toolbar together with the popup list names

Figure 16.3 shows a 3D solid model drawing of a machine part and Fig. 16.4 the UCS views of the part for each of the orthographic views as selected from the **UCS II** popup list.

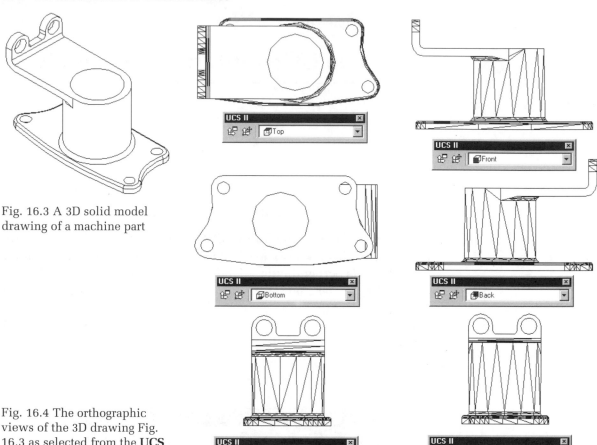

Fig. 16.3 A 3D solid model drawing of a machine part

Fig. 16.4 The orthographic views of the 3D drawing Fig. 16.3 as selected from the **UCS II** toolbar

The names of the tools in the **UCS** toolbar are shown in Fig. 16.5. The tools can also be called from the **Tools** pull-down menu. Figure 16.6 shows one of the sub-menus associated with the **UCS** tools in that menu. The tools can also be seen in the sequence of prompts appearing when either ucs is *entered* at the Command line or when the **UCS** tool is selected from the **UCS** toolbar:

Command: *enter* ucs *right-click*
Enter an option [New/Move/orthoGraphic/Prev/Restore/Save/ Del/Apply/?/World] <World>:

A comparison between the prompts and the names of the tools from the toolbar show the similarity.

The set variable UCSFOLLOW

The UCS will change to a selected view only if the set variable **UCSFOLLOW** is ON (or set to 1), as follows:

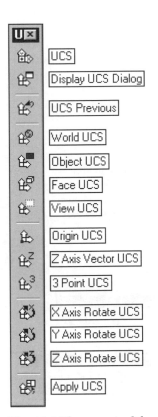

Fig. 16.5 The names of the tools in the **UCS** toolbar

Fig. 16.6 The **UCS** tools from the **Tools** pull-down menu

Command: *enter* ucsfollow *right-click*
New value for UCSFOLLOW <0>: *enter* 1 *right-click*
Command:

The UCS icon

The **UCS** icon will appear on screen if the set variable **UCSICON** is set to **ON** as follows:

Command: *enter* ucsicon *right-click*
Enter an option [ON/OFF/All/Norigin/ORigin] <OFF>: *enter* on
    right-click
Command:

And the icon will appear – usually at the left-hand bottom corner of the AutoCAD 2000 drawing area.

Figure 16.7 shows the variety of forms the icon can take according to various setting of the AutoCAD 2000 window.

It is advisable to experiment with settings in the UCS. It is important to be able to understand how the UCS works if successful 3D modelling is to be achieved.

The tools from the Solids toolbars

Two toolbars carry the **Solids** tool icons – **Solids** and **Solids Editing** (Fig. 16.8).

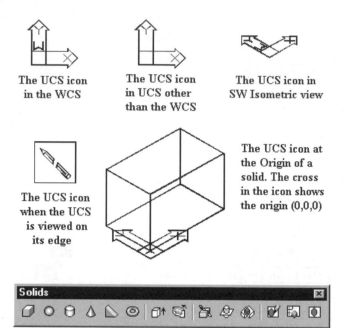

The UCS icon in the WCS

The UCS icon in UCS other than the WCS

The UCS icon in SW Isometric view

The UCS icon when the UCS is viewed on its edge

The UCS icon at the Origin of a solid. The cross in the icon shows the origin (0,0,0)

Fig. 16.7 The variety of forms of the **UCS** icon

Fig. 16.8 The **Solids** toolbars

Examples of the use of the Solids tools

In the examples given below only the coordinate points are shown against the sequences of prompts. *Enter* and *right-click* have not been included in each line of the sequences.

The names of the tools in the two **Solids** toolbars are shown in Fig. 16.9. In all the examples given below it has been assumed the tools have been called from the toolbars.

Example 1 – Box (Fig. 16.12)

Left-click on the **Box** tool from the **Solids** toolbar (Fig. 16.10):

Command:_box
Specify corner of box or [Center]: 130,200
Specify corner or [Cube/Length]: 310,100
Specify height: 30
Command: *right-click*
Specify corner of box or [Center]: 130,200,200
Specify corner or [Cube/Length]: 260,100,200
Specify height: 30
Command: *right-click*
Specify corner of box or [Center]: 130,200,30

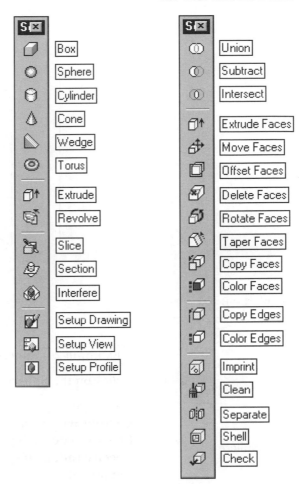

Fig. 16.9 The tools in the two
Solids toolbars – **Solids** and
Solids Editing

Fig. 16.10 Calling **Box**

Fig. 16.11 Calling **Union**

Specify corner or [Cube/Length]: 200,100,30
Specify height: 170
Command:

Select **SE Isometric** from the **View** pull-down menu
    Left-click on the **Union** tool from the **Solids Editing** toolbar (Fig. 16.11):

Command:_union
Select objects: *pick* one of the boxes **1 found**
Select objects: *pick* another of the boxes **1 found 2 total**
Select objects: *pick* the third of the boxes **1 found 3 total**
Select objects: *right-click*
Command: *enter* hi (for Hide) *right-click*
HIDE Regenerating drawing
Command:

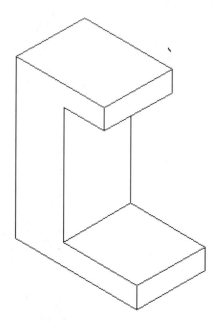

Fig. 16.12 Example 1 – Box

Fig. 16.13 Calling **Sphere**

Example 2 – Sphere (Fig. 16.15)

1. *Left-click* on the **Sphere** tool from the **Solids** toolbar (Fig. 16.13):

> **Command:_sphere**
> **Current wire frame density: ISOLINES=16**
> **Specify center of sphere <0,0,0>:** 160,180
> **Specify radius of sphere or [Diameter]:** 100
> **Command:**

2. Select **SE Top** from the **View** pull-down menu.
3. Construct a box 90 by 90 and 400 high central to the sphere.
4. Call the **Subtract** tool from the **Solids Editing** toolbar (Fig. 16.14).

> **Command:_subtract Select solids and regions to subtract from...**
> **Select objects:** *pick* the sphere
> **Select objects:** *right-click*
> **Select solids and regions to subtract...**
> **Select objects:** *pick* the box
> **Select objects:** *right-click*
> **Command:**

5. Call **Hide**:

> **Command:** *enter* hi (for Hide) *right-click*
> **HIDE Regenerating drawing**
> **Command:**

Fig. 16.14 Calling **Subtract**

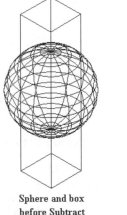

Fig. 16.15 Example 2 – Sphere

**Sphere and box
before Subtract**

**Sphere and box
after Subtract
and Hide**

Note

The first line of the **Sphere** prompts sequence is **Current wire frame density: ISOLINES=16**.

The default setting in AutoCAD 2000 is **4**. To set the variable **ISOLINES** to a different figure (to say 12):

Command: *enter* isolines *right-click*
Enter new value for ISOLINES: *enter* 12
Command:

Example 3 – Cylinder (Fig. 16.17)

1. Reset **ISOLINES** to 24
2. *Left-click* on the **Cylinder** tool from the **Solids** toolbar (Fig. 16.16):

Command:_cylinder
Current wire frame density: ISOLINES=24
Specify center for base of cylinder or [Elliptical] <0,0,0>:
     100,170
Specify radius for base of cylinder or [Diameter]: 80

Fig. 16.16 Calling **Cylinder**

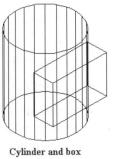

**Cylinder and box
before Subtract**

**Cylinder and box
after Subtract
and Hide**

Fig. 16.17 Example 3

Specify height of cylinder or [Center at other end]: 200
Command:

3. Construct a box $50 \times 140 \times 100$.
4. Place in **3D Views/Front**.
5. With **Move** move the box vertically upwards to centre of cylinder.
6. Place in **3D Views/SE Isometric**.
7. Call **Subtract** and subtract the box from the cylinder.

Example 4 – Cone (Fig. 16.19)

1. Reset **ISOLINES** to the default value of **4**.
2. *Left-click* on the **Cone** tool from the **Solids** toolbar (Fig. 16.18):

Command:_cylinder
Current wire frame density: ISOLINES=4
Specify center for base of cone or [Elliptical] <0,0,0>: 130,150
Specify radius for base of cone or [Diameter]: 80
Specify height of cone or [Apex]: 200
Command:

Fig. 16.18 Calling **Cone**

3. Construct a cylinder radius 100, height 100 with its centre at the right-hand quadrant of the cone.
4. Place in **SE Isometric** view:
5. Call **Union** and join the two solids together in a union.
6. Call **Hide**.

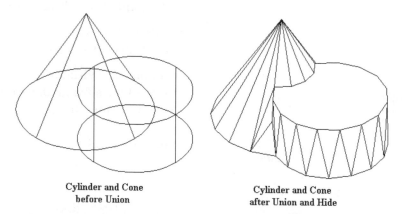

Fig. 16.19 Example 4

Cylinder and Cone
before Union

Cylinder and Cone
after Union and Hide

Example 5 – Wedge (Fig. 16.22)

1. *Left-click* on the **Wedge** tool from the **Solids** toolbar (Fig. 16.20):

Command:_wedge
Specify first corner of wedge or [Center] <0,0,0>: 60,220
Specify other corner or [Cube/Length]: 240,110
Specify height: 80
Command:

Fig. 16.20 Calling **Wedge**

Fig. 16.21 Calling **Intersect**

2. Construct a cone, in the centre of the wedge (150,165) of radius 50 and height 100.
3. Place in the **SE Isometric** view.
4. Call **Intersect** from the **Solids Editing** toolbar (Fig. 16.21).

    Command:_intersect
    Select objects: *pick* the wedge
    Select objects: *pick* the cone
    Select objects: *right-click*
    Command:

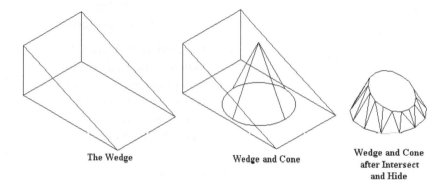

The Wedge   Wedge and Cone   Wedge and Cone after Intersect and Hide

Fig. 16.22 Example 5

Example 6 – Torus (Fig. 16.24)

1. Set **ISOLINES** to 16.
2. *Left-click* on the **Torus** tool from the **Solids** toolbar (Fig. 16.23):

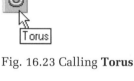

Fig. 16.23 Calling **Torus**

    Command:_torus
    Current wire frame density: ISOLINES=16
    Specify center of torus <0,0,0>: 130,160
    Specify radius of torus or [Diameter]: 110
    Specify radius of tube or [Diameter]: 10
    Command:

3. Place in the **SW Isometric** view.
4. Call **Hide**.

Fig. 16.24 Example 6

Fig. 16.25 Torus and cylinder acted upon by the three Boolean operators

Torus centred on a cylinder, followed by Union and Hide   Torus centred on cylinder, followed by Subtract and Hide   Torus centred on cylinder, followed by Intersect and Hide

The Boolean operators

Figure 16.25 shows three cylinders of radius 50 and height 100 with torii of radius 50 and tube radius 20 centred around the cylinder. Each of the pairs of solids have been acted upon by what are known as the **Boolean operators** – Union, Subtract and Intersect. The Boolean operators can be selected from the **Solids Editing** toolbar.

Example 7 – Extrude (Fig. 16.27)

1. Construct the two outlines shown in the left-hand drawing of Fig. 16.27 using the **Polyline** tool and working to any sizes.
2. *Left-click* on the **Extrude** tool from the **Solids** toolbar (Fig. 16.26):

Fig. 16.26 Calling **Extrude**

> **Current wire frame density: ISOPLANES=4**
> **Command:_extrude**
> **Select object:** *pick* one of the plines **1 found**
> **Select object:** *pick* the other pline **1 found 2 total**
> **Select object:** *right-click*
> **Specify height of extrusion or [Path]:** 150
> **Specify angle of taper for extrusion: <0>:** *right-click*
> **Command:**

3. Place in the **SW Isometric** view.
4. With the aid of **Subtract** subtract the inner extrusion from the outer.
5. Call **Hide**.

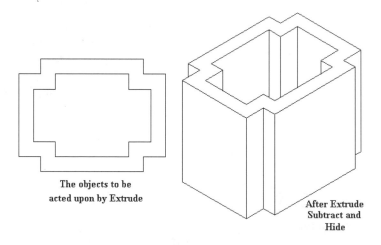

The objects to be
acted upon by Extrude

After Extrude
Subtract and
Hide

Fig. 16.27 Example 7

Example 8 – Extrude (Fig. 16.28)

This example follows the same procedures as for the seventh example, except that the **Path** option is used, the path in this example being an arc drawing in the **3D Views/Front** view. The left-hand drawing of Fig. 16.28 shows the object to be extruded and the

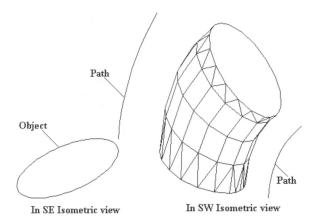

Fig. 16.28 Example 8

path along which it will be extruded. The right-hand drawing shows the extrusion after **Hid**e has been called.

Example 9 – Revolve (Fig. 16.30)

1. Set **ISOLINES** to 12.
2. *Left-click* on the **Revolve** tool from the **Solids** toolbar (Fig. 16.29):

Fig. 16.29 Calling **Revolve**

> **Command:_revolve**
> **Current wire frame density: ISOLINES=12**
> **Select objects:** *pick* the pline outline **1 found**
> **Select objects:** *right-click*
> **Specify start for axis of revolution or define axis by [Object/**
>   **X (axis)/Y (axis)]** *pick* start point
> **Specify end point of axis:** *pick*
> **Specify angle of revolution <360>:** *right-click*
> **Command:**

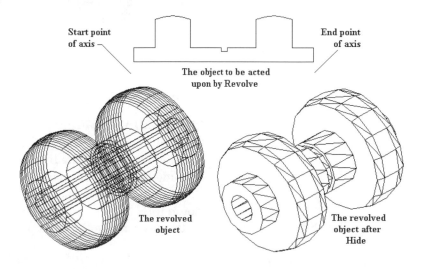

Fig. 16.30 Example 9

Example 10 – Revolve (Fig. 16.31)

1. Place screen in **3D Views/Front**.
2. Construct the pline outline as shown in Fig. 16.31.
3. Call **Offset** and offset the pline by 2.
4. Join the two plines at each end with plines and using **Pedit** to join the end plines to the offsets.
5. Call **Revolve** and revolve the pline through 180°.
6. Place in the **3D Views/NE Isometric**
7. Call **Hide**.

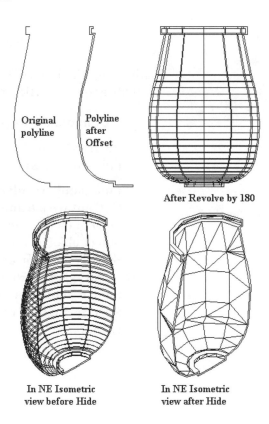

Original polyline

Polyline after Offset

After Revolve by 180

In NE Isometric view before Hide

In NE Isometric view after Hide

Fig. 16.31 Example 10

Example 11 – Slice (Fig. 16.33)

1. Place in **3D Views/Front**.
2. Construct the two pline outlines as shown in Fig. 16.33.
3. Extrude the outer pline by 40.
4. Extrude the inner pline by 20.
5. Place in **3D Views/Top**.
6. **Zoom** to **1**.
7. With **Move**, move the smaller extrusion to rest on the larger.

Slice

Fig. 16.32 Calling **Slice**

8. With **Copy**, copy the larger extrusion so that the copy is resting on to smaller extrusion.

9. Call **Union** and union the three extrusions together.

10. *Left-click* on the **Slice** tool from the **Solids** toolbar (Fig. 16.32):

> **Command:_slice**
> **Select objects:** *pick* the 3D solid just created **1 found**
> **Select objects:** *right-click*
> **Specify first point on slicing plane by [Object/Zaxis/View/XY/**
> **YZ/ZX/3points] <3points>:** *pick* first point (see Fig. 16.33)
> **Specify second point on plane:** *pick* second point
> **Specify third point on plane:** *enter* .xy *right-click*
> **of** *pick* third point **(need Z)** *enter* 1 *right-click*
> **Specify a point on the desired side of the plane or [Keep both**
> **sides]:** *pick* lower half
> **Command:**

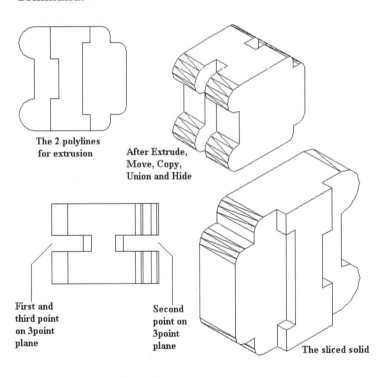

The 2 polylines
for extrusion

After Extrude,
Move, Copy,
Union and Hide

First and
third point
on 3point
plane

Second
point on
3point
plane

The sliced solid

Fig. 16.33 Example 11

Example 12 – Section (Fig. 16.35)

This example is a 3D model of the drawing given in Fig. 13.33 on page 204. The 3D model was created from a pline with the aid of the **Revolve** tool. The holes were created by arraying a suitably sized cylinder around the centre of the solid of revolution and then with **Subtract** subtracted them from the solid of revolution.

Section

Fig. 16.34 Calling **Section**

1. Place the drawing in **3D views/Top**.
2. *Left-click* on the **Section** tool from the **Solids** toolbar (Fig. 16.34):

> **Command:_section**
> **Select objects:** *pick* the solid drawing **1 found**
> **select objects:** *right-click*
> **Specify first point on slicing plane by [Object/Zaxis/View/XY/**
> **YZ/ZX/3points] <3points>:**
> **Specify second point on plane:** *pick* second point
> **Specify third point on plane:** *enter* .xy *right-click*
> **of** *pick* third point **(need Z)** *enter* 1 *right-click*
> **Command:**

A section outline is formed as shown in Fig. 16.35.

3. With **Move**, move the section plane outline away from the solid.
4. Place the drawing in a **3point UCS** with the UCS plane passing through the section plane line.
5. Call the **Boundary Hatch** dialogue box and hatch the section outline with a suitable hatch pattern. In the example given the pattern is **ANSI31** at a **Scale** of **2**.

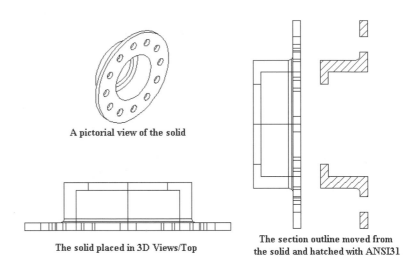

A pictorial view of the solid

The solid placed in 3D Views/Top

The section outline moved from
the solid and hatched with ANSI31

Fig. 16.35 Example 12

Notes

1. The tools described in this chapter have been shown as having been selected from either the **Solids** toolbar or from the **Solids Editing** toolbar. Or, they may be selected from the **Solids** sub-menu of the **Draw** pull-down menu as shown in Fig. 16.36. The **Boolean** operators – **Union**, **Subtract** and **Intersect** can be selected from the **Solids Editing** sub-menu of the **Modify** toolbar.

Fig. 16.36 Selecting **Solids** tools from the **Draw** pull-down menu

2. A few of the **Solids** tools can be *entered* at the Command line in an abbreviated form as follows:

   ext – Extrude
   rev – Revolve
   sec – Section
   uni – Union

3. Space in a book of this nature forbids describing many of the tools from the **Solids Editing** toolbar. The reader is advised however to experiment with these tools.

4. The three tools from the **Solids** toolbar – **Setup Drawing**, **Setup View**, **Setup Profile** will be described in the next chapter.

Questions

1. Frequent use can be made of using the **3D Views** from the **View** pull-down menu when constructing 3D solid drawings. Why is this so?

2. The alternative to using the **3D Views** is to use the **UCS**. How can the **UCS** be used in this manner?

3. The solids tools can be brought into action in various ways – can you name the methods of doing so?

4. When creating 3D solids which are based on circular parts or on arcs, it is important to set one of the set variables before calling the tool. Which variable is this?

5. Can you name the **Boolean** operators?

6. What is the purpose of the Boolean operators?

7. What is the purpose of the et variable **UCSFOLLOW**?

8. Why is the **Extrude** tool so important when constructing 3D solid drawings?

9. Why is the **Hide** tool important in the construction of 3D solid drawings?

10. The **Surfaces** tools and the **Solids** tools appear to produce similar 3D objects. What are the differences between 3D objects created with the two sets of tools?

   Notes

1. When constructing 3D solid models in AutoCAD 2000 it will be necessary to switch between various **3D Views** called from the **View** pull-down menu.

2. Instead of using the **3D Views**, the switching can be done between **UCS Orthographic** planes from the **Modify II** toolbar.

3. When switching either between **3D Views** or between **UCS** planes it will be necessary to **Zoom** to 1 (scale 1:1), otherwise the model tends to fill the drawing area.

4. If setting a **UCS** plane with 3 points, whether to obtain a new plane, or to **Slice** or **Section** an object, when using the filter **.xy**, only the figure 1 (one) need be *entered* in response to the **(need Z)** prompt.
5. Rather than work out the exact plane on which to position part of a model, it is easier to change to a new **3D View** or **UCS Orthographic** view and **Move** the part in that view.
6. The Boolean operators **Union** and **Subtract** will frequently be needed during constructions of 3D solid models. The **Intersect** Boolean tool is less likely to be used, but it is advisable for the reader to practise its use to understand how it functions.

Exercises

The illustrations associated with several of the exercises given below show the stages in constructing the 3D models in answer to the exercises. The following notes should help in obtaining good results when attempting the exercises.

1. To construct the 3D solid of the hook shown in the isometric drawing, top left-hand drawing of Fig. 16.37:

   a) Construct the outline of the central 2D drawing from circles and lines, use **Trim** as necessary, change to a closed polyline with **Polyline Edit** (pedit), use **Fillet** where necessary.
   b) With **Extrude** and **Subtract** complete the 3D solid shown in the **SW Isometric** view of the right-hand drawing of Fig. 16.37.

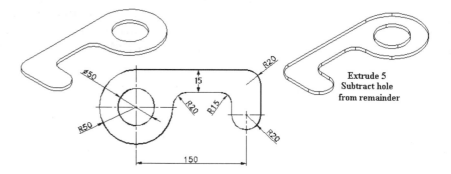

Fig. 16.37 Exercise 1

2. Figure 16.38 shows the stages for the construction of the 3D solid drawing given in the right-hand drawing of the illustration:

   a) Construct the polyline outline – left-hand drawing.
   b) Copy the outline to a new position.
   c) **Extrude** one of the plines to a height of 150.
   d) Place in **3D Views/Front** and in that view construct a semicircle.
   e) Use the semicircle as a **Path** for the second pline outline.

f) **Copy** the first extrusion and move all three extrusions to their correct positions relative to each other.

g) With **Union** union the three extrusions to form the 3D model.

h) Call **Hide**.

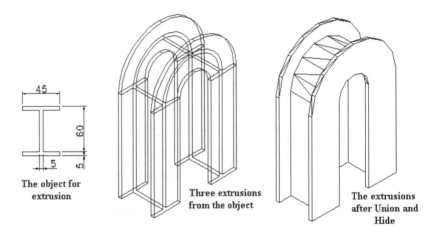

45

60

5

5

The object for
extrusion

Three extrusions
from the object

The extrusions
after Union and
Hide

Fig. 16.38 Exercise 2

3. Figure 16.39. To construct the 3D model:

a) On a common centre construct three cylinders – one of radius 15 and height 60; the second of radius 60 and height 50; the third of radius 90 and height 10.

b) Place in **3D Views/Front** and **Zoom** to **1**.

c) With **Move** move the radius 90 cylinder to rest on top of the radius 60 cylinder.

d) Place in **3D Views/SW Isometric** and with **Union** join the two larger cylinders to form a single solid model.

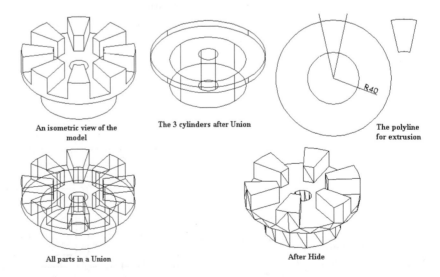

An isometric view of the
model

The 3 cylinders after Union

R40

The polyline
for extrusion

All parts in a Union

After Hide

Fig. 16.39 Exercise 3

e) With **Subtract** subtract the smallest cylinder from the solid.

f) Place in **3D Views/Front** and **Zoom** to **1**.

g) Form a **UCS** plane with **UCS 3point** along the top line of the solid. Then **Zoom** to **1**.

h) Construct the pline outline of one of the teeth of the solid and **Extrude** to 30.

i) With **Array** polar array the extrusion 5 times around the solid so far formed.

j) With **Union** join the 6 teeth to the remainder of the solid.

k) Call **Hide**.

4. Figure 16.40 gives sizes for the 3D model of this exercise. Stages in creating the 3D model for the exercise are given in Fig. 16.41.

a) Place in **3D Views/Front**. **Zoom** to **1**.

b) Construct the pline outline shown in the top left-hand drawing of Fig. 16.41.

c) With **Extrude** construct an extrusion from the pline of height 115.

d) Create a box fitting inside the extrusion of height 85.

e) Place in **3D Views/Top**. **Zoom** to **1**.

f) With **Move** move the box to lie between central to the extrusion.

g) Place in **3D Views/SE Isometric**. **Zoom** to **1**.

h) With **Subtract**, subtract the box from the extrusion.

i) Place in **3D views/Front**. **Zoom** to **1**.

j) With **Cylinder** create a cylinder of radius 25 and height 120 central to the arc of the extrusion.

k) Place in **3D Views/Top**. **Zoom** to **1**.

l) Place a cylinder of radius 20 and height 20 in the base of the extrusion.

m) Place in **3D Views/SE Isometric**. **Zoom** to **1**.

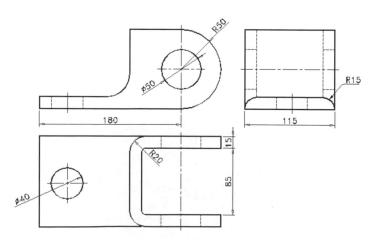

Fig. 16.40 Orthographic projection for exercise 4

n) **Subtract** the cylinders from the solid.
o) Call **Hide**.

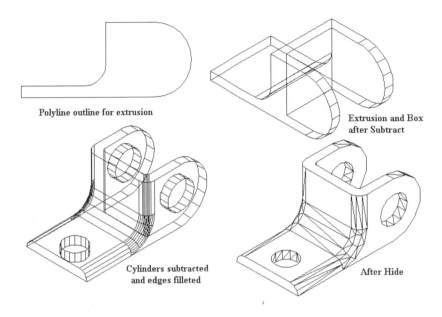

Polyline outline for extrusion

Extrusion and Box
after Subtract

Cylinders subtracted
and edges filleted

After Hide

Fig. 16.41 Exercise 4

5. Figure 16.42 is a plan view of the outlines for the first stage of extrusions for exercise 5.

a) Construct the outlines and circles of Fig. 16.42.
b) **Extrude** the outer pline to height 40; **Extrude** the inner pline to height 35; **Extrude** the circles to height 10.
c) Place in **3D Views/Front. Zoom** to **1**.
d) With **Move** move the inner extrusion up by **5**.
e) Place in **3D Views/SE Isometric. Zoom** to **1**.
f) Construct the pline outline for subtraction from the solid to date.
g) Place in **3D Views/Plan. Zoom** to **1**.
h) If necessary **Move** the last extrusion over the original extrusion.
i) Place in **3D Views/SE isometric. Zoom** to **1**.
j) **Subtract** the last extrusion from the 3D solid so far created.

Fig. 16.42 Dimensions for
outline for extrusions of
exercise 5

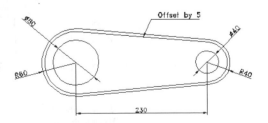

Offset by 5

⌀80
⌀40
R60
R40
230

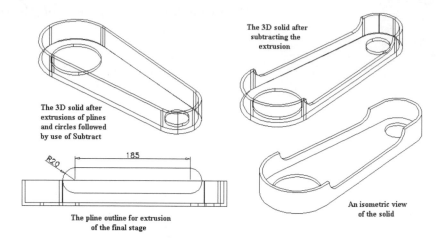

The 3D solid after subtracting the extrusion

The 3D solid after extrusions of plines and circles followed by use of Subtract

R20   185

The pline outline for extrusion of the final stage

An isometric view of the solid

Fig. 16.43 Stages in creating exercise 5

6. This model of a flange coupling was constructed as follows:
    a) **3D Views/Top. Zoom** to **1**.
    b) Construct the pline outline and circle of Fig. 16.44
    c) **Extrude** – Height 15.
    d) **Copy**, **Rotate** copy by 90°.
    e) **3D Views/Front** and **Move** copy vertically up by 135 units.
    f) **3D Views/Top. Zoom** to **1**.
    g) **Cylinder** – Radius 68; Height 150.

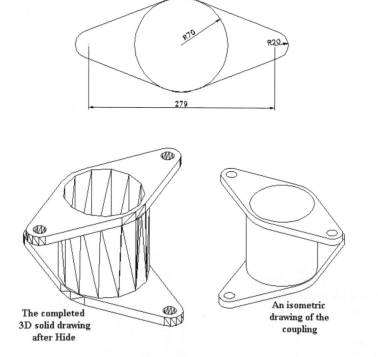

R70   R20

279

Fig. 16.44 Outlines for extrusions for exercise 6

The completed 3D solid drawing after Hide

An isometric drawing of the coupling

Fig. 16.45 Exercise 6

h) **Union** – cylinder to both extrusions.
i) **Cylinder** – Radius 60; Height 150.
j) **Subtract** cylinder from solid.
k) **3D Views/SW Isometric. Zoom** to **1**.
l) **Hide**.

Chapter 17

Further 3D model constructions

The Setup tools from the Solids toolbar

Three tools from the **Solids** toolbar which were not described in the previous chapter are **Setup Drawing**, **Setup View** and **Setup Profile**.

The Setup Drawing tool

1. Load a 3D solid model drawing – Fig. 17.1. The drawing shown has been acted upon by **Hide** but only for the purposes of this illustration.

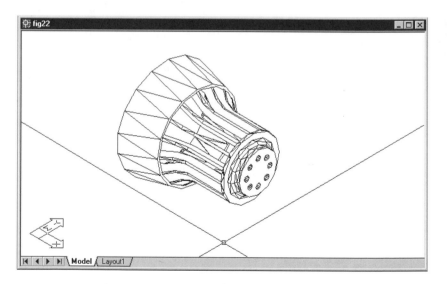

Fig. 17.1 A solid model drawing loaded into AutoCAD 2000

Fig. 17.2 Calling **Setup Drawing**

2. *Left-click* on the **Setup Drawing** tool (Fig. 17.2). The **Layout1** tab highlights and the **Page Settings – Layout1** dialogue box appears (Fig. 17.3).
3. If the settings in the dialogue box are suitable, *left-click* on the **OK** button. The dialogue box disappears and the drawing appears in the **Layout1** window (Fig. 17.4).

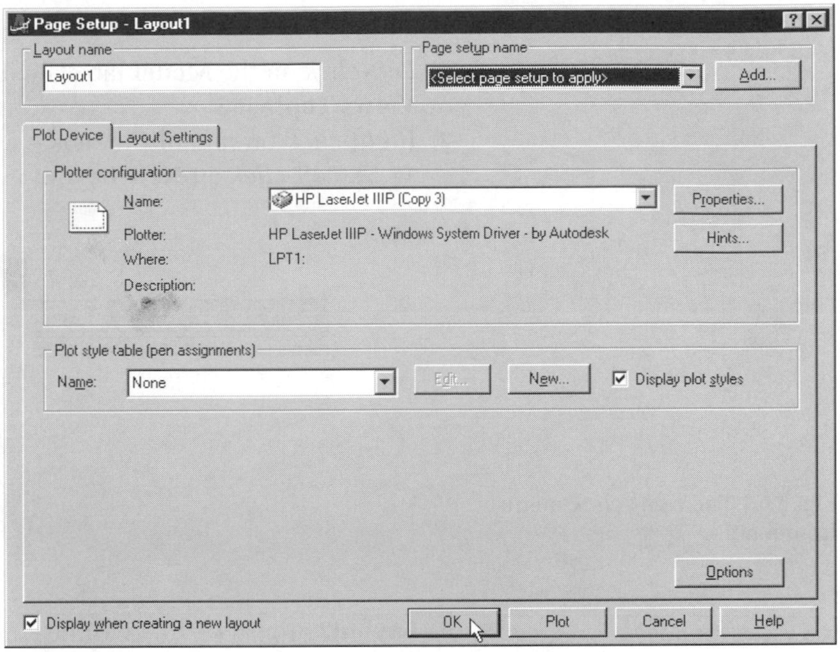

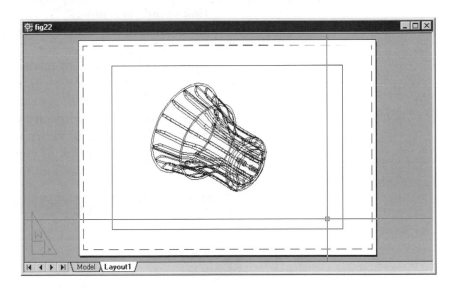

Fig. 17.3 The **Page Setup – Layout1** dialogue box

Fig. 17.4 The 2D drawing in **Layout1**

Notes

1. The drawing in **Layout1** is a 2D drawing, even though it is obtained from the 3D drawing in the **Model** window.
2. Note the **Paper Space** icon in the bottom left-hand corner of the window replacing the **UCS** icon.

The Setup View tool

1. *Left-click* on the **Model** tab. The drawing reappears in a plan (**3D Views/Top**) view.
2. *Right-click* on one of the tabs – a *right-click* menu appears (Fig. 17.5). *Left-click* on **New Layout** in the menu.

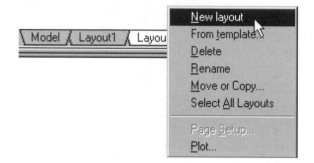

Fig. 17.5 The *right-click* menu from a tab

3. **Layout2** appears – this will be a plan (**Top**) view – Fig. 17.6.

>   **Command:_solview**
>   **Enter an option [UCS/Ortho/Auxiliary/Section]:** *enter* o *right-click*
>   **Specify side of view to project:** *left-click* on the right-hand side of the viewport outline
>   **Specify view center:** *pick* a suitable point
>   **Specify view center <specify viewport>:** *right-click*
>   **Specify first corner of viewport:** *pick*
>   **Specify opposite corner of viewport:** *pick*
>   **Enter view name:** *enter* end view *right-click*

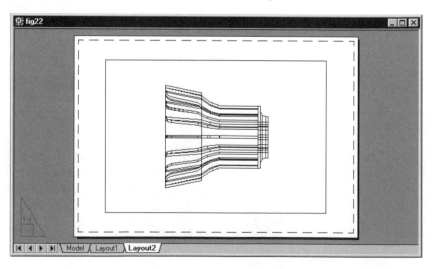

Fig. 17.6 **Layout2**

Fig. 17.7 Calling **Setup View**

UCS = 1 UCS will be saved with the view
Enter an option [UCS/Ortho/Auxiliary/Section]: *right-click*
Command:

Figure 17.8 shows the new view.

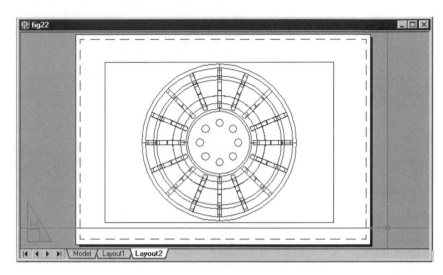

Fig. 17.8 The new view
produced with **Setup View**

The Setup Profile tool

1. *Left-click* on the **Layout1** tab.
2. Call **Setup Profile** (Fig. 17.9).

Fig. 17.9 Calling **Setup Profile**

Command:_solprof
A model space viewport must be active to use SOLPROF
(Use MVIEW and MSPACE commands)
Command: *enter* mv *right-click*
MVIEW
Specify corner of viewport or [ON/OFF/Fit/Hideplot/Lock/
    Object/Polygonal/Restore/2/3/4 <Fit>: *right-click*
Regenerating drawing
Command: *enter* ms *right-click*
MSPACE
Command: Call **Setup Profile**
Select objects: *pick* the drawing
Select objects: *right-click*
Display hidden profile lines on separate layer [Yes/No] <Y>:
    right-click
Project profile lines onto a plane [Yes/No] <Y>: *right-click*
Delete tangential edges [Yes/No]: <Y>: *right-click*
One solid selected
Command:

3. Make the layer **PV-255** (or similar **PV** layers) current.
4. Turn all other layers off. The profile only drawing appears in the viewport (Fig. 17.10).

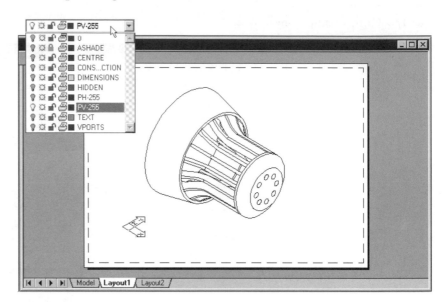

Fig. 17.10 The profile drawing and the **Layer Control** popup list

Other examples of layouts

1. Load a 3D solid model drawing and place in the **3D Views SW Isometric** view (Fig. 17.11).
2. *Left-click* on the **Layout1** tab. The **Page Setup – Layout1** appears. Check the settings and if correct *left-click* on the **OK** button. The drawing in **Layout1** appears (Fig. 17.12).

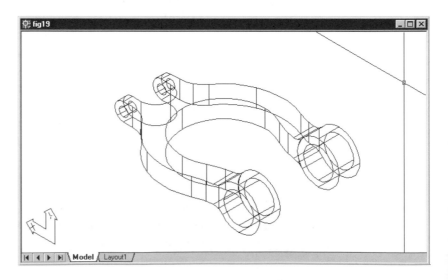

Fig. 17.11 The loaded 3D solid drawing

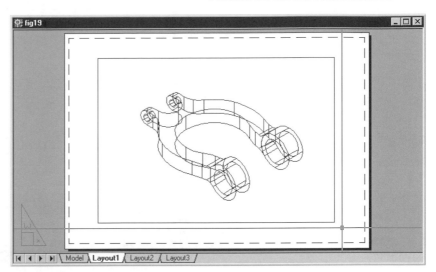

Fig. 17.12 The drawing in
Layout1

3. *Left-click* on the **Model** tab. Place in the **3D Views/Top** view. In the
   tabs *right-click* menu select **New layout.** The next layout tab
   appears – **Layout2**. *Left-click* on the **Layout2** tab. After checking the
   Page Setup – Layout2 dialogue box settings and *left-clicked* on the
   OK button, the **Layout2** screen appears with the top view (Fig.
   17.13).

4. *Left-click* on the **Model** tab. Place in the **3D Views/Right** view. In the
   tabs *right-click* menu select **New layout.** The next layout tab
   appears – **Layout3**. *Left-click* on the **Layout3** tab. After checking the
   Page Setup – Layout3 dialogue box settings and *left-clicked* on the
   OK button, the **Layout3** screen appears with the right view (Fig.
   17.14).

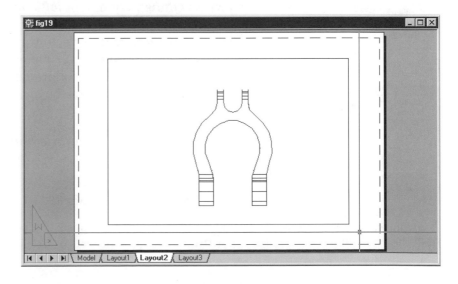

Fig. 17.13 The drawing in
Layout2

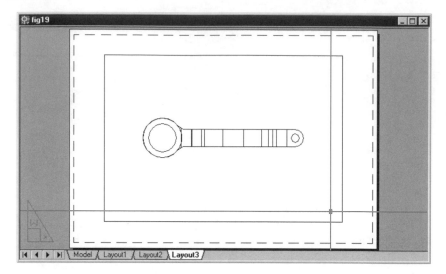

Fig. 17.14 The drawing in
Layout3

Note

1. It will be seen from the series of illustrations associated with these examples that a number of different views can be created from a 3D solid model loaded into the **Model** window.
2. Note that the drawings in **Layout** windows are 2D and have originated from the 3D drawing.

Viewports

The purpose of working in several viewports is to enable the operator to see the results of the constructions from several angles in different view, mostly isometric views. To set up a suitable viewport configuration, first *left-click* on **New Viewports...** in the **View** pull-down menu (Fig. 17.15) and select a suitable 2, 3 or 4 viewport layout from the selection given in the **Viewports** dialogue box which appears (Fig. 17.16). Figure 17.17 shows the result of first loading a 3D solid drawing followed by selecting a **Four: Left** layout from the **Viewports** dialogue box.

Note

In a multiple viewport layout, a *left-click* in any viewport makes that selected viewport current.

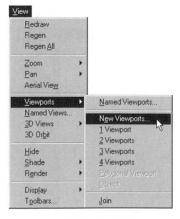

Fig. 17.15 Selecting **New Viewports...** from the **View** pull-down menu

Polygonal viewports

In a layout window, viewports can be created which are of a variety of outline shapes. A procedure is as follows:

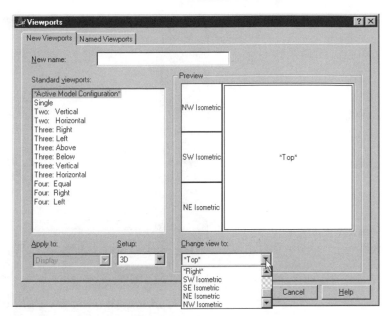

Fig. 17.16 The **Viewports** dialogue box

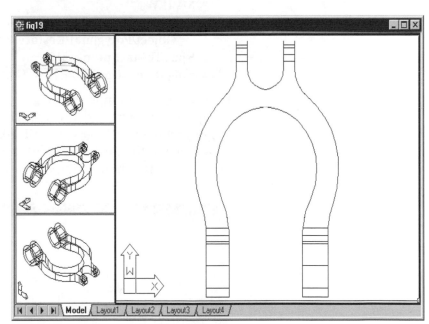

Fig. 17.17 The result of a **Four: Left** viewports selection with a different view in each viewport.

1. Load a 3D solid model drawing, place it in a **3D Views/SW Isometric** view. Figure 17.18 is an example, in this example a 3D drawing of a drill chuck key in a **Layout1** window.
2. With **Erase** remove the viewport – call erase, *pick* one of the edges of the viewport and the viewport with its contents disappears. However the data for recalling the drawing remains with **Layout1**.

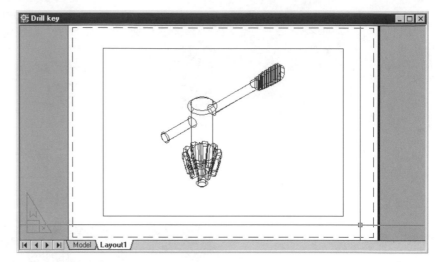

Fig. 17.18 A 3D drawing in
Layout1

3. Call **MVIEW**:

> **Command:** *enter* mv *right-click*
> **MVIEW**
> **Specify corner of viewport or [ON/OFF/Fit/Hideplot/Lock/**
> **Object/Polygonal/Restore/2/3/4] <Fit>:** *enter* p *right-click*
> **Specify start point:** *pick*
> **Specify next point or [Arc/Close/Length/Undo]:**

Following the prompts of this sequence, a variety of shapes for
viewports can be created. Figure 17.19 shows a rectangular viewport,
a viewport with outlines consisting of arcs and a circular viewport.

As each outline for a viewport is constructed, so the data for the
drawing restores the drawing within each viewport as it is completed.

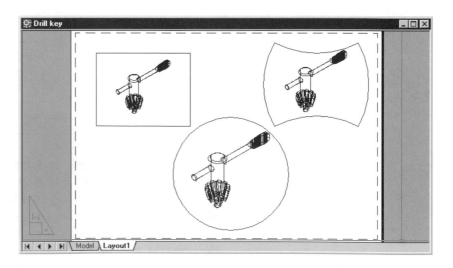

Fig. 17.19 Polygonal viewports

Other tools for constructing 3D models

Purge

When constructing 3D models the **Purge** tool should be used before finally saving the model drawing to file. Purging can save considerable file space on disk.

The tool can be called either from the **File** pull-down menu (Fig. 17.20) or by *entering* pu (or purge) at the Command line. The following shows a typical purging:

Fig. 17.20 Calling **Purge** from the **File** pull-down menu

Command: *enter* pu *right-click*
PURGE
Purge unused Blocks/Dimstyles/LAyers/LTypes/Plotstyles/SHapes/
    STyles/textSTyles/Mlinestyles/All: *enter* a (All) *right-click*
Purge block OVERHEAD? <N>: *enter* y (Yes) *right-click*
Purge layer DEFPOINTS? <N>: *enter* y (Yes) *right-click*
Purge layer HIDDEN? <N>: *enter* y (Yes) *right-click*
Purge layer CENTRE? <N>: *enter* y (Yes) *right-click*
No unreferenced blocks found.
No unreferenced layers found.
No unreferenced linetypes found.
No unreferenced text styles found.
No unreferenced shape files found.
No unreferenced dimension styles found.

No unreferenced mline styles found.
No unreferenced plotstyles found.
Command:

Fillet and Chamfer

Either of these two tools (described in Chapter 5) can be used as tools for modifying 3D solid model drawings. The tools are used in 3D Constructions in the same way as when working with the tools in 2D constructions.

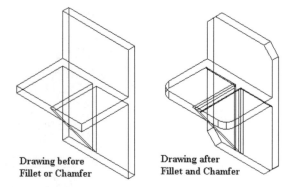

Fig. 17.21 An example of the use of the tools **Fillet** and **Chamfer**

Drawing before
Fillet or Chamfer

Drawing after
Fillet and Chamfer

Further examples of 3D Solid model drawings

Fig 17.22 shows the stages in constructing a 3D model of a spindle from a fan. The stages in the construction were as follows:

Stage 1: Construct in the **3D View/Right** the following solids:

1. A cylinder of radius 40 and height 25.
2. On the same centre, a cylinder of radius 15 and height 145.
3. On the same centre a cylinder of radius 10 and height 5.
4. On the same centre a cylinder of radius 5 and height 200.
5. A box 65 × 5 and of height 30.

Stage 2: Place the solids in the **3D Views/SW Isometric** just to check that the five solids have been constructed accurately.

Stage 3: Place in **3D Views/Front** and with **Move** move the solids to their correct positions. With **Copy**, copy the radius 10 cylinder from the left-hand end to the right-hand end.

Stage 4: Return to the **3D Views/Right** and with **Polar Array** array the boxes 6 times around the center of the cylinders.

Stage 5: Place the solids in **3D Views/SW Isometric** and with **Union** union all but the radius 5 cylinder into a single solid. With **Subtract**, subtract the radius 5 cylinder from the union.

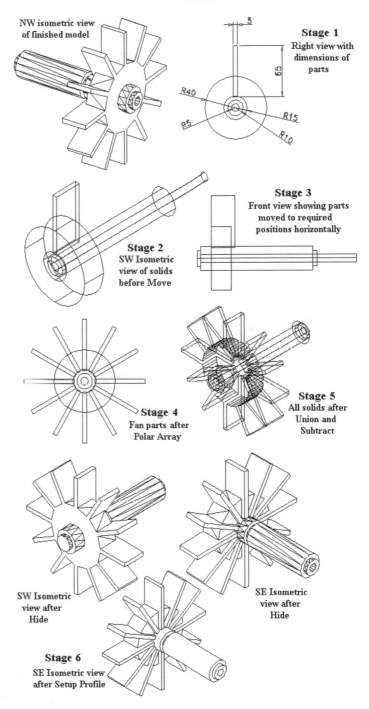

Fig. 17.22 An example of a 3D solid model drawing

Stage 6: In **3D Views/SE Isometric** and with **Setup Profile** change the solid into a profile only view.

Two other 3D solids are shown in **Hide** and **Setup Profile** views in Figs 17.23 and 17.24.

Figure 17.23: Made up from cylinders and extrusions. Some of the solids combined with **Union** and some parts removed with **Subtract**. Mostly constructed in **3D Views/Plan** with moves taking place in **3D Views/Front** and with the finished models in the **3D Views SW Isometric** position.

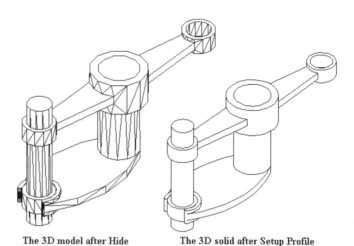

Fig. 17.23 An example of a 3D solid model drawing

The 3D model after Hide   The 3D solid after Setup Profile

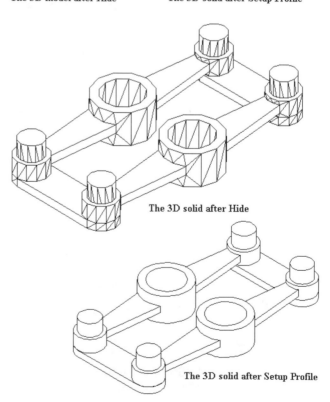

The 3D solid after Hide

Fig. 17.24 Another example of a 3D solid model drawing

The 3D solid after Setup Profile

Figure 17.24: The front and left-hand models, constructed from cylinders and extrusions, moved into position relative to each other, then combined with **Union** with parts removed with **Subtract**. The two solids were then copied to form the four linked solid model as shown.

The 3D Orbit tool

Load a 3D solid model drawing into the AutoCAD 2000 window. Call the **3D Orbit** tool from the **Standard** toolbar (Fig. 17.25). The 2000 window will appear as in Fig. 17.26.

Note the following in this window:

1. A circle centred on the 3D solid, with small circles at its quadrants.
2. In place of the usual cursor one of three cursors will be seen.
3. A compass in the bottom left-hand corner indicating the directions of the X, Y and Z.

Fig. 17.25 Calling **3D Orbit**

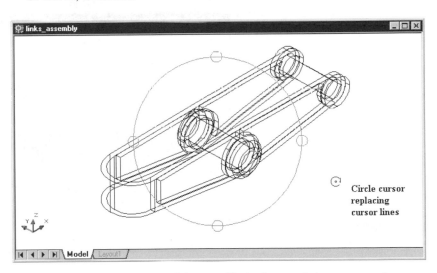

Fig. 17.26 Calling the **3D Orbit** tool with a 3D solid model drawing loaded

Move the cursor into one of the small circles and the cursor changes shape to an elliptical shape, vertical in the upper and lower quadrants and horizontal in the left and right quadrants. Move the cursor outside the main circle and it changes to a circular shape. Move the cursor inside the main circle and the cursor changes again into a pair of crossing ellipses. *Dragging* the cursors in these positions allows complete control over the position of the 3D solid in the window.

Figure 17.27 shows the three cursors with arrows and text explaining the *dragging* movement possible with the three cursors.

It is advisable to experiment with placing a 3D model on screen into a variety of positions under the control of the three cursors before attempting other possibilities with the tool.

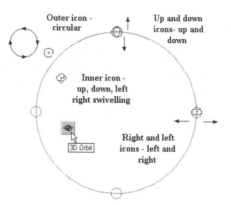

Fig. 17.27 The *dragging* movements of the three **3D Orbit** cursors

A *right-click* menu associated with the tool will show other uses for the tool. *Right-click* anywhere in the drawing area of the 2000 window when **3D Orbit** is in action and the *right-click* menu will appear (Fig. 17.28).

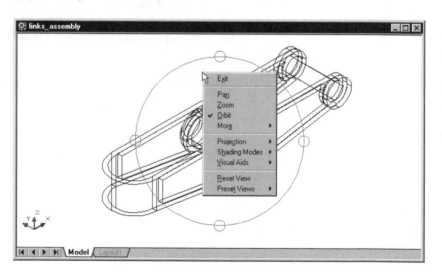

Fig. 17.28 The *right-click* menu of **3D Orbit**

Figure 17.29 shows all the sub-menus associated with the **3D Orbit** *right-click* menu. As can be seen, there is a large range of possibilities when using the tool. The reader is advised to experiment with the variety of possibilities.

Figure 17.30 shows the 3D solid repositioned with the tool after *dragging* the cursor placed inside the **3D Orbit** main circle.

Figure 17.31 shows the 3D solid after calling for one of the clipping planes to be adjusted. When **Adjust Clipping Planes** from the **More** sub-menu of the *right-click* menu is selected an **Adjust Clipping Planes** dialogue appears. *Dragging* the cursor icon in that window will show results in the 2000 window as the clipping planes are adjusted.

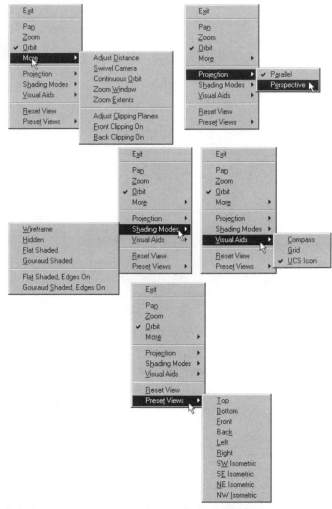

Fig. 17.29 The *right-click*
menu of **3D orbit** with all its
sub-menus

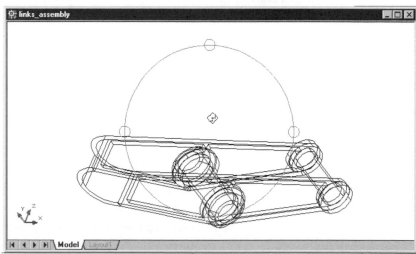

Fig. 17.30 A result of *dragging*
the inside cursor icon

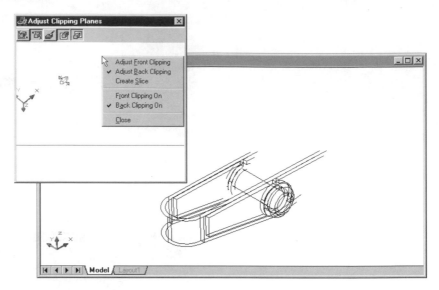

Fig. 17.31 A **Clipping Plane** in action

Questions

1. What is the purpose of using the **Setup Profile** tool?
2. Why should the **Purge** tool be used before saving a 3D model drawing to file?
3. Why is it often better practise to use a three or four viewport setup when constructing a 3D model drawing than to construct the drawing in a single viewport?
4. What is the essential difference between drawings in the **Model** window and drawings in the **Layout** windows?
5. Have you experimented with the various options available with the **3D Orbit** tool?
6. When working in a **Layout** window, can viewports and their contents be copied?
7. Can they be erased?
8. Can they be rotated?
9. Which do you prefer using when constructing 3D solids – the **UCS Presets** or the **3D Views** views?
10. How can a perspective views of a 3D model drawing be obtained in AutoCAD 2000?

Exercises

1. Figure 17.32 shows a dimensioned front view and a 3D solid model drawing of a rotating arm from a machine.

   Working to the dimensions given with the two drawings, construct a 3D solid model drawing of the arm.

When you have completed the 3D drawing, create a profile drawing of the model.

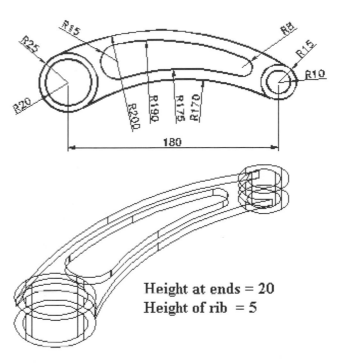

Height at ends = 20
Height of rib = 5

Fig. 17.32 Exercise 1

2. Figure 17.33 shows a profile only drawing of an assembly consisting of 3 parts hinged to each other by pins.

Also included in Fig. 17.33 are dimensioned views of the 3 parts. Working to the given dimensions, construct a 3D solid model drawing of the assembly, followed by creating a profile drawing of the assembly.

3. A two-view projection of a link is given in Fig. 17.34. Construct a 3D solid model drawing of the link working to the given dimensions. Then create a profile only drawing of the model.

4. Figure 17.35 consists of a profile only 3D drawing of a crank shaft. The lower drawing of Fig. 17.35 is a two-view projection of the crank shaft.

Construct a 3D solid model drawing of the crank shaft to the given dimensions, followed by creating a profile only view of your solid model.

5. Figure 17.36 shows a profile only drawing of a trolley designed to carry an electronics project.

Working to sizes of your own discretion construct a 3D solid model drawing similar to that shown, followed by using **Setup Profile** on your model to produce a profile only drawing similar to that shown.

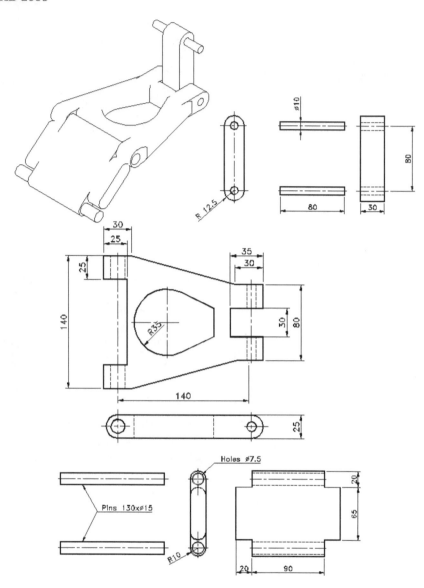

Fig. 17.33 Exercise 2

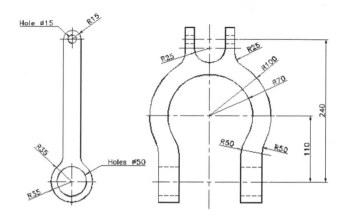

Fig. 17.34 Exercise 3

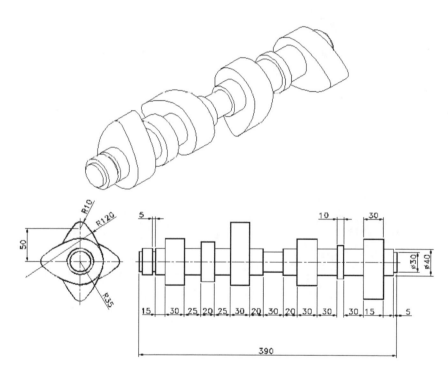

Fig. 17.35 Exercise 4

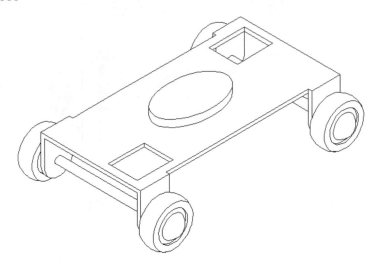

Fig. 17.36 Exercise 5

Chapter 18

The Rendering tools

Rendering

Fig. 18.1 The **Render** toolbar

Rendering is a system which produces realistic photographic like coloured images in the AutoCAD 2000 window from 3D solid drawings. In AutoCAD 2000 the sequence involved in rendering usually follows an order such as:

1. A 3D solid model drawing is constructed.
2. The model is usually placed in the **WCS** to allow lights to be included for illuminating the model.
3. Either colours or 'materials' are added to the model to give the rendering an appearance of having been made from suitable materials.
4. The model is placed in a suitable **3D Views** view.
5. The model is then rendered to produce the required realism to the solid model. Backgrounds and other effects can be included with the rendering if required.

Fig. 18.2 The names of the tools in the **Render** toolbar

The Render toolbar

Right-click in any toolbar on screen select the **Render** toolbar from the menu which appears. The **Render** toolbar appears on screen (Fig. 18.1). Figure 18.2 shows the names of the tools in the toolbar.

Rendering a 3D solid model drawing

To revise some aspects of the forms 3D solids can take in AutoCAD 2000, the three illustrations Figs 18.3 to 18.5 give examples of a 3D solid in a **3D Views** isometric position after construction has been completed (Fig. 18.3 – This is a *wireframe* of the solid); after calling

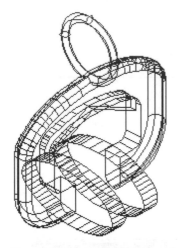

Hide (Fig. 18.4) and a **Setup Profile** view (Fig. 18.5). Figure 18.6 is included as a simple example of the rendering of the wireframe solid.

Fig. 18.3 A wireframe view of a 3D solid model

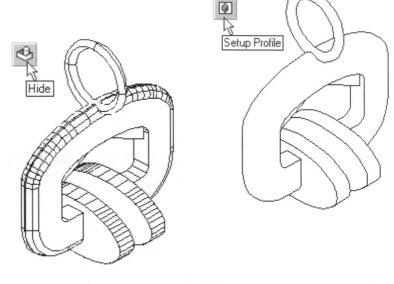

Figures 18.4 and 18.5 **Hide** and **Setup Profile** views of a 3D solid model

Fig. 18.6 A rendering of a 3D solid model

An example of the rendering of a 3D solid model

1. Load the model to be rendered into the AutoCAD 2000 window.
2. Place the solid in a **3D Views/Top** position – or in **UCS/W** (the **WCS**).
3. Move the solid to a position near the upper edge of the AutoCAD 2000 window. This enables suitable lighting to be placed on screen.
4. *Left-click* on the **Lights** tool icon in the **Render** toolbar. The **Lights** dialogue box appears (Fig. 18.7). In the dialogue box select **Point**

Light from the lights popup list, followed by a *left-click* on the **New…** button. The **New Point Light** dialogue box appears (Fig. 18.8).

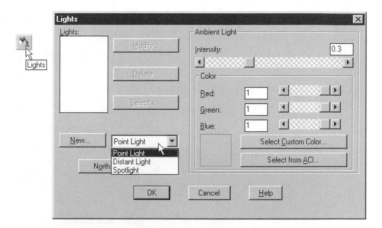

Fig. 18.7 The **Lights** dialogue box

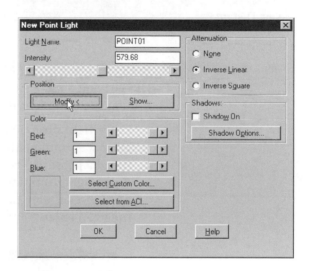

Fig. 18.8 The **New Point Light** dialogue box

5. *Enter* a name in the **Light Name:** box – in this example it is **POINT01** followed by a *left-click* on the **Modify…** button. The AutoCAD 2000 window reappears with the position of the light held at the centre of the window by a rubber band. At the Command line the following appears:

> **Command:_light** *enter* .xy *right-click*
> **of** *pick* a point central to the solid
> **(need Z)** *enter* 300 *right-click*

The **New Point Light** dialogue box reappears. *Left-click* on the **OK** button. The **Light** dialogue box appears.

6. In the dialogue box, select **Distant Light** from the popup list, followed by a *left-click* on the **New...** button. The **New Distant Light** dialogue box appears (Fig. 18.9).

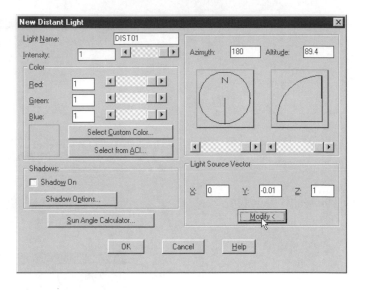

Fig. 18.9 The **New Distant Light** dialogue box

7. In the dialogue box *enter* a name for the light – in this case this is **DIST01** and *left-click* on the **Modify...** button. The Command line sequence continues with

> **Enter light direction TO <current>:** *enter* .xy *right-click*
> **of** *pick* a point central to the solid
> **(need Z)** *enter* 50 *right-click*
> **Enter light direction FROM <current>:** *enter* .xy *right-click*
> **of** *pick* a suitable point – see Fig. 18.10
> **(need Z)** *enter* 200 *right-click*

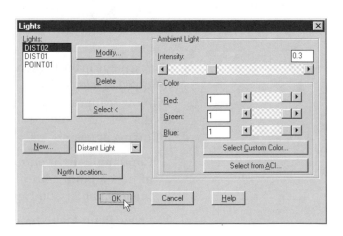

Fig. 18.10 The **Lights** dialogue box showing the completed lighting

The **New Distant Light** dialogue box reappears. *Left-click* on its **OK** button.

8. Repeat item 7 for a second distant light (**DIST02**). After finishing this sequence the **Lights** dialogue box reappears showing the names of the lights so far added to the drawing (Fig. 18.10). *Left-click* on the **OK** button and the lighting is completed.

Note the **Modify...** button in this dialogue box, allowing editing of the intensity and position of the lights.

Notes

1. In the **Lights** dialogue box, note the **Ambient Light** set to **0.3**. Ambient light is the general light surrounding us all. The figure can be set lower of higher and some experimentation is possible. In general in rendering in AutoCAD 2000 ambient lighting is best set at the default of 0.3.
2. The positioning of lighting as shown in this example will produce fairly good lighting results for most renderings. The lights were positioned as follows:

    Point light: Above the 3D solid. A general light which is spread from the point in all directions.
    Distant lights: One in front and slightly to the right and above the height of the 3D solid, a second to the left and above the height of the solid, but not as high as the first. Distant light throws light in the direction in which it is pointed − hence the prompts **Enter light direction TO** and **Enter light direction FROM**.

3. Extra lights may produce better lighting − for example a distant light behind and below a solid may highlight the outlines of the solid to good effect.
4. It is worth while experimenting with **Spotlights** which produce a beam of conical light − as the name implies. With spotlights it will be seen that two editing features − **Hotspot** and **Falloff** allow changes to the cone of the spot to be changed.
5. All lighting types can be changed as to their intensity and it is nearly always necessary to make such changes in order to obtain the best lighting effect for any particular 3D solid.

The lighting positions

Figure 18.11 shows the positions of the three lights for this example. The icons for the lights have been enlarged for the purpose of this illustration. Normally, when working in an A3 window as is common throughout this book, the icons will appear in position much smaller.

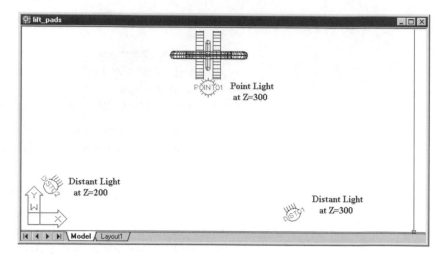

Fig. 18.11 The positions of the
three lights in this example

Rendering the solid model

The results of this lighting is shown in Fig. 18.6 on page 276. The
rendering is also shown in the Colour plate section, with a material
added to the solid (Plate XV). To render the solid:

1. Place the solid in the **3D Views/SW Isometric** position. **Zoom**
   window the solid to a suitable size.
2. Select the **Render** tool icon from the **Render** toolbar. The **Render**
   dialogue box appears (Fig. 18.12). Select **Photo Raytrace** from the
   Rendering type: popup list, followed by a *left-click* on the **Options...**
   button which brings up the **Photo Raytrace Render Options** dialogue
   box (Fig. 18.13). *Left-click* on the **OK** button and on the **Render**

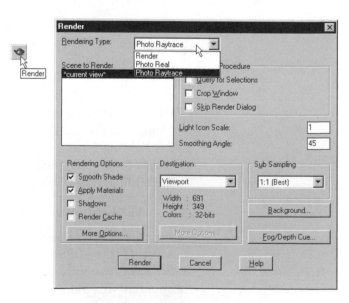

Fig. 18.12 The **Render**
dialogue box

button of the **Render** dialogue box and the 3D model renders. This is after accepting the default settings.

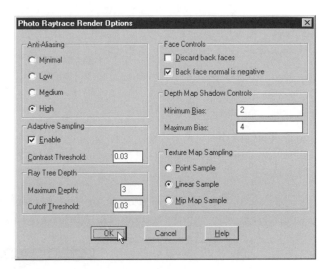

Fig. 18.13 The **Photo Raytrace Render Options** dialogue box

Fig. 18.14 The completed rendering

Attaching materials to a 3D solid drawing

AutoCAD 2000 includes a large materials library from which a variety of materials can be attached to 3D solid models or to their parts. As an example this example describes materials attached to a 3D solid drawing made up from four different solids in an assembly for a roller foot from a machine. The process followed the sequence:

1. Open the drawing in AutoCAD 2000 and place in **3D Views/Isometric** (Fig. 18.15).

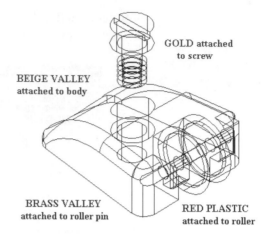

Fig. 18.15 the drawing of the roller foot opened in AutoCAD 2000

2. *Left-click* on the **Materials Library** tool icon from the **Render** toolbar The **Materials Library** dialogue box appears (Fig. 18.16).

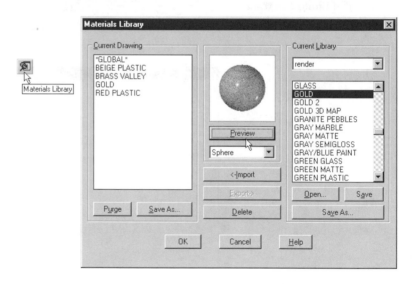

Fig. 18.16 The **Materials Library** dialogue box

3. From the **Current Library** list select the following four materials in turn.

BEIGE VALLEY; BRASS VALLEY; GOLD; RED PLASTIC.

As each is selected *left-click* on the **<-Import** button and the imported material name then appears in the **Current Drawing:** list. A *left-click* on any material in either list, followed by a *left-click* on the **Preview** button causes the selected material to appear in the preview window showing how it will appear in a drawing when rendered. Note the box below the **Preview** button. This contains a small popup list from which either **Cube** or **Sphere** can be chosen for showing the appearance of the chosen material in the preview window. Figure 18.17 shows the **Materials Library** dialogue box, with the **GOLD** material being previewed. When all four materials have been selected, *left-click* on the **OK** button of the dialogue box.

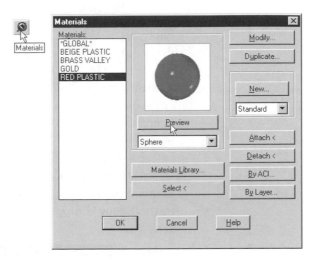

Fig. 18.17 The **Materials** dialogue box

4. *Left-click* on the **Materials** tool icon in the **Render** toolbar. The **Materials** dialogue appears showing the four materials selected from the **Current Library** list in the **Materials Library** dialogue (Fig. 18.17). Selecting each material name in turn, *left-click* on the **Attach** button. The dialogue box will disappear allowing the operator to *pick* the solid to which the material will be assigned. Figure 18.15 shows these attachments.
5. Now *left-click* on the **Render** tool icon from the **Render** toolbar and render the model. Figure 18.18 shows the resulting rendering. This

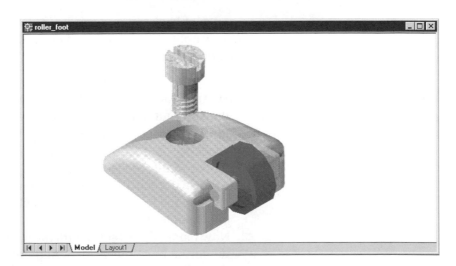

Fig. 18.18 The rendering in four materials of a 3D solid drawing

rendering is also shown in the colours of the attached materials in the colour plate section.

Scenes

Each 3D solid can be placed in different views and assigned a different set of materials. Note that materials can be detached from solids by using the **Detach** button of the **Materials** dialogue box. If a variety of views with different materials attached is required, a *left-click* on the **Scenes** tool icon in the **Render** toolbar brings up the **Scenes** dialogue box (Fig. 18.19). A *left-click* on the **New...** button brings a secondary dialogue box (**New Scenes**) on screen. *Enter* a suitable name for the scene in the **Scene Name:** box, followed by a *left-click* on the **OK** button and the view with its materials, lighting is saved to that scene name. Scenes can be recalled from their names in the **Scene** dialogue box when required.

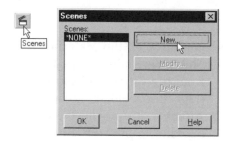

Fig. 18.19 The **Scenes** dialogue boxes

Background

A range of backgrounds can be included with a rendered 3D solid. An example of an added background scene is shown in Fig. 18.20. To include a background in a scene:

1. *Left-click* on the **Background** tool icon from the **Render** toolbar, or on the **Background** button in the **Render** dialogue box. The **Background** dialogue box appears (Fig. 18.21).
2. In the dialogue box, cancel the tick in the **AutoCAD Background** check box and *left-click* in the **Find File...** button. This brings the **Background Image** dialogue on screen. Select the directory **AutoCAD 2000/Textures** and from the **Files of type:** box select ***.tga**. In the list of tga files, select **cloud**, followed by a *left-click* on the **Open** button.
3. Now render the 3D solid with the result as shown in Fig. 18.20. The rendering in colour is also included in the Colour Plates section (Plate XIV).

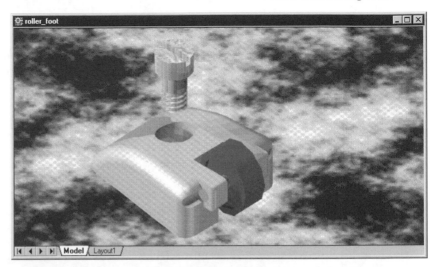

Fig. 18.20 A 3D model
rendered against a background

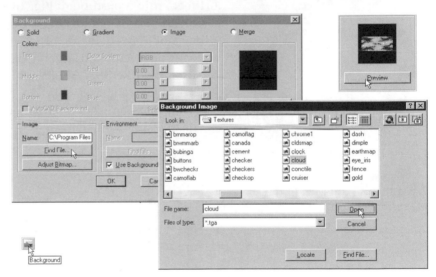

Fig. 18.21 The **Background**
dialogue boxes

Questions

1. Have you tried using the **Landscape Library**? Or the **Landscape New** tool?

2. Render a 3D solid and then *left-click* on the **Statistics** tool icon in the **Render** toolbar. Will you regularly use the table shown when the tool is called each time you construct a 3D solid, followed by rendering?

3. When adding lights to a scene which includes a 3D solid model, when would you consider placing a Distant Light behind and below the model?

4. What is the difference between a Distant Light and a Spotlight?

5. Backgrounds can be included in scenes in which 3D models have been created. How is a background selected and applied?
6. If a material is attached to a 3D model drawing, can it be detached?
7. What is meant by **Ambient Light**?
8. What is the default setting for the intensity of **Ambient Light**?
9. Can a profiled 3D solid model be rendered?
10. Can you explain the term 'rendering'?

Exercises

If you have saved the 3D models constructed in response to the exercises from Chapter 16, open them, add lighting and materials and render each in turn.

1. Figure 18.22 is a rendering of the pulley wheel shown in the orthographic projection of Fig. 18.23.

    Construct a 3D solid model drawing based on the views and dimensions given in Fig. 18.23; place in one of the isometric viewing positions; add suitable lighting; attach a suitable material, for example **BRASS VALLEY** and render your model.

    Save your rendered solid to a scene. Change the isometric viewing position, render the model again and save the second scene to a suitable name.

Fig. 18.22 A rendering of the 3D solid exercise 1

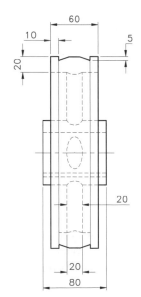

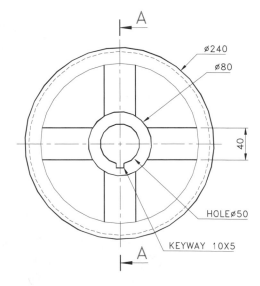

Fig. 18.23 Details of shapes and dimensions of the 3D model for exercise 1

2. Figure 18.24 is an orthographic projection of an arm designed to carry a pivot through the holes at each end.

Working to the dimensions given in this projection, construct a 3D solid model drawing of the arm. Include two pins, the left-hand pin of length 120, the right-hand pin of length 80 with the arm.

Add lighting and materials to the three parts of the solid. Place the solid in one of the isometric viewing positions and render the solid. Save the rendered drawing to a scene name. Repeat in another isometric viewing position and save this second view to a named scene.

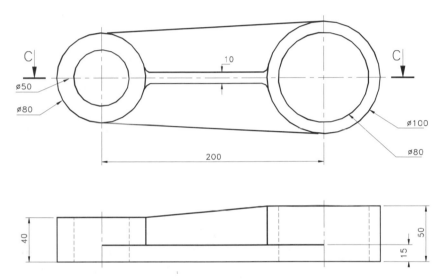

Fig. 18.24 Exercise 2 – a two-view orthographic projection

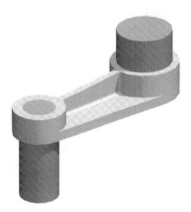

Fig. 18.25 A rendering of the 3D solid exercise 2

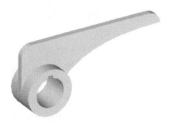

Fig. 18.26 A rendering of the 3D solid exercise 4

3. Figure 18.26 shows a rendering of the 3D solid model constructed to the views and dimensions given in the orthographic projection of Fig. 18.16.

   Construct a 3D solid model drawing to the views and sizes given in Fig. 18.27. Add lights; attach a material and render your drawing in a suitable isometric viewing position.

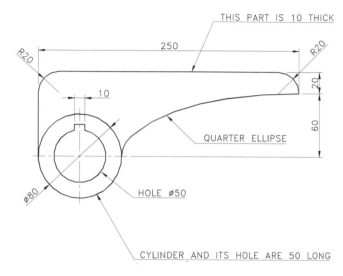

Fig. 18.27 Exercise 3 – a two-view orthographic projection

4. Figure 18.28 is a rendering of the gear plate cover described in the orthographic projection of Fig. 18.29.

   Construct a 3D solid model drawing of the cover to the dimensions given with Fig. 18.29. Add lights, attach a material, place in a suitable viewing position and render your drawing.

Fig. 18.28 A rendering of the 3D solid exercise 4

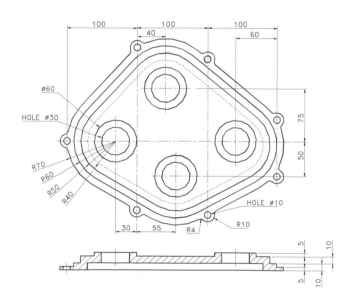

Fig. 18.29 Exercise 4 – a two-view orthographic projection

The Internet

The Internet

AutoCAD 2000 includes features for accessing the Internet to obtain up-to-date information for **Help** and for the sending and receiving of drawings through URLs (User Resource Locators). The **Help** information available for AutoCAD 2000 can be seen with a *left-click* on **Help** in the menu bar, followed by another on **AutoCAD on the Web**, followed by selecting from the sub-menu which appears (Fig. A.1)

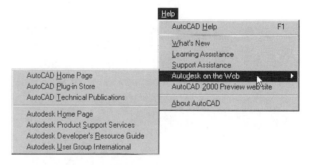

Fig. A.1 The AutoCAD on the Web sub-menu from the **Help** pull-down menu

AutoCAD 2000 drawings can be sent or received over the Internet via URLs.

The HTML language

HTML (HyperText Markup Language) is a reasonably simple computer language designed for the setting up of pages which can be sent or received via the **www** (World Wide Web) system on the Internet. Pages made up using HTML must be sent via a Web server on an URL. In general, to set up a server is rather expensive for the single user of AutoCAD 2000. Space can, however, usually be rented or hired if necessary from some firms who have Web servers.

Although the HTML language is an easily learned and easy to use computer language, it is beyond the scope of this book to describe the language and how pages can be set up in HTML for sending and receiving information via the Internet.

URLs

A URL is an address on a server to which and from which AutoCAD drawings can be sent or received. In order to be able to send or receive to or from a URL, it is necessary for the computer in use to have a Web Browser such as Microsoft Internet Explorer loaded ready for use. It is advisable to have the latest version of such a Browser in use to obtain the best results.

URL addresses

A URL address consists of three parts. Taking as an example:

> **http://www.autodesk.com/acaduser**:
> **http://** – is the service descriptor.
> **www.autodesk.com/** – is the Internet address at which the required resource is to be found.
> **acaduser** – location at the Internet address where the resource can be found.

Another common service descriptor is **ftp:** There are others.

When sending or receiving AutoCAD 2000 drawings over the Internet the **ftp** protocol as the service descriptor is usually used because this protocol will handle large files such as many AutoCAD drawings can become, more efficiently than when the **http** descriptor is used.

Passwords

In order to ensure privacy it is necessary to use passwords to protect what is sent or received by the World Wide Web. The request for *entering* a password will frequently be seen when using URLs. When typing in a password, the letters or numbers being *entered* will show in password boxes as asterisks, further guarding against anybody learning the password being *entered*.

Notes

1. Addresses and passwords are usually case sensitive.
2. In the examples which follow, the URL addresses are all fictional and are only shown here to indicate how the process of sending and/or receiving AutoCAD drawings to and from the Internet are processed.
3. A server is a machine which stores pages (and, in our case, drawings) which can be chosen and then sent or received via the

Internet. It is also a machine which while always running can send or receive pages in file form as and when requested to do so.

4. AutoCAD drawings can sent by a server or received from a server.

Receiving/sending drawing files between servers

Figure A.2 is a diagrammatic illustration showing how the design office of a construction firm based in England can send drawings to and from various teams working on projects all over the world. The central design office and each of the teams working away from the central office are equipped with computer servers for sending and receiving drawing files via the Internet using the ftp protocol. The drawings can be sent/received in a very short period of time and this facility is particularly effective when modifications to existing drawings are required or when teams away from the home office wish to query drawings and be sent modifications if needed.

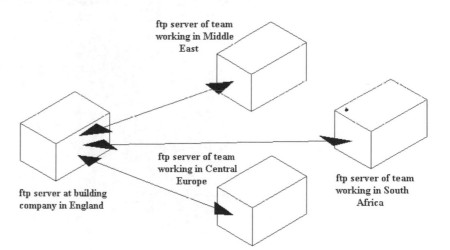

Fig. A.2 Sending/receiving drawing files between servers

Example – receiving a drawing from a server

1. *Left-click* on **Open** in the **File** pull-down menu. In the **Select File** dialogue box which then appears, *left-click* on the **Search the Web** icon (Fig. A.3).
2. In the **Browse the Web** dialogue box which appears, in the **File name:** box *enter* a file name such as that shown in Fig. A.4.
3. The **Dial up Connection** dialogue box appears seeking a **User name:** and a **Password:** without which the connection to the **Web site** cannot be made. *Enter* the name and password and *left-click* on the **Connect** button (Fig. A.5).

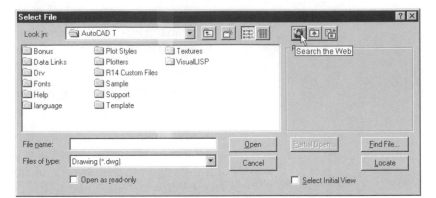

Fig. A.3 The **Search the Web** icon in the **Select File** dialogue box

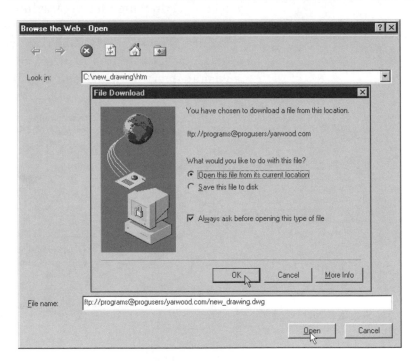

Fig. A.4 The **Browse the Web** dialogue box

Fig. A.5 The **Dial up Connection** dialogue box

4. The **Dialling Progress** dialogue box appears showing how dialling is progressing (Fig. A.6).

Fig. A.6 The **Dialling Progress**
dialogue box

5. When the connection has been made, the **File Download** dialogue box (Fig. A.7) showing the progress of the downloading from the distant server.

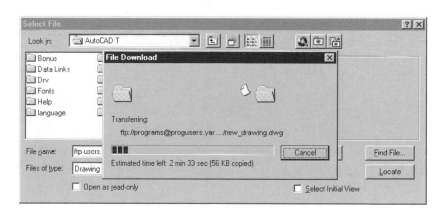

Fig. A.7 The **File Download**
dialogue box

6. When the file has been completely downloaded, the drawing appears on screen from where it can be saved with a file name in the computer in use.

Example – sending a drawing to a server

The process follows the same procedure as when receiving a drawing except that the file is saved to a ftp file name in the **Save Drawing As** dialogue box (Fig. A.8). The *left-click on* the **Browse the Web** icon and enter user name and password in the appropriate dialogue boxes and the drawing can be sent to the distant server.

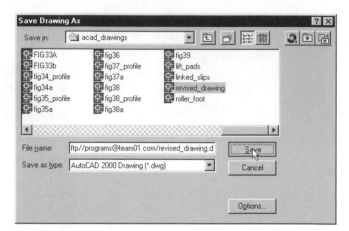

Fig. A.8 First stage in sending
a drawing to a distant server

Printing and plotting

Introduction

AutoCAD 2000 allows a large number of different printers or plotters to be configured for plotting or printing drawings constructed within its drawing area. To see this availability, *left-click* on **Plotter Manager...** in the **File** pull-down menu (Fig. B.1). The **Plotter** window appears (Fig. B.2). *Double-click* on the **Add-A-Plotter Wizard** icon and the **Add a Plotter Wizard** appears. *Left-click* on the **Next...** button and again when the second dialogue box appears and it will be seen from the two lists of plotter/printer manufacturers and their products that a selection can be made from a very comprehensive number of machines. In this book however we will only be concerned with the Windows default printer which in the computer used to produce the pages of this book is a **HP LaserJetIIIp** laser printer. When the software files for AutoCAD 2000 are loaded in Windows 95, 98 or NT, the default printer/plotter is automatically loaded.

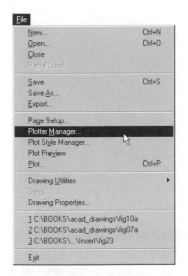

Fig. B.1 Selecting **Plotter Manager...** from the **File** pull-down menu

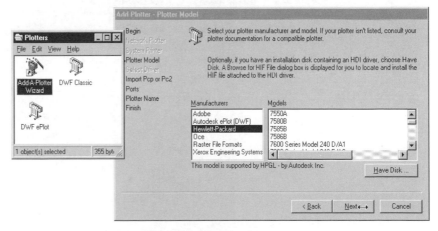

Fig. B.2 The **Plotter** window and the **Add a Plotter Wizard**

Printing or plotting a drawing

Note it is the default Windows printer (HP LaserJetIIIp) that is used throughout this description of printing (or plotting) a drawing.

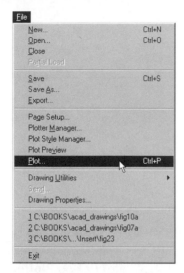

Fig. B.3 Calling **Plot...** from the **File** pull-down menu

1. Open the drawing to be printed.
2. Select **Plot...** from the **File** pull-down menu (Fig. B.3). The **Plot** dialogue box appears (Fig. B.4).

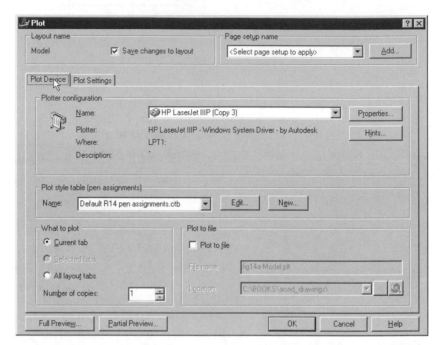

Fig. B.4 The **Plot** dialogue box

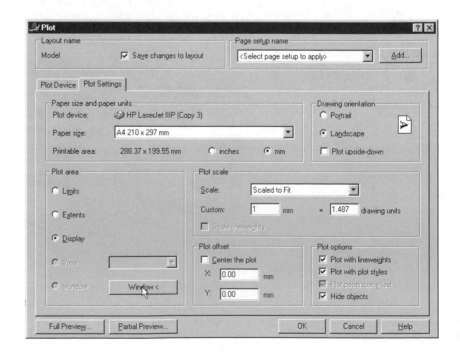

Fig. B.5 The **Plot Settings** dialogue box

3. If the drawing is a 3D solid model and it is desired to hide objects behind the front of the drawing, make sure the **Hide objects** check box is checked on (tick in box). Hidden lines will then be automatically hidden in the print/plot.
4. Check whether the **Plot device**, **Paper size** and **Drawing orientation** are set correctly, then *left-click* on the **Plot Settings** label at the top of the dialogue box. The **Plot Settings** dialogue box appears (Fig. B.5).
5. *Left-click* on the **Window<** button and following prompts at the Command line window the area of the drawing to be plotted. The **Plot Settings** dialogue reappears.
6. *Left-click* on the **Full Preview<** button and the a preview window appears showing how the drawing will print on the selected paper (Fig. B.6).

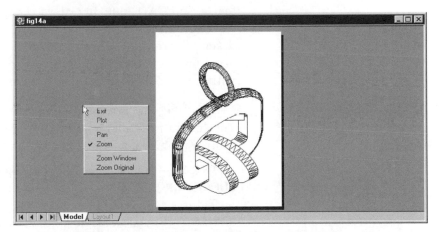

Fig. B.6 The drawing in the **Full Preview** window

7. If the preview appears satisfactory *right-click* and in the *right-click* menu which appears, *left-click* on **Exit**. When the **Plot** window reappears, *left-click* on its **OK** button and the drawing will print to the printer/plotter attached to the computer.

Glossary of tools

Introduction

Many of the tools shown in this glossary have not been described in the pages of this book. This book is intended for those learning how to use AutoCAD 2000. In order to keep the book to a reasonable size on the grounds of cost to the reader, it has been necessary to restrict description of tool usage to those considered to be essential to the beginner. It is hoped this glossary will encourage readers to experiment with those tools (commands) not described earlier.

Note

The letters in brackets after the tool (command) name show the abbreviation or key shortcuts for the tool.

3DARRAY – Creates an array of 3D models in 3D space

3DFACE (3F) – Creates a 3 or 4 sided 3D mesh behind which other features can be hidden

3DMESH – Creates a 3D mesh in 3D space

3DSIN – Brings the **3D Studio File Import** dialogue box on screen

3DSOUT – Brings the **3D Studio Output File** dialogue box on screen

3DORBIT (3D0) – Allows manipulation of 3D models on screen

ABOUT – Brings the **About AutoCAD** bitmap on screen

ALIGN – Allows selected entities to be aligned to selected points in 3D space

AMECONVERT – Converts AME solid models (from Release 12) into AutoCAD 2000 solid models

APPLOAD – Brings the **Load/Unload Applications** dialogue box to screen

ARC (A) – Creates an arc

AREA – States in square units of the area selected from a number of points

ARRAY (AR) – Creates **Perpendicular** or **Polar** arrays in 2D

ASE – Brings the **dbConnect Manager** on screen

ATTDEF – Brings the **Attribute Definition** dialogue box on screen

ATTEDIT – Allows editing of attributes from the Command line

AUDIT – Checks and fixes any errors in a drawing

BHATCH (H) – Brings the **Boundary Hatch** dialogue box on screen

BLIPMODE – Sets blips on or off (1 or 0)

BLOCK – Brings the **Block Definition** dialogue box on screen

BMAKE (B) – Brings the **Block Definition** dialogue box on screen

BMPOUT – Brings the **Create BMP File** dialogue box

BOX – Creates a 3D solid box

BOUNDARY (BO) – Brings the **Boundary Creation** dialogue box on screen

BREAK (BR) – Breaks an object into parts

CAL – For the calculation of mathematical expressions

CHAMFER (CHA) – Creates a chamfer between two entities

CHPROP (CH) – Brings the **Properties** window on screen

CIRCLE (C) – Creates a circle

CONE – Creates a 3D model of a cone

COPY (CO) – Creates a single or multiple copies of selected entities

COPYCLIP (Ctrl+C) – Copies a drawing, or part of a drawing for inserting into a document from another application

COPYLINK – Forms a link between an AutoCAD drawing and its appearance in another application such as a word processing package

CYLINDER – Creates a 3D cylinder

DBLIST – Creates a database list in a Text window for every entity in a drawing

DDATTDEF (AT) – Brings the **Attribute Definition** dialogue box to screen

DDATTE (ATE) – Edits individual attribute values

DDATTEXT – Brings the **Attribute Extraction** dialogue box on screen

DDCHPROP – Brings the **Properties** window on screen

DDCOLOR (COL) – Brings the **Select Color** dialogue box on screen

DDEDIT (ED) – Select text and the **Edit Text** dialogue box appears

DDIM (D) – Brings the **Dimension Style Manager** dialogue box on screen

DDINSERT (I) – Brings the **Insert** dialogue box on screen

DDMODIFY – Brings the **Properties** window on screen

DDOSNAP (OS) – Brings the **Drafting Settings** dialogue box on screen

DDPTYPE – Brings the **Point Style** dialogue box on screen

DDRMODES (RM) – Brings the **Drafting Settings** dialogue box on screen

DDUCS (UC) – Brings the **UCS** dialogue box on screen

DDUNITS (UN) – Brings the **Drawing Units** dialogue box on screen

DDVIEW (V) – Brings the **View** dialogue box on screen

DEL – Allows a file (any file) to be deleted

DIM – Starts a session of dimensioning

DIM1 – Allows the addition of a single addition of a dimension to a drawing

Note

There are a large number of set variables controlling methods of dimensioning. These are not included here.

DIST (DI) – Measures the distance between two points in coordinate units

DIVIDE (DIV) – Divides an entity into equal parts

DONUT (DO) – Creates a donut

DSVIEWER – Brings the **Aerial View** window on screen

DTEXT (DT) Creates dynamic text. Text appears in drawing area as it is entered

DVIEW (DV) – Instigates the dynamic view prompts sequence. It is preferable in AutoCAD 2000 to use **3dorbit**

DXBIN – Brings the **Select DXB File** dialogue box on screen

DXFIN – Brings the **Select File** dialogue box on screen

DXFOUT – Brings the **Save Drawing As** dialogue box on screen

EDGESURF – Creates a 3D mesh surface from four adjoining edges

ELLIPSE (EL) – Creates an ellipse

ERASE – Erases selected entities from a drawing

EXIT – Ends a drawing session and closes AutoCAD down

EXPLODE (X) – Explodes a block or group into its various entities

EXPLORER – Brings the Windows 95 Explorer on screen

EXPORT (EXP) – Brings the **Export Data** dialogue box on screen

EXTEND (EX) – To extend an entity to another

EXTRUDE (EXT) Extrudes a closed polyline

FILLET (F) – Creates a fillet between two entities

FILTER – Brings the **Object Selection Filters** dialogue box on screen

GROUP (G) – Brings the **Object Grouping** dialogue box on screen

HATCH – Allows hatching by the *entry* responses to prompts

HATCHEDIT (HE) – Allows editing of associative hatching

HELP – Brings the **Help Topics** dialogue box on screen

HIDE (HI) – To hide hidden lines in 3D models

ID – Identifies a point on screen in coordinate units

IMAGEADJUST (IAD) – Allows adjustment of images

IMAGEATTACH (IAT) – Brings the **Select Image File** dialogue box on screen

IMAGECLIP – Allows clipping of images

IMPORT – Brings the **Import File** dialogue box on screen

INSERT (I) – Brings the **Insert** dialogue box on screen

INSERTOBJ (INS) – Brings the **Insert Object** dialogue box

INTERFERE – Creates an interference solid from selection of several solids

INTERSECT (IN) – Creates an intersection solid from a group of two or more solids

ISOPLANE (Ctrl/E) – Sets the isoplane when constructing an isometric drawing

LAYER (LA) – Brings the **Layer and Linetype** dialogue box on screen

LAYOUT – Allows editing of layouts

LENGTHEN (LEN) – Lengthen an entity on screen

LIGHT – Brings the **Lights** dialogue box on screen

LIMITS – Sets the drawing limits in coordinate units

LINE (L) – Creates a line

LINETYPE (LT) – Brings the **Linetype Manager** dialogue box on screen

LIST (LI) – Lists in a text window details of any entity or group of entities selected

LOAD – Brings the **Select Drawing File** dialogue box on screen

LOGFILEOFF – The Text window contents are no longer recorded

LOGFILEON – The Text window contents are recorded

LTSCALE (LTS) – Allows the linetype scale to be adjusted

MATLIB – Brings the **Materials Library** dialogue box on screen

MEASURE (ME) – Allows measured intervals to be placed along entities

MENU – Brings the **Select Menu File** dialogue box on screen

MENULOAD – Brings the **Menu Customization** dialogue box on screen

MIRROR (MI) – Creates an identical mirror image to selected entities

MIRROR3D Mirrors 3D models in 3D space in selected directions

MLEDIT – Brings the **Multiline Edit Tools** dialogue box on screen

MLINE (ML) – Creates mlines

MLSTYLE – Brings the **Multiline Styles** dialogue box on screen

MOVE (M) – Allows selected entities to be moved

MSLIDE – Brings the **Create Slide File** dialogue box on screen

MSPACE (MS) – Changes from Paperspace to Modelspace

MTEXT (MT or T) – Brings the **Multiline Text Editor** on screen

MVIEW (MV) – When in PSpace brings in MSpace objects

MVSETUP – Allows drawing specifications to be set up

NEW (Ctrl+N) – Brings the **Create New Drawing** dialogue box on screen

NOTEPAD – For editing files from the Windows 95 **Notepad**

OFFSET (O) – Offsets selected entity by a stated distance

OOPS – Cancels the effect of using **Erase**

OPEN – Brings the **Select File** dialogue box on screen

ORTHO – Allows ortho to be set ON/OFF

PAN (P) – Pans the R14 drawing editor in any direction

PBRUSH – Brings Windows 95 **Paint** on screen

PEDIT (PE) – Allows editing of polylines

PFACE – Allows the construction of a 3D mesh through a number of selected vertices

PLAN – Allows a drawing in 3D space to be seen in plan (UCS World)

PLINE (PL) – Creates a polyline

PLOT (Ctrl+P) – Brings the **Plot** dialogue box to screen

POINT (PO) – Allows a point to be placed on screen

POLYGON (POL) – Creates a polygon

POLYLINE (PL) – Creates a polyline

PREFERENCES (PR) – Brings the **Options** dialogue box on screen

PREVIEW (PRE) – Brings the print/plot preview box on screen

PSFILL – Allows polylines to be filled with patterns

PSIN – Brings the **Select Postscript File** dialogue box on screen

PSOUT – Brings the **Create Postscript File** dialogue box on screen

PSPACE (PS) – Changes Modelspace to Paperspace

PURGE (PU) – Purges unwanted data from a drawing before saving to file

QSAVE – Quicksave. Saves the drawing file to its current name in AutoCAD 2000 format

QUIT (Q) – Ends a drawing session and closes down AutoCAD

RAY – A construction line from a point

RECOVER – Brings the **Select File** dialogue box on screen to allow recovery of selected drawings as necessary

RECTANG (REC) – Creates a pline rectangle

REDEFINE – If an AutoCAD Command name has been turned off by **Undefine** turns the command name back on

REDO – Cancels the last **Undo**

REDRAW (R) – Redraws the contents of the AutoCAD 2000 drawing area

REDRAWALL (RA) – Redraws the whole of a drawing

REGEN (RE) – Regenerates the contents of the R14 drawing area

REGENALL (REA) – Regenerates the whole of a drawing

REGION (REG) – Creates a region from an area within a boundary

RENAME (REN) – Brings the **Rename** dialogue box on screen

RENDER (RRE) – Brings the **Render** dialogue box on screen

REPLAY – Brings the **Replay** dialogue box on screen from which bitmap image files can be selected

REVOLVE (REV) – Forms a solid of revolution from outlines

REVSURF – Creates a solid of revolution from a pline

RMAT Brings the **Materials** dialogue box on screen

ROTATE (RO) – Rotates selected entities around a selected point

ROTATE3D – Rotates a 3D model in 3D space in all directions

RPREF (RPR) – Brings the **Rendering Preferences** dialogue box on screen

RULESURF – Creates a 3D mesh between two entities

SAVE (Ctrl+S) – Brings the **Save Drawing As** dialogue box on screen

SAVEAS – Brings the **Save Drawing As** dialogue box on screen

SAVEIMG – Brings the **Save Image** dialogue box on screen

SCALE (SC) – Allows selected entities to be scaled in size – smaller or larger

SCENE – Brings the **Scenes** dialogue box on screen

SCRIPT (SCR) – Brings the **Select Script File** dialogue box on screen

SECTION (SEC) – Creates a section plane in a 3D model

SETVAR (SET) – Can be used to bring a list of the settings of set variables into an AutoCAD Text window

SHADE (SHA) – Shades a selected 3D model

SHAPE – Inserts an already loaded shape into a drawing

SHELL – Allows MS-DOS commands to be entered

SKETCH – Allows freehand sketching

SLICE (SL) – Allows a 3D model to be cut into two parts

SOLID (SO) – Creates a filled outline in triangular parts

SOLPROF – Creates a profile from a 3D solid model drawing

SPELL (SP) – Brings the **Check Spelling** dialogue box on screen

SPHERE – Creates a 3D solid model sphere

SPLINE (SPL) – Creates a spline curve through selected points

SPLINEDIT (SPE) – Allows the editing of a spline curve

STATS – Brings the **Statistics** dialogue box on screen

STATUS – Shows the status (particularly memory use) in a Text window

STLOUT – Saves a 3D model drawing in ASCII or binary format

STRETCH (S) – Allows selected entities to be stretched

STYLE (ST) – Brings the **Text Styles** dialogue box on screen

SUBTRACT (SU) – Subtracts one 3D solid from another

TABLET (TA) – Allows a tablet to be used with a pointing device

TABSURF – Creates a 3D solid from an outline and a direction vector

TBCONFIG – Brings the **Toolbars** dialogue box on screen to allow configuration of a toolbar

TEXT – Allows text from the Command line to be entered into a drawing

THICKNESS (TH) – Sets the thickness for the Elevation command

TOLERANCE – Brings the **Geometric Tolerance** dialogue box on screen

TOOLBAR (TO) – Brings the **Toolbars** dialogue box on screen

TORUS (TOR) – Allows a 3D torus to be created

TRIM (TR) – Allows entities to be trimmed up to other entities

TYPE – Types the contents of a named file to screen

UNDEFINE – Suppresses an AutoCAD command name

UNDO (U) (Ctrl+Z) – Undoes the last action of a tool

UNION (UNI) – Unites 3D solids into a single solid

VIEW – Brings the **View** dialogue box on screen

VPLAYER – Controls the visibility of layers in paperspace

VPOINT – Allows viewing positions to be set by x,y,z entries

VPORTS – Brings the **Viewports** dialogue box on screen

VSLIDE – Brings the **Select Slide File** dialogue box on screen

WBLOCK (W) – Brings the **Create Drawing File** dialogue box on screen

WEDGE (WE) – Creates a 3D solid in the shape of a wedge

WMFIN – Brings the **Import WMF File** dialogue box on screen

WMFOPTS – Brings the **Import Options** dialogue box on screen

WMFOUT – Brings the **Create WMF** dialogue box on screen

XATTACH (XA) – Brings the **Select Reference File** dialogue box on screen

XLINE – Creates a construction line

XREF (XR) – Brings the **Xref Manager** dialogue box on screen

ZOOM (Z) – Brings the zoom tool into action

allows blank optical disks to have data written onto them only once.

Set Variables

Introduction

AutoCAD 2000 is controlled by over 280 set variables, many of which are automatically set when making entries in dialogue boxes. Many are also automatically set or read only variables depending upon the configuration of AutoCAD 2000.

Below is a list of those set variables which are of interest in that they often require to be set by *entering* figures or letters at the Command line. To set a variable, enter its name at the Command line and respond to the prompts which are seen.

To see all the set variables, *enter* set (or setvar) at the Command line:

Command: *enter* set *right-click*
SETVAR Enter variable name or ?: *enter* ? *right-click*
Enter variable name to list <*>: *right-click*

and a Text window opens showing a list of the first of the variables. To follow on the list press the **Return** key when prompted.

ANGDIR – Sets angle direction. **0** counter-clockwise; **1** clockwise
APERTURE – Sets size of pick box in pixels
BLIPMODE – Set to **1** marker blips show; set to **0** no blips
CMDDIA Set to **1** enables **Plot** dialogue boxes: set to **0** disables **Plot** dialogue box

Note

DIM variables – There are between 50 and 60 variables for setting dimensioning, but most are in any case set in the **Dimension Styles** dialogue box or as dimensioning proceeds. However one series of the **Dim** variables may be of interest:
DIMBLK – Sets a name for the block drawn for an operator's own arrowheads. These are drawn in unit sizes and saved as required
DIMBLK1 – Operator's arrowhead for first end of line
DIMBLK2 – Operator's arrowhead for other end of line

DRAGMODE – Set to **0** no dragging; set to **1** dragging on; set to **2** automatic dragging

DRAGP1 – Sets regeneration drag sampling. Initial value is 10

DRAGP2 – Sets fast dragging regeneration rate. Initial value is 25

EDGEMODE – Controls the use of **Trim** and **Extend**. Set to **0** does not use extension mode; set to **1** uses extension mode

FILEDIA – Set to **0** disables dialogue boxes; set to **1** enables dialogue boxes

FILLMODE – Set to **0** entities created with **Solid** are not filled; set to **1** they are filled

MBUTTON PAN – Set to **0** no *right-click* menu with the Intellimouse. Set to **1** Intellimouse *right-click* menu on

MIRRTEXT – Set to **0** text direction is retained; set to **1** text is mirrored

PELLIPSE – Set to **0** creates true ellipses; set to **1** polyline ellipses

PICKBOX – Sets selection pick box height in pixels

PICKDRAG – Set to **0** selection windows picked by two corners; set to **1** selection windows are dragged from corner to corner

QTEXTMODE – Set to **0** turns off Quick Text; set to **1** enables Quick Text

SAVETIME – Sets Automatic Save time. Initially 120. Set to **0** disables Automatic Save time

SHADEDGE – Set to **0** faces are shade, edges are not highlighted; set to **1** faces are shaded, edges in colour of entity; set to **2** faces are not shaded, edges in entity colour; set to **3** faces in entity colour, edges in background colour

SHORTCUTMENU – For controlling how *right-click* menus show:

0 all disabled; **1** Default menus only; **2** Edit mode menus; **4** Command mode menus; **8** Command mode menus only when options are currently available. Adding the figures enables more than one option.

SKETCHINC – Sets the **Sketch** record increment. Initial value is **0.1**

SKPOLY – Set to **0** and **Sketch** makes line; set to **1 and** Sketch makes polylines

SURFTAB1 – Sets mesh density in the M direction for surfaces generated by the **Surfaces** tools

SURFTAB2 – Sets mash density in the N direction for surfaces generated by the **Surfaces** tools

TEXTFILL – Set to **0** True Type text shows as outlines only; set to **1** True Type text is filled

TILEMODE – Set to **0** Paperspace enabled; set to **1** tiled viewports in Modelspace

TOOLTIPS – Set to **0** no tool tips; set to **1** tool tips enabled

TRIMMODE – Set to **0** edges not trimmed when **Chamfer** and **Fillet** are used; set to **1** edges are trimmed

UCSFOLLOW – Set to **0** new UCS settings do not take effect; set to **1** UCS settings follow requested settings

UCSICON – Set **OFF** and the UCS icon does not show; set to **ON** and it shows

Glossary of computer terms

This glossary contain some of the more common computing terms.

Application – The name given to software packages which perform the tasks such as word processing, Desktop Packaging, CAD etc.

ASCII – The American National Standard Code for Information Interchange. A code which sets bits for characters used in computing.

Attribute – Text appearing in a drawing, sometimes linked to a block

Autodesk – The American company which produces AutoCAD and other CAD software packages.

Baud rate – A measure of the rate at which a computer system can receive information (measured in bits per second).

BIOS – Basic Input-Output System. The chip in a PC that controls the operations performed by the hardware (e.g. disks, screen, keyboard etc.).

Bit – Short for binary digit. Binary is a form of mathematics that uses only two numbers: 0 and 1. Computers operate completely on binary mathematics.

Block – A group of objects or entities on screen that have been linked together to act as one unit.

Booting up – Starting up a computer to an operating level.

Bus – An electronic channel that allows the movement of data around a computer.

Byte – A sequence of 8 bits.

C – A computer programming language.

Cache – A section of memory (can be ROM or RAM) which holds data that is being frequently used. Speeds up the action of disks and applications.

CAD – Computer-aided design. The term should not be used to mean computer aided drawing.

CAD/CAM – Computer-aided design and manufacturing;

CD-ROM – Computer disc read only memory. A disk system capable of storing several hundred Mbytes of data – commonly 640 Mbytes. Data can only be read from a CD-ROM, not written to it.

Chips – Pieces of silicon (usually) that drive computers and into which electronic circuits are embedded.

Command Line – In AutoCAD 2000, the Command Line is a window in which commands are entered from the keyboard and which contains the prompts and responses to commands.

Clock speed – Usually measured in MHz (Megaherz) – this is the measure of the speed at which a computer processor works.

Clone – Refers to a PC that functions in a way identical to the original IBM PC.

CMOS – Complimentary metal oxide semiconductor. Often found as battery-powered chips which control features such as the PC's clock-speed.

Communications – Describes the software and hardware that allow computers to communicate.

Compatibility – Generally used as a term for software or programs able to run on any computer that is an IBM clone.

Coprocessor – A processor chip in a computer which runs in tandem with the main processor chip and can deal with arithmetic involving many decimal points (floating-point arithmetic). Often used in CAD systems to speed up drawing operations.

CPU – Central processing unit. The chip that drives a PC.

Data – Information that is created, used or stored on a computer in digital form.

Database – A piece of software that can handle and organise large amounts of information.

Dialogue box – A window that appears on screen in which options may be presented to the user, or requires the user to input information requested by the current application.

Directories – The system in MS-DOS for organising files on disk. Could be compared with a folder (the directory) containing documents (the files).

Disks – Storage hardware for holding data (files, applications etc.). There are many types: the most common are hard disks (for mass storage) and floppy disks (less storage) and CD-ROMs (mass storage).

Display – The screen allowing an operator to see the results of his work at a computer.

DOS – Disk operating system. The software that allows the computer to access and organise stored data. MS-DOS (produced by the Microsoft Corporation) is the DOS most widely used in PC's.

DTP – Desktop publishing. DTP software allows for the combination of text and graphics into page layouts which may then be printed.

Entity – A single feature in graphics being drawn on screen – a line, a circle, a point. Sometimes linked together in a block, when the block acts as an entity.

EMS – Expanded memory specification. RAM over and above the original limit of 640 Kbytes RAM in the original IBM PC. PCs are now being built to take up to 128 (or even more) Mb RAM.

File – Collection of data held as an entity on a disk.

Fixed disk – A hard disk that cannot usually be easily removed from the computer as distinct from floppy disks which are designed to be easily removable.

Floppy disk – A removable disk that stores data in magnetic form. The actual disk is a thin circular sheet of plastic with a magnetic surface, hence the term 'floppy'. It usually has a firm plastic case.

Flyout – A number of tool icons which appear when a tool icon which shows a small arrow is selected from a toolbar.

Formatting – The process of preparing the magnetic surface of a disk to enable it to hold digital data.

ftp – File Transfer Protocol. An Internet protocol used to fetch a required resource from the World-Wide Web (www) server.

Giga – Means 1,000,000,000. In computer memory terms really 1,000 Mb (megabytes) – actually 1,073,741,824 bytes because there are 1024 bytes in a kilobyte (Kb).

GUI – Graphical user interface. Describes software (such as Windows) which allows the user to control the computer by representing functions with icons and other graphical images.

Hardcopy – The result of printing (or plotting) text or graphics on to paper or card.

Hard disk – A disk, usually fixed in a computer, which rotates at high speed and will hold large amounts of data often up to 1 gigabyte.

Hardware – The equipment used in computing: the computer itself, disks, printers, monitor etc.

HTML – HyperText Markup Language. A computer language for setting up pages which can be sent via the Internet

http – HyperText Transfer Protocol. An Internet protocol used to fetch a required resource from the World-Wide Web (www) server.

Hz (herz) – The measure of 1 cycle per second. In computing terms, often used in millions of Herz – (megaherz or MHz) as a measure of the clock speed.

IBM – International Business Machines. An American computer manufacturing company – the largest in the world.

Intel – An American company which manufactures the processing chips used in the majority of PCs.

Internet – A network of computers linked in a world-wide system by telephone.

Joystick – A small control unit used mainly in computer games. Some CAD systems use a joystick to control drawing on screen.

Kilo – Means 1000. In computing terms 1K (kilobyte) is 1024 bytes.

LAN – Local area network. Describes a network that typically link PCs in an office by cable where distances between the PCs is small.

LED – Light emitting diode.

Library – A set of frequently used symbols, phrases or other data on disk, that can be easily accessed by the operator.

Light pen – Used as a stylus to point directly at a display screen sensitive to its use.

Memory – Any medium (such as RAM or ROM chips), that allows the computer to store data internally that can be instantly recalled.

Message box – A window containing a message to be acted on which appears in response when certain tools or command are selected.

MHz – Megahertz – 1,000,000 herz (cycles per second).

Mouse – A device for controlling the position of an on-screen cursor within a GUI such as Windows.

Microcomputer – A PC is a microcomputer; a minicomputer is much larger and a mainframe computer which is larger still. With the increase in memory possible with a microcomputer, the term seems to be dropping out of use.

Microsoft – The American company which produces Windows and MS-DOS software.

MIPS – Millions of instructions per second. A measure of a computer's speed – it is not comparable with the clock speed as measured in MHz, because a single instruction may take more than a cycle to perform.

Monitor – Display screen.

MS-DOS – Microsoft Disk Operating System.

Multitasking – A computer that can carry out more than one task at a time is said to be multitasking. For example in AutoCAD Windows printing can be carried out 'in the background', while a new drawing is being constructed.

Multi-user – A computer that may be used by more than one operator.

Networking – the joining together of a group of computers allowing them to share the same data and software applications. LANs and WANs are examples of the types of networks available.

Object – A term used in CAD to describe an entity or group of entities that have been linked together.

Operating System – Software and in some cases hardware, that allows the user to operate applications software and organise and use data stored on a computer which allow the hardware of a computer to operate application software.

PC – Personal computer. Should strictly only be used to refer to an IBM clone, but is now in general use.

Pixels – The individual dots on a monitor display.

Plotter – Produces hardcopy of, for instance, a drawing produced on a computer by moving a pen over a piece of paper or card.

Printer – There are many types of printer: dot-matrix, bubble-jet and laser are the most common. Allows material produced on a computer (graphics and text) to be output as hardcopy.

Processor – The operating chip of a PC. Usually a single chip, such as the Intel 80386, 80486 or Pentium chip.

Programs – A set of instructions to the computer that has been designed to produce a given result.

RAM – Random access memory. Data stored in RAM lost when the computer is switched off, unless previously saved to a disk.

RGB – Red, green blue.

ROM – Read only memory. Refers to those chips from which the data stored can be read, but to which data can not be written. The data on a ROM is not lost when a computer is switched off.

Scanner – Hardware capable of being passed over a document or drawing and reading the image into a computer.

Software – Refers to any program or application that is used and run on a computer.

SQL – Structured query language. A computer programming language for translating and transferring data between an application such as AutoCAD and a database.

Tools – Tools, are usually selected from icons appearing in toolbars. A tool represent a command.

Toolbar – Toolbars contain a number of icons, representing tools.

Tooltip – When a tool is selected by a *left-click* on its icon, a small box appears (a Tool Tip) carrying the name of the tool.

UNIX – A multiuser, multitasking operating system (short for UNICS: uniplexed information and computing systems).

URL – Uniform Resource Locator

VDU – Visual display unit.

Vectors – Refers to entities in computer graphics which are defined by the coordinates of end points of each part of the entity.

VGA – video graphics array. Screen displays with resolution of up to 640 x 480 pixels in 256 colours. SVGA (Super VGA) will allow resolutions up to 1024 x 768 pixels.

Virtual memory – A system by which disk space is used as if it were RAM to allow the computer to function as if more physical RAM were present. It is used by AutoCAD (and other software), but can slow down a computer's operation.

WAN – Wide area network. A network of computers that are a large distance apart – often communicating by telephone.

Warning box – A window containing a warning or request which the user must respond to, which appears when certain circumstances are met or actions are made.

WIMP – Windows, icons, mice and pointers. A term used to describe some GUIs.

Windows – An area of the computer screen within which applications such as word processors may be operated.

Workstation – Often used to refer to a multiuser PC, or other system used for the purposes of CAD (or other applications).

WORM – Write once read many. An optical data storage system that allows blank optical disks to have data written onto them only once.

www – World-Wide Web.

WYSIWYG – What you see is what you get. What is seen on the screen is what will be printed.

Index